Populism in Asian Democracies

Global Populisms

Series Editors

Amy Skonieczny, *San Francisco State University*
Amentahru Wahlrab, *The University of Texas at Tyler*

Editorial Board

Roland Benedikter, *EURAC Research, Center For Advanced Studies*
Lenka Buštíková, *Arizona State University*
Angelos Chryssogelos, *London Metropolitan University*
Benjamin De Cleen, *Vrije Universiteit Brussel*
Carlos de La Torre, *University of Florida*
Emmy Eklundh, *King's College London*
Federico Finchelstein, *The New School for Social Research*
Chris Hudson, *RMIT University*
Paul James, *Western Sydney University*
Erin Kristin Jenne, *Central European University*
David Macdonald, *University of Guelph*
Jennifer McCoy, *Georgia State University*
Cynthia Miller-Idriss, *American University*
Benjamin Moffitt, *Australian Catholic University*
Dirk Nabers, *Kiel University*
Danielle Resnick, *International Food Policy Research Institute (IFPRI)*
Matthew Rhodes-Purdy, *Clemson University*
Larbi Sadiki, *Qatar University*
Colin Snider, *The University of Texas at Tyler*
Manfred Steger, *University of Hawai'i at Mānoa*
Frank Stengel, *Kiel University*
Kurt Weyland, *The University of Texas at Austin*

VOLUME 01

The titles published in this series are listed at *brill.com/gpop*

Populism in Asian Democracies

Features, Structures, and Impacts

Edited by

Sook Jong Lee
Chin-en Wu
Kaustuv Kanti Bandyopadhyay

BRILL

LEIDEN | BOSTON

The Asia Democracy Research Network is supported by the National Endowment for Democracy (NED) since 2015.

Cover illustration: photo by Chris Slupski, from Unsplash.com

Library of Congress Cataloging-in-Publication Data
Names: Lee, Sook Jong, editor. | Wu, Chin-en, editor. | Bandyopadhyay, Kaustuv Kanti, editor.
Title: Populism in Asian democracies : features, structures, and impacts / Edited by Sook Jong Lee, Chinen Wu and Kaustuv Kanti Bandyopadhyay.
Description: Leiden ; Boston : Brill, [2021] | Series: Global populisms, 2666-2280 ; Volume 1 | Includes index.
Identifiers: LCCN 2020046136 (print) | LCCN 2020046137 (ebook) | ISBN 9789004444348 (hardback) | ISBN 9789004444461 (ebook)
Subjects: LCSH: Populism–Asia. | Democracy–Social aspects–Asia. | Comparative government–Asia. | Income distribution–Social aspectsAsia. | Asia–Politics and government.
Classification: LCC JQ36 .P68 2021 (print) | LCC JQ36 (ebook) | DDC 320.56/62095–dc23
LC record available at https://lccn.loc.gov/2020046136
LC ebook record available at https://lccn.loc.gov/2020046137

Typeface for the Latin, Greek, and Cyrillic scripts: "Brill". See and download: brill.com/brill-typeface.

ISSN 2666-2280
ISBN 978-90-04-44434-8 (hardback)
ISBN 978-90-04-44446-1 (e-book)

Copyright 2021 by Sook Jong Lee. Published by Koninklijke Brill NV, Leiden, The Netherlands. Koninklijke Brill NV incorporates the imprints Brill, Brill Hes & De Graaf, Brill Nijhoff, Brill Rodopi, Brill Sense, Hotei Publishing, mentis Verlag, Verlag Ferdinand Schöningh and Wilhelm Fink Verlag. Koninklijke Brill NV reserves the right to protect this publication against unauthorized use. Requests for re-use and/or translations must be addressed to Koninklijke Brill NV via brill.com or copyright.com.

This book is printed on acid-free paper and produced in a sustainable manner.

Contents

Acknowledgments   VII
List of Figures and Tables   IX
Notes on Contributors   X

Introduction: Populism in Asian Democracies   1
Sook Jong Lee, Chin-en Wu, and Kaustuv Kanti Bandyopadhyay

PART 1
Progressive Populism

1 South Korea's Tamed Populism: Popular Protests from Below and Populist Politics from the Top   21
Sook Jong Lee

2 Populism in Taiwan: A Bottom-Up Model   38
Chin-en Wu and Yun-han Chu

PART 2
Authoritarian Populism

3 Contemporary Populism and Democratic Challenges in the Philippines   61
Francisco A. Magno

4 Judicial Populism and Its Impact on the Quality of Democracy in Pakistan   80
Aasiya Riaz

PART 3
Redistributive Populism

5 Populism in Contemporary Indian Politics   97
Kaustuv Chakrabarti and Kaustuv Kanti Bandyopadhyay

6 Populism in Thailand 121
  Thawilwadee Bureekul, Ratchawadee Sangmahamad, and
   Nuchaprapar Moksart

7 Populism as a Phenomenon: Signs of Populism in Mongolian
  Development 136
  Gerelt-Od Erdenebileg, Ariunbold Tsetsenkhuu, and Ganbat Damba

8 The Changing Nature of Populism in Malaysia 147
  Faiz Abdul Halim and Aira Azhari

PART 4
Ethnic and Religious Populism

9 Populism in Indonesia: Learning from the 212 Movement in Response to
  the Blasphemy Case against Ahok in Jakarta 165
  Sri Nuryanti

10 Hegemonic Populism: Sinhalese Buddhist Nationalist Populism in
  Contemporary Sri Lanka 176
  Pasan Jayasinghe

11 Populism in Myanmar 197
  Myat Thu

  Conclusion: Sources and Features of Asian Democracies 211
  Chin-en Wu, Sook Jong Lee, and Kaustuv Kanti Bandyopadhyay

  Index 227

Acknowledgments

This book is a product of collaboration between the members of the Asia Democracy Research Network (ADRN). When academics, practitioners, and civil society leaders gathered at the Community of Democracies non-governmental forum in Ulaanbaatar in 2013, participants agreed to the idea of promoting democracy in the Asian region through democratic research cooperation. The ADRN was created from this idea and launched in 2015 with its inaugural workshop in Seoul. This network of democracy research institutions has grown to include 23 university centers and think tanks from 14 countries. The first project to which all members were invited to contribute research on their countries was this study of populism. As global democracy continues to suffer from rising populism and exclusive nationalism, the demand for comparative studies on Asian populism from both scholars and policy makers has also grown. The group held two workshops to present and discuss our findings, and ultimately 11 country cases were collected. We tried to identify the prominent features and structures of populism for each country while also comparing the region as a whole with other regions.

This book would not have come to fruition without support and assistance from a great many people. First of all, I would like to thank all the chapter contributors for their tireless dedication and enthusiasm in collaborating. The fantastic cooperation of co-editors Chin-en Wu and Kaustuv Kanti Bandyopadhyay was critical to completing the manuscript. Second, without Jinkyung Baek, ADRN's hardworking project manager, the painstaking process of book publication would have been far more challenging. Natalie Grant's careful and attentive editing helped polish the text, and Sea Young Kim also offered her hand in the final stages of editing. Lastly, I would like to thank the two anonymous reviewers for offering constructive comments which helped us better align this book with the conceptual discussion in academia. Jennifer Obdam and Debbie De Wit at Brill assisted greatly throughout the process of preparing the manuscript. Amentahru Wahlrab at the University of Texas at Tyler should also be mentioned for his encouragement in staying the course so that this book could be published.

The ADRN's collaborative research and other related activities would not be possible without the generous and continued funding of the National Endowment for Democracy. NED President Carl Gershman has been an enthusiastic supporter of Asian democracies and has worked tirelessly to form bridges between Asia and the international community of democracies. Its Associate Director for Asia, Lynn Lee, has been a great friend of our network members.

The Seoul-based East Asia Institute has played the role of ADRN secretariat, and its President Yul Sohn has also strongly supported the ADRN's activities.

There must be more studies on Asian democracy. Despite some cross-national gaps in democratic achievements within the region, Asian countries are steadily democratizing on a firm foundation of economic and social development. Understanding the region from a democratic perspective is important in measuring the quality of global democracy. We hope this book can contribute to the understanding of the region in global populism studies. The ADRN will continue to identify important themes in democracy studies and contribute to practitioners working for democracy and good governance.

On behalf of contributors
Sook Jong Lee

Figures and Tables

Figures

2.1 China's influence on the region and on Taiwan. (Source: Asian Barometer Survey Fourth Wave, 2015, http://www.asianbarometer.org/ (accessed June 10, 2020)) 43

2.2 Views of China and perceived democratic supervision. (Source: Asian Barometer Survey Fourth Wave, 2015, http://www.asianbarometer.org/ (accessed June 10, 2020)) 45

8.1 What worries Malaysians in 2017? (Source: Ipsos Malaysia, "What Worries Malaysia: Post GE 2018," *Ipsos*, August 16, 2018, https://www.ipsos.com/en-my/what-worries-malaysia-post-ge-2018 (accessed October 1, 2018)) 153

8.2 Malaysia general elections XIV outlook: prospects and outcome. (Source: Merdeka Centre for Opinion Research, "Survey, Kuala Lumpur: National Voter Sentiments: Excerpt of Principal Indicators," *Merdeka Center*, 2019) 153

8.3 Malaysians optimistic about economic outlook following recent government initiatives. (Source: Nielsen, July 12, 2018) 154

Tables

4.1 Trust in institutions 90

6.1 Timeline of populist policies implemented by each government in the period between 2001 and 2018 124

C.1 Types of populism and their primary sources in Asia 214

Notes on Contributors

Aira Azhari
is a research manager at the Democracy and Governance Unit, IDEAS. She holds a Bachelor of Law from the University of Liverpool, UK and a Master of Law (Public International Law) from the London School of Economics and Political Science. She has provided analysis on political and economic issues to the Malaysian and international press, including Channel News Asia and the BBC.

Kaustuv Kanti Bandyopadhyay
is the director of Participatory Research in Asia, New Delhi, working on participation, democratic governance, and civil society development for more than three decades. He has 25 years of professional experience working with universities, research institutions, and CSO s. He serves on the Steering Committee of ADRN and the Asia Democracy Network (ADN). He holds a PhD in anthropology for his work with the Parhaiya tribes of Chotanagpur in India.

Thawilwadee Bureekul
is the director of the Research and Development Office at King Prajadhipok's Institute (KPI), Thailand, where she is involved in the planning, management, implementation, and coordination of the Institute's research projects. In addition to her role at KPI, she is a professor at several universities in Thailand, including the Asian Institute of Technology, Thammasat University, Burapha University, Mahidol University, and Silpakorn University. She succeeded in proposing "Gender Responsive Budgeting" in the Thai Constitution and she was granted the "Woman of the Year 2017" award as a result.

Kaustuv Chakrabarti
is a senior program officer at Participatory Research in Asia (PRIA), New Delhi. Kaustuv is working on the issues of civic space, multi-stakeholder partnerships, South-South Cooperation, and building civil society organization (CSO) capacities. He has been passionately engaged with PRIA's work on civic space both at the Asian and South Asian level. He co-authored *Civic Space under Siege: Experiences from South Asia*; the "State of Democracy: India" report in 2018, and the synthesis report on "Civic Space in Asia: Emerging Issues and Policy Lessons from Six Asian Countries 2018." He has an MA in globalization and development from the Institute of Development Studies at the University of Sussex, UK.

NOTES ON CONTRIBUTORS

Yun-han Chu

is a distinguished research fellow of the Institute of Political Science at Academia Sinica and Professor of Political Science at National Taiwan University. He serves concurrently as president of the Chiang Ching-kuo Foundation for International Scholarly Exchange. He is the founding director of the Asian Barometer Survey, a regional network of surveys on democracy, governance, and development covering more than 18 Asian countries. Professor Chu received his PhD in political science from the University of Minnesota and joined the faculty of National Taiwan University in 1987.

Ganbat Damba

is currently Chairman of the Board, APEserved as the Ambassador of Mongolia to Germany and was the former director of the Institute for Strategic Studies of the National Security Council of Mongolia. Previously, he served as the managing director of the Academy for Political Education of Mongolia. He earned his PhD in political science at the Academy of Sciences of Mongolia.

Gerelt-Od Erdenebileg

is associate professor of the Mongolian National University of Education (MNUE), Ulaanbaatar, Mongolia. He specializes in research on internal party democracy, party development and electoral system in Mongolia. Previously, he served as the national project manager in the UNDP Mongolia. He completed his PhD in political science at the Mongolian National University of Education in 2009.

Faiz Abdul Halim

has been an assistant researcher at the Democracy and Governance Unit, the Institute for Democracy and Economic Affairs (IDEAS), a public policy research organization based in Kuala Lumpur, Malaysia. He holds a BA degree in political science from the International Islamic University of Malaysia.

Pasan Jayasinghe

is a researcher at the Centre for Policy Alternatives (CPA) in Colombo, Sri Lanka. He is involved with research and advocacy work primarily covering constitutional reform, electoral law, and transitional justice. He also acts as the Information Officer for the CPA, responsible for its Right to Information Act compliance and policy. Pasan holds BA, LLB, and MA degrees, and has previously worked as a policy advisor for the New Zealand government.

Sook Jong Lee

is a professor of public administration at Sungkyunkwan University, Seoul, South Korea, and senior fellow of the East Asia Institute. She has been directing the Asian Democracy Research Network (ADRN) since its formation in 2015, leading a network of research organizations across Asia to promote democracy with the support of the National Endowment for Democracy. Her recent publications include *Transforming Global Governance with Middle Power Diplomacy: South Korea's Role in the 21st Century* (ed. 2016), and *Keys to Successful Presidency in South Korea* (ed. 2013 and 2016).

Francisco A. Magno

teaches Political Science and Development Studies at De La Salle University (DLSU), Manila, Philippines. He is the Founding Director of the DLSU Jesse M. Robredo Institute of Governance. He served as president of the Philippine Political Science Association from 2015 to 2017. He completed his PhD in political science at the University of Hawaii.

Nuchaprapar Moksart

is a researcher assigned to the Research and Development Office at KPI. Her research includes social policy and political economy theory. She also writes on socioeconomic issues.

Sri Nuryanti

is a researcher at the Center for Political Studies, the Indonesian Institute of Sciences, Jakarta, Indonesia. She is the former Election Commissioner of the Indonesian General Election Commission 2007–12, where she successfully oversaw the Parliamentary election and Presidential election 2009, as well as local elections from 2007 to 2012. She is an active participant in various academic activities at the national as well as the international level. She is a Co-Secretary General of the Asia Pacific Peace Research Association and the Executive Council member of the International Peace Research Association. She is director in charge of the Electoral Research Institute, Jakarta, Indonesia.

Aasiya Riaz

is joint director at PILDAT, the leading Pakistani think tank she co-founded in 2001, and she leads PILDAT's projects and activities. Trained in the field of media and political communication at the London School of Economics, UK, Aasiya has also worked with the mainstream press and electronic media in Pakistan as a political analyst. She has been a Reagan-Fascell Democracy Fellow at the National Endowment for Democracy, as well as a distinguished fellow at the Center on Democracy, Development, and the Rule of Law at the Stanford University.

Ratchawadee Sangmahamad

is a researcher assigned to the Research and Development Office at KPI. Her research focuses on citizenship, gender, and election studies. Her publications include *Value Culture and Thermometer of Democracy* (with Thawilwadee Bureekul), *Thai Citizens: Democratic Civic Education* (with Thawilwadee Bureekul and Eugenie Mario), and many articles.

Myat Thu

led a student protest for democracy, human rights, and educational reform in 2000 at Pyay Technological University in Pyay, Bago Division and was arrested and sentenced to seven years in prison. He was released in 2002 and resumed his studies, to receive his BE in Engineering from Yangon Technological University. In 2011 he founded Yangon School of Political Science (YSPS). He received a Chevening Scholarship in 2012 and graduated from London School of Economics and Political Science with an MSc in political theory in 2013. He was a visiting scholar at St. Anthony's College, University of Oxford in 2018. He currently serves as the Chairperson of YSPS.

Ariunbold Tsetsenkhuu

is a researcher at the Academy of Political Education of Mongolia and the Institute of Strategic Studies of the National Security Council of Mongolia. His research focuses on the interactions between the media and political forces.

Chin-en Wu

is an associate research fellow at the Institute of Political Science at Academia Sinica, Taiwan. He received his PhD from the University of Michigan. He serves as one of the co-PIs of the Asian Barometer Survey. His main research interests include political economy, democratization, and the relationship between regime type and economic reforms.

Introduction: Populism in Asian Democracies

Sook Jong Lee, Chin-en Wu, and Kaustuv Kanti Bandyopadhyay

While populism has long existed as a research topic in social science, scholarly and policy attention to populism to date has been primarily based on its rise in Western societies. Globalization is generally considered the root cause of rising populism in the West. The integrative and innovative forces of globalization have intensified competition and broadened economic inequalities between the skilled and adaptable and the unskilled and less adaptable labor force. Faced with the increased movement of people, usually from developing to developed countries, globalization is also viewed by the populations of advanced economies as detrimental to cultural and social integrity. Regardless of whether or not such claims are valid, people claim that globalization is a primary instigator of unequal economic opportunity and "threatened" national identity, soliciting their governments and politicians to exercise sovereign power over the public issues raised by globalization. This anti-globalist nationalism is strongly echoed in populist sentiments. The convoluted political process of Brexit and the anticipated economic problems caused by the United Kingdom's leaving the European Union (EU) may alter the calculus of leaving the regional body for other member states.

In addition to this anti-globalist populism in the West, another frontline of populism is operating against conventional mainstream parties. Despite its pathological symptoms, populism is a form of democracy. By making the majority of people the only legitimate source of power over elite representatives or transnational governance, populism plays people's call for democracy. It also shares the healthy elements of participatory democracy, where citizens tend to engage more actively in politics and public decision-making processes. Populism turns bad when it tries to weaponize politics against minority groups. The failure of mainstream political parties to account for social discontent is a more immediate cause of the rise of populism. Disenchantment with the government or major parties is not a new phenomenon. Political scientists have observed a growing mistrust of political elites and the establishment since the 1980s. What distinguishes recent years from the past is that populism is more focused and effectively mobilized to influence politics. Right-wing populists have founded new political parties that have gained substantial support. Even in the United States, where two major parties dominate, the Tea Party movement and the rise of Donald Trump embody the intra-party populism of the

© LEE, WU, AND BANDYOPADHYAY, 2021 | DOI:10.1163/9789004444461_002

Republican Party, just as the rise of Bernie Sanders reflects populism within the Democratic Party. One of the important consequences of rising populism in Western politics, therefore, has been the destabilization of politics and governance.

While anti-globalist and anti-establishment pictures of Western populism are familiar, the concept of populism in Asia is more difficult to grasp. If Western populism is largely regarded as a post-modern and post-democracy phenomenon reacting against transnational governance and diluted national identity, many Asian countries are still undergoing democratization and are opting for further globalization. This is not to say that the region is free of populism. In fact, democratization has been accompanied by the rise of populism in this region. Asian populism is unleashed as countries further open up their society and undertake political reforms toward democracy. This book identifies different patterns of populism in the region by examining how the existing social cleavages of Asian countries have contributed to their populist politics. It also maintains that the impact of populism upon Asian democracies is comprised of both negative and positive analyses, in contrast to the West, where it is viewed as a predominantly negative force. In this way, this comparative study on Asian populism sheds light on how the quality of democracy could be improved within the region.

1 The Rise of Asian Populism

Populism is a contested concept. Scholars have used the term in reference to a political discourse, ideology, leadership or strategy. As a research concept, populism is overly inclusive to the degree that countless political phenomena and social movements have been deemed populist. The *Oxford Handbook of Populism* (2017) is conscious of this difficult problem of rigorously defining populism. Instead of offering a single definition, the book groups studies of populism into ideational, political-strategic, and socio-cultural approaches. As a supporter of the ideational approach, Cas Mudde defines populism as a thin-centered ideology that divides society into two homogeneous and adversarial groups—"the pure people" versus "the corrupt elite"—and asserts that politics should express the general will of the people.[1] In a similar vein, Jan-Werner

---

1 Cas Mudde, "The Populist Zeitgeist," *Government and Opposition* 39, no. 4 (2004): 541–563, at 543; Cas Mudde, "Populism: An Ideational Approach," in *The Oxford Handbook of Populism*, ed. Cristobal Rovira Kaltwasser et al. (Oxford, UK: Oxford University Press, 2017), 27–47, at 29.

Muller argues that populism is not only anti-elitist but also needs to be anti-pluralist, claiming exclusive moral representation. Namely, populism is a kind of identity politics that champions the people as morally superior and opposes pluralism as a tool of elites.[2] Both these definitions share elements of anti-globalism and an "us" vs. "them" dichotomy to which populism operates externally and internally respectively. Populist leaders claim that they represent the general will of the people. When populism targets political and business elites, it does so based on a people-centered and anti-elite ideology. When populism attacks ethnic or religious minorities, it is regarded as an illiberal and anti-plural ideology.

On the other hand, scholars who view populism as a political strategy consider populism to comprise methods and instruments used for winning and exercising power.[3] If the ideational approach centers on the people, the political-strategic approach focuses on how a political ruler sustains government support and public obedience. A typical tactic of a ruler in power is to implement economically redistributive policies to govern the people. Daron Acemoglu, Georgy Egorov and Konstantin Sonin argue that politicians seek reelection by selecting the left spectrum of median voter "populist" policies to signal that they are not beholden to the interests of the right. Politicians are more likely to exercise such tendencies when they are perceived by the public as corrupt and when the policy preferences of median voters and right-wing interests display greater polarization.[4] Since an anti-elite ideology can be easily combined with a political leader's strategy to gain or maintain power, ideational and strategic approaches are not mutually exclusive. Lastly, the socio-cultural approach regards populism as a low-brow discourse than can undermine legalistic and institutionally mediated authority.[5] It looks at the interactive communication between the people and the political leadership. In terms of political discourse, the low-brow culture based on excessive emotions and unscientific claims are visible in many cases of populism. The socio-cultural approach can be easily mixed with both ideological and political

---

2   Jan-Werner Muller, *What is Populism?* (Philadelphia: University of Pennsylvania Press, 2016); "Populism and Constitutionalism," in *The Oxford Handbook of Populism*, ed. Christobal Rovira Kaltwasser et al. (Oxford, UK: Oxford University Press, 2017), 590–606.

3   Kurt Weyland, "Populism: A Political-Strategic Approach," in *The Oxford Handbook of Populism*, ed. Cristobal Rovira Kaltwasser et al. (Oxford, UK: Oxford University Press, 2017), 55, 59.

4   Daron Acemoglu, Georgy Egorov, and Konstantin Sonin, "A Political Theory of Populism," *Quarterly Journal of Economics* 128, no. 2: 771–805.

5   Pierre Ostiguy, "Populism: A Socio-Cultural Approach," in *The Oxford Handbook of Populism*, ed. Cristobal Rovira Kaltwasser et al. (Oxford, UK: Oxford University Press, 2017), 73–74, 84–85.

approaches if cognitive and emotional aspects are the only narratives of populism in consideration.

Paul Kenny advocates an organizational approach to populism, defining the phenomenon as "the charismatic mobilization of a mass movement in pursuit of political power."[6] He argues that populists do not need to have deeply institutionalized links with supporters through interest groups and civil society organizations. Therefore, populism is a form of efficient and low-cost political mobilization where ties between voters and bureaucratic or clientelist parties do not exist or have decayed.[7]

The above-mentioned approaches are all useful depending on which aspects of populism are the focus of analysis. Most contributors of this book take an ideational approach by considering populism to be an anti-elite ideology and, at the same time, pay attention to the mass mobilization facilitated by the institutional power devolution that has accompanied democratic transition in Asia.

From the comparative perspective, a worthy question to consider is whether populism is practiced distinctively across different regions. Mudde and Cristóbal Rovira Kaltwasser categorize populism into two regional subtypes including exclusionary populism in Europe and inclusionary populism in Latin America, which correspond to rightist and leftist populism respectively. Both regional subtypes are considered to be civic responses to globalization and its negative impacts.[8] In the West, globalization is increasingly considered an elite ideology that does not serve the interest of the masses. Leftist populism in Southern Europe, for example, is highly critical of multilateral transnational institutions because of the belief that EU institutions contributed to the devastating aftermath of the 2012 European debt crisis. Financial meltdowns following the crisis empowered leftist economic populism in Greece and Spain to resist strong restructuring demands from EU headquarters in Brussels. Leftist parties Syriza and Podemos, which emerged in Greece and Spain respectively amid the Euro Crisis, denounced the EU's austerity and neoliberal policies. Their leaders, Alexis Tsipras and Pablo Iglesias, believe that two distinct groups of illegitimate elites stand against the people whom they arguably represent: the corrupt elites in Greece and those within the wider European

---

6 Paul D. Kenny, *Populism in Southeast Asia* (Cambridge, UK: Cambridge University Press, 2018), 1.

7 Kenny, *Populism in Southeast Asia*, 3.

8 Cas Mudde and Cristóbal Rovira Kaltwasser, "Exclusionary vs. Inclusionary Populism: Comparing Contemporary Europe and Latin America," *Government and Opposition* 48, no. 2 (2013): 147–174.

and global political economic scenes. Even as the leaders of the Syriza and Podemos parties object to austerity measures, however, they continue to demand financial support from the EU to distinguish themselves from Eurosceptics.

In addition to leftist populism, the wave of migration into Europe that peaked during the Syrian refugee crisis of 2015–2016 led to a rise in identity-driven rightist populism against regional integration. Moreover, the rise of globalization and the accessibility of information to the public have also led to a rise in human migration. Yet networks for human transport, while they may be largely beneficial for those in need, are also susceptible to criminal activities such as human trafficking. More importantly, sudden influxes of heterogeneous populations carry the potential to trigger negative sentiments among native populations against foreigners. As such, Western and Eastern Europe—unlike Latin America and Southern Europe—harbor more right-wing populist sentiments that prioritize cultural identity over economic insecurity due to their continued inflows of refugees.[9]

While there are few studies on Asian populism, populism in Southeast Asia has been drawing increased attention in scholarly literature. William Case offers a model for analyzing populism in Southeast Asia which centers on elite-level relations and social coalition. He argues that the elites in Thailand, Indonesia, and the Philippines have exploited opportunities for populist mobilization. But populism in these three countries has led to different outcomes in their respective democracies; it has brought about democracy's breakdown in Thailand, survival in Indonesia, and slippage in the Philippines. With the same three countries as the subjects for his case study,[10] Kenny approaches populism from an electoral politics perspective. He argues that severed ties

---

9   For decades, Jean-Marie Le Pen of the France's National Front pushed an extreme rightwing message with anti-Semitic elements. To broaden the party base, his daughter, Marine Le Pen, shifted the party toward an anti-immigration, anti-Islam stance and embraced anti-EU nationalism. Austria's former right-wing party, the Freedom Party, took on an anti-immigration, anti-EU platform as well. Germany's Eurosceptic Alternative for Germany, founded in 2013, is also a far-right party, which emerged as the third largest party after the 2017 federal election. Viktor Orban, after winning his second term as Prime Minister in 2010, transformed Hungary so that it not only embraces anti-migrant nationalism, but also has become an illiberal democracy infringing press freedom. Brexit was also based on significant anti-migrant and anti-EU sentiments, in response to which politicians hastily called a referendum and then proceeded to mangle the subsequent process. The Trump administration is implementing harsh anti-immigration policies with the building of a wall, forcible separation of immigrant families, and placement of refugees and asylum-seekers in detention camps. President Trump has vilified immigrants as criminals and drug smugglers.

10   William Case, *Populist Threats and Democracy's Fate in Southeast Asia: Thailand, the Philippines, and Indonesia* (New York: Routledge, 2017).

between voters and bureaucratic or clientelist parties have enabled populists to mobilize electoral support directly from the people.[11] This point is shared by most contributors of this book in their analyses of the rise of populism in Asia. They also view the region's democratization, while it has denounced its authoritarian past, as being responsible for discrediting existing institutions. The differences between Northeast Asian countries and Southeast Asia, however, need to be highlighted. Although many disillusioned voters are turning their backs on electoral politics, major political parties in South Korea and Taiwan still hold a crucial gatekeeping role. With an electoral system that gives an advantage to bigger parties, a presidential candidate from one of two major parties is usually elected in both countries. Once a president is elected, both pro- and anti-president forces tend to bypass political parties and engage directly in popular politics. When an election is approaching, however, these grassroot political forces come together to align with the less disfavored political party rather than presenting a better alternative.

Populism in Asia takes diverse subtypes that cannot be simply summarized as either exclusionary or inclusionary. Progressive elements of populist politics in South Korea and Taiwan that are discussed in this book are certainly more inclusive than those of other regional populist movements. Progressive populist elements in these two countries specifically target the corrupt and inept elites, despite alienating people who do not share the same political views. The economic populist policies for redistribution in India, Malaysia, and Thailand are also essentially inclusive in terms of their response to the needs of the poor. On the other hand, religious and ethnic populism in Myanmar, Sri Lanka, and Indonesia is considered exclusionary because it discriminates against minority groups. The unjust targeting of individuals framed as "criminals" by the authoritarian leader in the Philippines is also seen as an exclusionary practice of populism although it is not based on issues related to ethnic identity. As discussed in the book, populist politics in countries such as Mongolia and Pakistan are more difficult to characterize as either inclusive or exclusive due to the distinctive populist styles of their respective leaderships. Owing to existing variances in the inclusiveness and exclusiveness of populism across the Asian region, contributors of this book find bottom-up or top-down populism to be more fitting and useful in explaining the diversity of populism in Asia.

Vertical populism between leaders and people can take two forms. The first form of vertical populism is bottom-up and people-centered. People directly express their demands while being critical of their governments and

---

11   Kenny, *Populism in Southeast Asia.*

INTRODUCTION: POPULISM IN ASIAN DEMOCRACIES

legislatures for being corrupt or incompetent. The second form is top-down, in which political leaders within the ruling system mobilize populism under the tenets of anti-establishmentarianism to seize power. Mudde and Kaltwasser argue that populism in opposition, that is usually bottom-up, is less harmful than populism in government, that is often top-down mobilization.[12] If "us" vs. "them" exclusionary politics exist horizontally between social groups without or with less involvement from political leaders, one can identify this as horizontal populism. Horizontal populism is usually accompanied by hate speech, discrimination, and even violence such as terrorism and extra-judicial killings against specific ethnic or religious minority groups. Although vertical and horizontal interactions in populism are often found to coexist, it is better to distinguish them for analytical purposes in order to identify the primary source of populism in different contexts. If bottom-up populism is more commonly found in mature democracies where it is the public that increasingly views elected politicians and technocrats as corrupt or incapable, top-down populism is more prevalent in flawed democracies where political leaders instrumentalize populist movements to meet their ends. One may simplify this to say that horizontal populism undermines pluralist democracy by negating diversity while vertical populism destabilizes elitist representative democracy. If the state or ruling elites mandate the majority group's cultural and political hegemony or even go so far as to intervene or plan physical violence against minority groups, anti-pluralist populism backed up by repressive governments is likely to undermine democracy in the most serious way.

If there is anything fundamentally absent from Asian populism, it is anti-globalization sentiment. Compared with other regions, in Asia regional bodies tend to be less coherent and transnational rules and norms are weaker. Asian countries are known to be highly nationalistic, which often prevents them from adhering to any meaningful form of regionalism. However, nationalism does not necessarily lead to protectionism and anti-globalism. On the contrary, many Asian countries have tried to link their economies with external markets and consider globalization an integral part of modernization. Even in the case of migration, exclusive populism in Asia has emerged against long-term settlers rather than new migrants. Populous Asia sends countless migrants outside the region. According to the International Organization for Migration's *World*

---

12   Cas Mudde and Cristóbal Rovira Kaltwasser, "Populism and (liberal) Democracy: A
      Framework for Analysis," in *Populism in Europe and the Americas: Threat or corrective for
      democracy?*, ed. Mudde and Kaltwasser (Cambridge, UK: Cambridge University Press,
      2012), 1–26, at 23–25.

Migration Report 2018, of the world's 244 million international migrants—which accounts for 3.3 percent of the world's population—Asians comprised nearly 40 percent as of 2015.[13] Since migrants tend to move to higher-income countries mainly for work, half the total number of Asian migrants (59 million) resides in other countries within the region. Of the top 20 migration corridors for Asian countries, migrant flows from India and Pakistan—countries which are still affected by their partition—to the Gulf Cooperation Council countries take up the majority. Other migration trends in South and East Asia include a steady flow of people from Myanmar to Thailand and Bangladesh as the Rohingya and other political targets seek refugee status. Since high-income Northeast Asian countries including South Korea, Japan, and Taiwan implement strict migration control, other advanced Asian economies such as Malaysia and Singapore have become notable destinations for regional migrants. Yet the temporary nature of migrant workers combined with the strict control that host countries exercise over them has prevented the rise of anti-migrant populism. Overall, the impact of migration on populism in East and South Asia is not significant at the time of writing.

2 Types of Asian Populism

This book deals with cases of populism in Asia. Each case study illustrates something of a prototype of country-specific populism. Each prototype has been drawn from three elements: the country's own democratization history, distinctive social composition, and specific socio-political context. While the country-specific pattern of populism is certainly evolving, one can anticipate the path-dependent nature of populism. Namely, future populism in each country is likely to mimic its basic form. Focusing on the nature of issues upon which populism is mobilized, individual country cases are grouped into political populism, authoritarian populism, redistributive populism, and ethnic/religious populism. This grouping aids comparative study by addressing salient common features of populism among the country cases while carefully highlighting their points of divergence. At the same time, less distinctive cases of populism within a country should not be dismissed for failing to fit within the dominant framework of populism in Asia.

---

13   Marie McAuliffe and Martin Ruhs, "World Migration Report 2018" (Geneva: International Organization for Migration, 2017).

INTRODUCTION: POPULISM IN ASIAN DEMOCRACIES

2.1 *Political Populism: Progressive and Authoritarian*

Political populism centers on people's movements against corrupt elites and ill-conceived government policies. While economic conditions certainly influence this kind of political populism, they remain in the background without developing into typical labor or welfare issues. Political populism can take two directions in terms of vertical people–government relations. This oppositional movement is based on the liberal values of active citizenship, which demand that elected officials and government leaders be held accountable. Accordingly, despite transitional political instability, this type of populism ultimately serves democratic consolidation. South Korea and Taiwan are clearly bottom-up cases of populism. Since they are largely led by a progressive force pushing for socio-political changes, they can be labelled progressive populism from an ideological point of view. As the two most developed democracies among the countries dealt with in this book, civil society in these countries has been vibrant ever since their respective transitions to democracy in the late 1980s. Chapters 1 and 2 in this volume report that anti-establishment popular movements have emerged since the late 1990s in South Korea and since the Ma Ying-jeou period (2008–2016) in Taiwan. Led by active civil society organizations, citizens from all walks of life tend to participate in street demonstrations to oppose corrupt or unresponsive governments. Populist protests in South Korea and Taiwan are first mobilized by oppositional forces against the establishment and, if successful, extend to the political center. Political issues of corruption or power abuse often resonate strongly across political lines among people of both countries.

Foreign affairs-wise, public concern over national sovereignty vis-à-vis control by the United States and mainland China, powerful states with deep historical ties to South Korea and Taiwan respectively, provide an impetus to oppose conservative governments. For the Taiwanese, China issues are not limited to risky economic integration, but are closely linked to national identity. The fundamental difference between South Korea and Taiwan is the emergence of a populist party in Taiwan, where popular movements led to the creation of the White Force (WF) and the New Power Party (NPP). However, in South Korea, popular citizen movements have not led to the transformation of civilian power into a sustainable political force through the formation of a political party. In this structural context, liberal governments of these countries tend to ride on populism critical of the remnants of the authoritarian legacy under the previous conservative governments.

On the other hand, populism in the Philippines and Pakistan can be characterized as authoritarian populism in which political leaders or ruling elites mobilize popular support in order to strengthen their influence. In the Philippines, populism has been a recurrent but become salient social feature after Rodrigo Duterte took power. As mayor of Davao City, Duterte emerged on the national stage in the 2016 presidential election with a promise to shake up the political establishment. His signature campaign to wage war against criminality was not at the top of the list of national concerns. But Duterte successively framed criminality as the key campaign issue by saying that he would execute 100,000 criminals and dump their bodies in Manila Bay. Within two years in office as President, his anti-drug campaign had killed more than 4,500 people without due process. The authors of Chapter 3, on the Philippines, argue that high levels of inequality, easily manipulated social media, and weak institutions led to the rise of Duterte, who has also introduced redistributive policies such as tertiary education subsidies, exemptions to irrigation fees for small land holding farmers, and a doubling of the salary of police officers. Under Duterte's authoritarian populism, the media has been dominated by government propaganda and the free press has been under attack. To check the functioning of public institutions critical of his programs, Duterte threatened to abolish the Commission on Human Rights and restrict the Office of the Ombudsman, not to mention his marginalization of opposition party leaders. Duterte's populism is a typical case of populism by an authoritarian leader with a much greater negative than positive impact.

Pakistan poses an interesting case of populism from the top. In Pakistan, a judicial body formed from established institutions is seeking populist engagement with the people. This goes against the common sense of courts as the least politicized government entity. For example, Justice Saqib Nisar, Chief Justice of Pakistan, likened the role of the judiciary to a *baba* (a village elder). Allowed by the Constitution, the Supreme Court maintains original jurisdiction over matters of public importance and enforcement of the fundamental rights of every citizen of Pakistan. Using this *suo motu* power, Pakistan's judiciary has been increasingly active in public affairs. This is a newly added role for the courts. In the past, the Supreme Court had legitimized military coups and frequently disqualified prime ministers at the army's demand by invoking the doctrine of state necessity. Still serving the military as "tools for the generals," judges have now become eager to brief the public on any issue or incident that arises. The usage of *suo motu* largely began from the era of Chief Justice Iftikhar Muhammad Chaudhry, whose forced dismissal by General Pervez Musharraf in 2007 brought about the resisting Lawyers Movement. After being reinstated, he and his colleagues used *suo motu* on issues of fundamental rights and constitutionalism to define their judicial identity. The popular legacy of the judiciary has continued. But with the rise of social and electronic media, judges have begun to seek constant public media spotlight and care about maintaining a positive reputation. The Supreme Court's agenda is also influenced by television. The executive body's lack of response to high-level corruption has also resulted in the judiciary overstepping into the executive domain. The author argues that this judicial populism reinforces the admonishment of politicians by military leaders as corrupt and immoral and helps to weaken representative democracy in Pakistan. To use a more critical expression, "a military–judiciary nexus" has been created to manage and undercut a popularly elected party.

2.2 *Redistributive Populism*

Redistributive populism is economic populism used by politicians or governments as part of election campaigns or welfare policy packages. It is a preemptive spending of public money rather than spending in response to public pressure. Spending programs often exceed the state's fiscal capability. In this sense, redistributive populism is another form of top-down populism. The cases of India and Thailand belong to this category. Chapter 5, on India, describes the rich history of populism going back to Gandhi's self-sufficient agro-artisanal village movement of the colonial period, and later Indira Gandhi's populism of the 1970s, pledging work for poor people. The subcontinent-based populism has also embraced popular struggles in the form of opposing caste inequalities, addressing environmental damage, and protecting the livelihood of farmers. The more contemporaneous populism of India is rooted in the liberal reforms of the 1990s which resulted in uneven economic benefits following economic growth. Many redistributive populist measures have been introduced such as guaranteeing wage employment in rural areas, cooked food subsidies in Tamil Nadu, free laptops to students in Uttar Pradesh, and the demonetization that invalidated 500 and 1,000 rupee notes to attack black money. This long-practiced redistributive populism by the government was meant to redress the political contradiction of uneven development so that an anti-elitist, people-centered approach could be introduced. However, Prime Minister Narendra Modi's political mobilization added some anti-pluralist sentiments. After a series of corruption scandals in the ruling Indian National Congress, in the 2014 election Modi and his Bhartiya Janata Party campaigned to replace corrupt elites and end India's dynastic politics. The government in Modi's home base of Gujrat relies on sub-national populism based on the Gujarati identity pitted against the ineffectual elites in New Delhi.

In Thailand, the revered monarchy has been a traditional giver to the poor and underprivileged. During Thaksin Shinawatra's government (2001–06), redistributive populism was used widely. It was meant to alleviate poverty and also to win elections. Redistributive policies included the 30-baht healthcare scheme, community village funds, agrarian debt relief, One Tambon One

Product, and so on. Compared with India, Thailand's government-led redistributive populism is characterized by its top-down nature flowing from a benevolent political leader. Following the corruption scandal that emerged after Thaksin sold shares of his corporation for more than a billion tax-free dollars to foreign investors, a citizen movement against him, called the People's Alliance for Democracy or "Yellow Shirts" launched mass protests accusing him of corruption, abuse of power, and autocratic tendencies. After Thaksin was overthrown and his party was outlawed, however, he continued to influence Thai politics through the People's Power Party that ruled in 2008 and its successors the Pheu Thai Party and the United Front for Democracy against Dictatorship, known as the Red Shirts movement. Under a mandate from poor and rural Thais, Thaksin, who exiled himself after being ousted by the military coup of September 2006, managed to get his sister Yingluck Shinawatra elected in 2011. Redistributive populism for the poor and farmers continued until she was removed from office on May 7, 2014 by a Constitutional Court decision. The Pheu Thai Party reemerged as the biggest party in terms of constituent seats in the March 2019 election, which was the first popular election after the military coup five years before. Despite this victory, the party could not take power due to the strange ballot system of taking a reduction of the number of constituency seats from the number of proportional seats.

Mongolian economic populism is a mixture of growth-oriented economic catching up and an element of redistributive populism. Mongolian populism manifests as election campaign promises of making the country "rich" and similar empty or exaggerated promises. Once elected, politicians spend national revenue to fulfill their campaign promises or pursue their personal interests. Populism has also changed the political culture of Mongolia. Politicians now portray themselves as "sons of the people" standing up for the nation, and they try to appeal to national sentiment by heavily utilizing media outlets and social media to create a populist public image. This popularization of politics only diverts public attention from important public agendas and ultimately weakens party politics in Mongolia.

Malaysia is a mixture of redistributive populism and democratic reforms from the top. Popular discourses are delineated by political parties rather than grassroots movements. The author of Chapter 8 argues that the Pakatan Harapan (PH)'s campaign manifesto in the 2018 general election relied on populist language to direct much of the blame to Prime Minister Najib Rajak, the United Malays National Organisation (UMNO), and the Barisan National coalition for covering up the 1Malaysia Development Berhad scandal (when Prime Minister Najib was accused in 2015 of stealing huge amounts of money from this state investment fund and was pressed to resign) and introducing an unpopular goods and services tax. The PH campaigned against the cronyism and kleptocracy of elites and won the election to the surprise of many. While the PH's manifesto borrowed populist concepts and language, the author maintains its content and subsequent government policies are designed to encourage a move toward a more plural system which is further decentralized and institutes greater checks and balances on the government. It does not make use of a moral "people" versus a corrupt "elite." If there is a penchant for political Islam and Malay nativist sentiments, these have been exploited by the UMNO and Malaysian Islamic Party leaders. With the country's diverse ethnic make-up and strong interest in socioeconomic issues, however, the author contends that identity-driven populism is less likely to dominate Malaysian politics.

2.2.1 Ethnic and Religious Populism

Ethnic and religious populism is dominant in Indonesia, Sri Lanka, and Myanmar. The Western counterpart of this type of populism is usually called "rightist" populism and is opposed to influxes of migrants and refugees. As these countries lack such mass migrant inflows, their ethnic or religious populism tends to reflect ethnic composition that already exists. Ethnic and religious populism can occur both vertically and horizontally. Dominant ethnic or religious groups attack minority groups often independently of government and political parties to assert their hegemony in civil society. Overriding this horizontal populism at the social level, government and ruling elites utilize populist identity politics to maintain or strengthen their political control.

Indonesia is the largest Muslim majority country in the world with a population of more than 260 million. While the country is home to more than 300 ethnic groups, 87 percent of the population adheres to Islam. Only about 10 percent of the population are Christian, followed by the much smaller religious minorities of Hindus, who comprise 1.7 percent, and Buddhists, who comprise a mere 0.7 percent of the country. As Indonesia's motto "unity in diversity" signifies, Indonesian Islam has been known to be mild and tolerant of religious minority groups. For example, when Islamic mass rallies took place in Jakarta in 2016 accusing Christian Basuki Tjahaja Purnama (Ahok) of blasphemy, it was regarded as an abnormal occurrence.

The 2016 Ahok blasphemy incident in Indonesia started with a Facebook video uploaded by one person with the title of "Blasphemy against Religion?" The video went viral immediately and many Muslims were offended by Ahok's statement arguing that the Quranic verse Al-Ma'idah 51 was used as a tool to deceive the public. Ahok, a member of the nation's Christian minority, explained that he meant to say that the verse could be used to prevent people from voting for him in the Jakarta gubernatorial election of February 2017, and he apologized. Regardless, on October 11, the Indonesian Ulama Council issued a fatwa stating that Ahok had insulted Islam and also clarified that the verse is in fact a mandate to choose only Muslim leaders. After the issuance of this fatwa, Muslim groups such as the Islamic Defenders Front and the National Movement Guards Fatwa of the Indonesian Ulama Council launched mass rallies demanding that Ahok be detained. The number of demonstrators increased to the millions on December 2, and this event provided the name "212 movement" for subsequent protests defending Islam. The Jakarta protest was succeeded by another big rally in February 2017. Ahok lost the February election and three months later was sentenced to two years in prison. The 212 movement was honored by locals as a series of peaceful protests defending their religion rather than Islamic populism undermining religious minorities. The author of Chapter 9 argues that that the mass rallies relied on the narrative of the *ummah* (Islamic community) to unify society, and this Islamic populism was a temporal phenomenon which coalesced over the blasphemy issue. Indonesia's defensive Muslim populism is different from the cases of Sri Lanka and Myanmar in two respects. First of all, the Indonesian government was criticized by protestors for not arresting Ahok quickly, but there have been no signs of the government utilizing these popular protests politically as is often seen in cases of authoritarian populism. Second, while the Blasphemy Law was upheld, Ahok's blasphemy remains an incident that did not expand into exclusionary politics against other religious minorities. The freedom of the secular state from the dominant religion and the diverse multi-ethnic background of the country seem to tame Indonesia's Islamic populism. The following two cases are very different.

In Sri Lanka, Sinhalese make up 75 percent of the population. The second largest ethnic group are the Tamils, who make up about 15 percent of the population, followed by the Sri Lankan Moors, who comprise about 9 percent. Religion-wise, 70 percent of the population are Sinhalese Buddhists followed by 12.6 percent Hindus, 9.7 percent Muslims, and 7.4 percent Christians. Unlike Indonesia, the overlap between ethnicity and religion is greater for the Sinhalese Buddhists. In Myanmar, the Bamar majority ethnic group accounts for 68 percent of the total population followed by 9 percent Shan, 7 percent Karen, and 4 percent Rakhine. Theravada Buddhists, who make up 88 percent of the population, span multiple ethnic groups beyond the Bamar. Christians and Muslims make up just 6.2 percent and 4.3 percent of the population respectively. While these distinctive demographic and social compositions provide a ready basis for the impulsive populism of the ethnic/religious majority, the ebb and flow of populism begs the question of why movements arise.

INTRODUCTION: POPULISM IN ASIAN DEMOCRACIES

Chapter 10, on Sri Lanka, argues that the country after independence as gradually recast under Sinhalese Buddhism so that the state's explicit role became that of protecting and promoting Buddhism. This Sinhalese statism provoked Tamil separatist nationalism and subsequently led to the armed conflict between the Sri Lanka government and Tamil insurgents that lasted over three decades. It was Mahinda Rajapaksa's regime (2009–2015) that turned Sinhalese Buddhist nationalism more intentionally toward populism. By defeating the Liberation Tigers of Tamil Ealam in 2009, he was portrayed as the "nation's father," equivalent to the Sinhalese king Dutugamunu who defeated the Tamil King Elara in historical myth. Rajapaksa personified the Sinhalese state, and opposition to his agenda was treated as treason. While Rajapaksa's mobilization of dichotomous politics between traitors and patriots illustrates a typical strategy of authoritarian populism, the violence of Sinhalese Buddhists against Muslims emerged independently with the end of the war. The existing Sinhalese Populist Party and the newly formed Bodu Bala Sena (Buddhist Power Army) became the progenitors of postwar anti-Muslim politics and violence. This Sinhalese Buddhist populism continued with repeated attacks on minorities even after a more liberal government replaced Rajapaksa in 2015. Attempts at redress provisions for minorities and modest decentralization policies adopted by the new government have failed to date. Ethno-religious populism in Sri Lanka shows the powerful social currents along which the authoritarian government aligns for power and, at the same time, the reform government has to compromise or capitulate.

As in Sri Lanka, Buddhism has been essential to Burmese national identity and nationalism. Not only anti-Muslim movements but also anti-Christian sentiments were high as part of anti-colonial movements, and anti-Hindu sentiments encouraged anti-Indian riots. To be a true Burmese, one has to be a Buddhist. There are two kinds of Buddhist institutions, the official Mahana, which the government controls, and the Mabatha, which is more influential over the majority of people. Mabatha monks and the 969 movement groups are ultra-nationalistic and have propagated religious populism, but they have generally been checked one way or another. The author of Chapter 11, on Myanmar, argues that this religious populism became significantly active and violent only after the military and its Union Solidarity and Development Party (USDP) co-opted the Mabatha as a political strategy to win in the 2010 elections. Following years of authoritarian rule, the Myanmar military dictatorship was so widely disfavored that the military-backed USDP had no popular base. After Aung San Suu Kyi was released and free elections were introduced in 2010, the USDP attacked the National League for Democracy (NLD) as a "Muslim peacock," which was effective to the point that the NLD rejected any

Muslim candidates in the next election. The NLD's fear of strong anti-Muslim sentiment have kept the party and Aung San Suu Kyi herself quiet over the mass killings of the Rohingyas in Rakhine State. The Rohingyas were massacred by Burmese troops in September 2017, and the ongoing systematic killings and mass rapes have driven about 700,000 Rohingyas into exile in Bangladesh and India. Under this strong Buddhist nationalism, the reform-oriented NLD government has not been able to do much to stop ethnic cleansing, despite the fierce condemnation of international society.

3   Democracy and Populism in Asia

Democratization in many Asian countries has been accompanied by rising populism. This is quite logical and understandable. The essential theory of populism is that sovereign power comes from the people, which is also a fundamental principle of democracy. In an absolutely closed society, a dictator can rule a country through sheer terror or other forms of violent oppression with no concern for popular support. Once a society has become open to democracy, typically starting with free elections, however flawed, political leaders require popular support if they seek to acquire or maintain power. Authoritarian leaders may be tempted to mobilize populism in order to legitimize their power as having the enthusiastic consent of the people. In a substantially democratized society, democratically elected political leaders are likely to follow their rational-legal authority with no need to rely on populist appeals. Even in mature procedural democracies, however, politicians may be tempted to rely on populism if society is highly polarized or is facing a sudden shock such as an influx of migrants or refugees. Therefore, one can argue that populism accompanies democratization, but populism does not disappear as democracy consolidates. Rather, populism can emerge at any stage of democratization. Most chapters of this book support this argument. The rise of populism in South Korea, Taiwan, and Thailand overlaps with the deepening stages of democracy when citizens re empowered, and populism in Myanmar has emerged since the country began transition to democracy.

How does populism influence a country's quality of democracy? Outsider views become negative when populism is related to violence. According to the Economist Intelligence Unit's *2017 Democracy Index*, the only "full democracies" in the Asia and Australasia regions are Australia and New Zealand, while 13 countries belong to "flawed democracies," six are "hybrid regimes," and seven are "authoritarian regimes." Among the eleven Asian countries this book deals with, South Korea (8.00), Taiwan (7.73), India (7.23), the Philippines (6.71),

Malaysia (6.54), Mongolia (6.50), Sri Lanka (6.48), and Indonesia (6.39) are classified as "flawed democracies" while Pakistan (4.71) and Thailand (4.63) are classified under "hybrid regimes." Myanmar (3.83) was the only country categorized as an "authoritarian regime." It is certain that the rising popular oppression against religious and ethnic minorities have soured outsider views. The cases of Indonesia and Myanmar are salient. Once a rising Muslim democracy, Indonesia slid to 68th position from 48th in the EIU rankings of democracy with the decline of free speech and minority rights. The arrest of the incumbent Jakarta governor Ahok in 2017 for alleged blasphemy and the rise of religious identity politics caused this slide. Myanmar (ranked 120th) sank deeper into authoritarianism by losing its previous gains, which had it at 4.20 in 2016, sliding back to 3.83 in 2017. The repression of the minority Rohingya Muslim community and the refugee crisis in mid- to late 2017 caused the country to score a mere 2.06 in the category of civil liberties.

While anti-pluralistic populism as seen in the Philippines, for example, is clearly viewed negatively by democracy watchers and contributes to negative assessments of democratic performance, other aspects of populism are more difficult to judge. Redistributive populism that responds to the relatively deprived classes can be defended as making governments accountable to the poor, despite its fiscal unsustainability and ineffectiveness in reducing poverty in the longer term. Further, economically less sanguine popular policies impact democracy negatively. The authors of Chapters 5 and 6, on India and Thailand respectively, have emphasized the negative effects of redistributive populism such as clientelism and corruption, yet also recognize its positive effects such as filling the gaps resulting from uneven development or even increasing trust in government. When the key stakeholder of a power bloc replaces a populist government without a democratic electoral process, redistributive populism can result in the unintended consequence of democratic reversal. An extreme example is Thailand's breakdown. Thailand's military launched a 12th coup in May 2014 against the government of Prime Minister Yingluck Shinawatra. Martial law was lifted in 2015 and the first post-coup election took place on March 24, 2019. The political chaos of mass demonstrations followed by military intervention caused Thailand's democracy score to fall continuously from 6.81 in 2008 to 4.63 in 2017. Despite the return to democratic elections in 2019, the flaws of the electoral system which allocates 250 seats out of the total 750 to the military leaves Thailand's highly polarized politics prone to popular revolt.

Citizen-led popular movements are bottom-up vertical populism. Independent civil society organizations and grassroots urban dwellers tend to lead this kind of popular movement. As featured in the cases of South Korea and Taiwan, the two most mature democracies out of the cases this book deals with, this bottom-up populism is strongly anti-elitist, opposing unresponsive technocratic public decision making or power abuse of strong presidents. This type of voluntary people-led popular movement is usually cheered as contributing to participatory democracy. Candlelight protests are emblematic of South Korea's peaceful mass protests, and they are praised for promoting government accountability and responsiveness. Accordingly, bottom-up anti-elite populism or popular movements are likely to contribute to correcting the problem of democratic deficit. When they are guarded by liberal values, the positive impacts are greater. At the same time, both authors recognize the consequential negative impact this type of populism can have by weakening stable representative democracy and the role of technocrats.

On the other hand, exclusive populism based on ethnic or religious cleavages, whether socially driven or manipulated by the state, is harmful to democracy as it undermines minority rights, pluralist values, and the rule of law. The impact of redistributive populism on democracy is more mixed. It can contribute to the short-term reduction of poverty and increase government responsiveness to the underprivileged. When redistributive populist schemes are used excessively to win votes during election campaigns, they can distort election results and undermine the commitment of the elites to democracy.

PART 1

Progressive Populism

CHAPTER 1

South Korea's Tamed Populism: Popular Protests from Below and Populist Politics from the Top

Sook Jong Lee

1   Introduction

The rise of populism throughout the world has drawn much attention. Rightist populism in advanced economies, including many European countries and the United States in particular, has alarmed democracy researchers.[1] Roberto Stefan Foa and Yascha Mounk have coined the phrase "deconsolidation of democracy" to describe the dangerous trend of declining support for democracy in the US.[2] Many scholars have attributed the difficulties of governing to economic decline and divisive migration issues, and they argue that poor government performance in dealing with these issues has delegitimized many democracies.[3] Regardless of whether we characterize the situation as a sustained decline or merely a temporary setback, the crisis of democracy in the West at the time of writing in 2020 is not only threatening democracy at home but also contributing to a global downturn of democracy. Domestically, populist

---

1 Michael Bröning, "The Rise of Populism in Europe: Can the Center Hold?," *Foreign Affairs*, last modified June 3, 2016, http://www.foreignaffairs.com/articles/europe/2016-06-03/rise-populism-europe (accessed June 8, 2020); Matthew Goodwin, *Right Response: Understanding and countering populist extremism in Europe* (London: Chatham House, 2011), https://www.chathamhouse.org/sites/files/chathamhouse/r0911_goodwin.pdf (accessed June 8, 2020); Thomas Greven, *The Rise of Right-Wing Populism in Europe and the United States: A comparative perspective* (Berlin: Friedrich Ebert Stiftung, 2016), http://fesdc.org/fileadmin/user_upload/publications/RightwingPopulism.pdf (accessed June 9, 2020); Sook Jong Lee, "The Rise of Korean Youth as a Political Force: Implications for the US–Korea Alliance," in *Brookings Northeast Asia Survey 2003–2004*, ed. Richard C. Bush et al. (Washington, DC: Center for Northeast Asian Policy Studies, Brookings Institution, 2004), 15–30.
2 Roberto Stefan Foa and Yascha Mounk, "The Danger of Deconsolidation," *Journal of Democracy* 27, no. 3 (2016): 5–17; Roberto Stefan Foa and Yascha Mounk, "The Signs of Deconsolidation," *Journal of Democracy* 28, no. 1 (2017): 5–15.
3 Larry Diamond, "Facing up to the Democratic Recession," *Journal of Democracy* 26, no. 1 (2015): 141–155; Francis Fukuyama, "Why is Democracy Performing So Poorly?," in *Democracy in Decline?*, ed. Larry Diamond and Marc F. Plattner (Baltimore, MD: Johns Hopkins University Press, 2016), 11–24.

© SOOK JONG LEE, 2021 | DOI:10.1163/9789004444461_003

protests and the successful entry of populist parties into legislatures are undermining the political stability of European democracies. Trumpism has transformed already polarized American politics into tribalism, with members of opposite sides treating their opponents as enemies. This rightist populism is antagonistic to transnational institutions as well as to international rules and norms. As politically disrupted democracies fail to actively promote the liberal international order, authoritarian states have become emboldened in breaking international rules and expanding their influence, and Western democracies have ceased to make unified efforts to support democracy throughout the world.

However, this seemingly negative influence of populism on democracy calls for deeper debate, since populism is after all claiming that the majority of people deserve better governance. In developing countries where democracy is not yet fully institutionalized, popular movements demanding that the interests of ordinary citizens be addressed can help to promote democratization. This chapter reviews major concepts and issues in the study of populism and then applies them to the case of South Korea, where popular movements have been strong since the late 1990s. Several popular protests as well as populist politics will be examined and discussed to illustrate ways in which South Korean populism is unique and how it plays out in terms of its influence on the quality of the country's democracy.

2   Concepts and Functions of Populism

While the concept of populism has been widely applied to diverse forms of political mobilization, scholars and experts of political science have attempted to clarify the specific conditions that underlie populist movements. Ernesto Laclau deserves scholarly attention since he challenged the study of populism as "the denigration of the masses" and outlined the logics behind populism as a constructive political concept.[4] Rather than offering a concise definition of populism, he delineates three preconditions for the emergence of populism: (1) the formation of an internal antagonistic frontier separating "the people" from those in power; (2) an equivalent articulation of demands that make the emergence of "the people" possible; and (3) the integration of these various demands into a stable system of signification, provided that the first two preconditions

---

4   Preface and Part I of Ernesto Laclau, *On Populist Reason* (London: Verso, 2005).

have reached a point of political mobilization.[5] According to Laclau, social environments are developed either via the people's assertion of particularities—the "logic of difference"—or via their upholding of shared common qualities through the surrender of particularities—the "logic of equivalence." With the equivalential logic cutting across new and more heterogeneous social groups, a plurality of demands constitutes a broader social subjectivity to form "popular demands" and "the people." Such extension of the equivalential articulation allows for a wider embracement of heterogeneous social demands. However, if the popular identity shared amongst the people falls short of maintaining the chain of equivalence and its acceptance of the diverse social demands, the chain loses its significance and becomes an empty signifier.[6]

Laclau's insightful conceptualization is useful for understanding the rise and fall of populism, and especially for studying how the logic of equivalence applies to political groups domestically. South Korea poses an interesting case study where Laclau's equivalential logic only applies to the integration of social groups within a set political boundary, and not for cross-cutting occurrences between different political groups. This is due to the strong political dichotomy within South Korea along complicated and intertwined lines of left versus right ideologies, generational gaps, and regional identities. The conservative political society accredits the past authoritarian regime for bringing successful economic development, cherishes the market based social order, and is guarded by the national security concern of deterring the North Korean threat. On the other hand, the liberal and progressive elements of society denounce the authoritarian past, demand that government do more for social justice, and favor reconciliation with North Korea. Divisions within the domestic political environment are further complicated by popular "fandomism"—a new South Korean phenomenon for political commentators becoming popular, like entertainers with a large group of loyal fans—which continues to emerge around favored political leaders in each society.

One aspect of democratization in South Korea is that the elites do not care for the welfare of the common people. The country's rapid modernization was led by elite bureaucrats and business leaders, and people believed their lives had been improved by national economic success. However, economic disparities and social opportunity gaps widened over time, and now people feel, the younger generation in particular, that they are excluded from the benefits

---

5   Laclau emphasizes the unit of populism should be "demand," much smaller than the group, to become the signifier of a wider universality. For the preconditions of populism, see *On Populist Reason*, 72–83.

6   Laclau, *On Populist Reason*, 95–96.

of growth and that the establishment is not capable of changing society for a better life. As Cas Mudde states, there is anti-elitist populism based on a thin ideology dividing society between "the pure people" and "the corrupt elite."[7] At the same time, "the people" is divided in South Korea along regional lines and the "thick" national security ideology surrounding the issues of alliance with the United States and how to engage North Korea. These two forces have been represented by two major parties that are competing for power in Korean politics. While both forms of political society claim that they are the ones who represent the general will of the people in order to legitimize their group's demands in governing the country, popular political discourse often favors antagonistic sentiments against the rich and the established. As such, populist politics—as a "permanent shadow of modern representative democracy"—occurs when ruling elites and the legislature have failed to represent the will of the majority.[8] Since populism is based on the principle of popular sovereignty, which is an integral element of democracy, populism cannot be deemed undemocratic or anti-democratic.

There is a strong influence of morality discourse in legitimizing popular protests in South Korea under the vertical divide between the "moral" people and the "immoral" elites or the system. Accompanying the country's democratization, popular protests have been frequent in South Korea since the late 1990s, aiming to restore the people's rights over those of the arrogant government or the corrupt system. They have also evolved over the years to take on peaceful forms, which can continue for longer durations, even several months. The South Korean model of "candlelight movements" is representative of such peaceful popular protest. These bottom-up social movements addressing public issues have been essentially inclusive due to South Korea's ethnically homogeneous nature. Therefore, rightist populist attacks against migrants and ethnic minorities do not occur in South Korea, despite a gradual increase in the number of multicultural families. On the other hand, populist movements are more likely to be inspired by nationalistic and patriotic sentiments, as when the South Korean public feels that their national pride has been damaged by the Japanese, Chinese, or the US government. These positive aspects

---

7   Cas Mudde, "Populism: An Ideational Approach," in *The Oxford Handbook of Populism*, ed. Cristóbal Rovira Kaltwasser et al. (Oxford, UK: Oxford University Press, 2017), 27–47; Cas Mudde, "The Populist Zeitgeist," *Government and Opposition* 39, no. 4 (2004): 543. See also Cas Mudde and Cristóbal Rovira Kaltwasser, *Populism in Europe and the Americas: Threat or corrective for democracy?* (Cambridge, UK: Cambridge University Press, 2012).

8   Jan-Werner Müller, *What Is Populism?* (Philadelphia: University of Pennsylvania Press, 2016), 11.

of popular movements in South Korea contribute to the weakening of political parties and politicization of public institutions.

From the perspective of democracy, populism is a double-edged sword. As Mudde and Cristóbal Roviar Kaltwasser maintain,[9] populism can be a corrective or a threat to the quality of democracy. Populism's positive effects include its ability to bring about participation through the inclusion of marginalized groups by giving them a voice and a way to mobilize; its provision of an ideological bridge that supports the building of important social and political coalitions, often across class lines; and its increasing of democratic accountability. On the other hand, populism can become a threat to the quality of democracy by contravening the checks and balances of power and separation of powers, limiting minority rights, making compromise and consensus difficult, undermining the legitimacy and power of institutions and governing bodies, and, ultimately, ironically contracting the effective democratic space. The way in which populism affects democracy, then, depends on the context. Mudde and Kaltwasser examine this context by establishing two criteria, whether populists are in opposition or in power, and whether the democratic regime is consolidated or unconsolidated.[10] They argue that populism within the opposition has only a minor impact on the quality of democracy since it has little room to maneuver, and it has the positive effect of giving a voice to groups with less representation. On the other hand, populism within the government brings about more negative effects. This threat is more serious for unconsolidated democracies, where checks and balances are not strongly institutionalized, compared with consolidated democracies where the embedded separation of powers can check populist forces.

This chapter examines South Korean populism and its influence on the quality of democracy. It argues that oppositional popular movements from below have strongly influenced democratic politics by serving the public interest in political reform. When government relies on populist demands for its legitimacy, however, it can harm democratic institutions and weaken governability in the end. Although South Korea is one of the few consolidated democracies in Asia, the separation of powers and horizontal accountability among the executive branch, the legislature, and the judiciary are not yet fully institutionalized. Nevertheless, South Korea's polarized political society places every government under social scrutiny and thereby prevents populism at the top from developing into authoritarian rule. This unique nature of South

---

9   Mudde and Kaltwasser, *Populism in Europe and the Americas*, 18–22.

10   Mudde and Kaltwasser, *Populism in Europe and the Americas*, 18–22.

Korea's politics allows its populism to remain "tamed," leaving no chance for populists to undermine democracy there.

3   The Case of South Korea

South Korean politics do not necessarily merit the label of populism per se if one employs a populist model based solely on the experiences of European or Latin American societies. There have been neither clear economic divides nor ethnic or other cultural divides that have led to explosive popular protests or movements. "Populism" has a negative connotation in South Korea and is usually applied to irresponsible public policies that waste taxpayer money. Politicians often attack one another by charging that their position is populist. Although the government and political parties in South Korea certainly engage in populist redistributive politics, the degree has not generally been considered to be excessive.[11] What is distinctive about South Korea is its vertical structure of political populism from both below and above. For the operational definition of populism in the Korean context, I will define populism as politics expressing the popular will of the people based on anti-establishment feelings and distrust of public institutions. South Korean populist politics can be led by people mobilized from below and they can also be maneuvered by the powerful. Since populism is used in this chapter as a neutral term, its impact on the quality of Korean democracy differs depending on the situation.

South Korean populism from below is usually oppositional rather than supportive of the government. Past occasions when people were mobilized to retrieve power have led to the reversal of government decisions and even the impeachment of a president. Unlike the hypothesis of Mudde and Kaltwasser, populism within the opposition has been influential in changing politics in South Korea. The country's development has been guided by a meritocratic elite bureaucracy, but a plebiscitary transformation has been underway with democratization since the late 1990s. This change is related to the active organization of civil society after the democratic transition from authoritarian rule in 1987. The influence of civil society organizations grew through the 1990s and the 2000s in forming a reform agenda in society and in mobilizing people to participate in street protests. With increasing technological development

---

11   With COVID-19, government spending to protect people out of work and to offer a basic income, excessive redistributive spending emerged as a hot potato from the spring of 2020.

individual political participation is even bypassing intermediary civil society organizations. South Korea's highly digitalized social environment has given its vocal citizens the power to mobilize public opinion. These days, Political leaders must cultivate a direct link with the people to claim legitimacy and maintain a favorable public reputation.

Candlelight protests have emerged as a way to represent popular movements from below, where people from all walks of life are voluntarily mobilized to express the will of the majority. While civil society organizations often play a core role in initiating and sustaining such protests, the success of such protests depends on the mass participation of ordinary citizens. Public anger and moral indignation are powerful drivers that mobilize people onto the streets. On the other hand, politicians can use populist tactics to strengthen their power over their opponents. This type of populism, which emanates from the top, aims to rationalize government decisions by claiming that the public supports them. The chapter refers to popular protestor movements as "popular protests from below" if they are sustained over a relatively long span of time, in order to distinguish them from "populist politics from the top." If popular protests or movements reject ties with political parties or any appearance of partisanship in order to claim their genuine upholding of civic virtue and care for the public interest, the form of populist politics practiced by those in power remains partisan essentially. The latter type of populist politics is more toxic to Korean democracy than purely voluntary oppositional popular protests from below and has not helped citizen protest movements translate into institution building for good governance. The following section discusses these different modes of popular movements and populist politics.

4   Popular Protests from Below

Like many other democracies, Korean society is plagued by rising inequality. People are anxious and extremely sensitive to the perceived lack of social mobility. They also view their society as ridden with high levels of social conflict, between the rich and poor, employers and employees, conservatives and progressives, older and younger generations, men and women, and so on. There are growing populist attitudes among South Koreans as they lose patience with their political system and become increasingly prone to take to the streets to protest. David Beetham argues there are three dimensions necessary to deem power as legitimate: conformity to rules that have legal validity, the presence of justifiable rules in terms of shared beliefs, and legitimation through expressed consent.[12] Rules are upheld not just for their impartial application but also for their end result in improving welfare and embodying social justice. In Korean society, the justifiability of rules is often challenged since many people believe that the rich and powerful can bend them as they please. This sense of injustice creates an undercurrent of resentment against the hereditarily privileged class such as *chaebol* families. *Chaebols* are conglomerates controlled by a founding family and passed from one generation to another. These economically powerful conglomerates have repeatedly colluded with government and political leaders who have the regulatory power to influence their businesses. The repeated bribe scandals from chaebol to politicians give a popular image of an unjust society where the rich can accumulate wealth immorally.

Political parties in Korea have not effectively coalesced around these negative social undercurrents and so have developed responsive but sustainable policies. Michael Bröning points out that from about 2010 mainstream liberal and conservative parties in Europe alienated traditional supporters as they moved closer to the ideological center, which made their disenchanted supporters easy targets for populists.[13] On the contrary, Korean political parties have been moving further toward ideological extremes rather than the center, resulting in a paralyzed legislature and the subsequent rise of public mistrust. Moreover, the voting system wherein the majority of legislative members are elected from a simple plurality has made the two major political parties, who easily win elections due to electoral rules, less attentive to public discontent. Dismissing their legislature as incompetent, people tend to run to the executive government directly to fix social problems. The legacy of the developmental state also makes South Koreans think that the executive side of the government is responsible for and able to resolve most public issues. Therefore, popular demands are usually made directly to the president and his or her administration rather than to representatives in the National Assembly. Both at the central and the local level, major protests are usually undertaken with the aim of influencing government decisions.

Korean civil society has been very active in expressing the public will. Domestically, civic activism is praised as a healthy sign of participatory democracy.[14]

---

12 David Beetham, *The Legitimation of Power,* 2nd ed. (Basingstoke and New York: Palgrave Macmillan, 2013).

13 Bröning, "The Rise of Populism in Europe."

14 Measuring participatory democracy can be controversial. The Varieties of Democracy Index ranked the participatory component of South Korea in 2016 lower than the other four components: electoral, liberal, deliberative, and egalitarian. This is because the criteria index uses direct populace votes (such as referendums and plebiscites) and the independence of local and regional government together with civil society participation: see

People can use institutionalized channels created by public authorities to insert their opinions into the policy-making process, and they can also employ the alternative measure of going out into the streets to make demands or just show their opposition to current policies. The latter method of "expressive politics" has been increasingly used. Downtown street demonstrations and the resulting traffic jams have become ordinary weekend events on the streets near Seoul City Hall, Gwanghwamun Plaza, and Seoul Station. According to one newspaper, downtown Seoul is a "heaven for demonstrations" with 30 rallies every day. Police reported that there were 37,478 demonstrations between January and July 2018, an increase of 58 percent compared with the previous year.[15] Progressive governments, including the Moon Jae-in administration since May 2017, have taken a more liberal stance toward public demonstrations than conservatives. Some of these street protests have been peaceful while others have been violent, leading to physical clashes with police.

Several largescale candlelight protests deserve particular attention for our understanding of South Korean populism. Candlelight protests are distinguished from conventional demonstrations put on by labor unions, farmer associations, and other interest groups, although in theory these groups can employ the use of candles in their protests as well. Unbounded by special interest groups, candlelight protests are usually indicative of popular protests driven by public interest causes. While they draw the same thousands of people to the streets, some are more populist while others are more reflective. Three candlelight protests are examined here to explore the different political contexts. Each of them has had a significant impact on South Korea's governance. If people in the first two cases were disapproving of specific government policies, people in the last candlelight protest movement discussed here rejected the existing system itself as unjust.

4.1   *The SOFA Revision Candlelight Protests*

Following the outbreak of the Korean War in 1950 and subsequent influx of American soldiers, the Korean government signed a new wartime Status of Forces Agreement (SOFA) that recognized the exclusive jurisdiction of the US

Frida Anderson and Valeriya Mechkova, *Country Report South Korea* (Gothenburg: The Varieties of Democracy Institute of University of Gothenburg, 2016) to evaluate participation. If expressive activities on the streets and in cyberspace were used, however, South Korea's democracy would be assessed to have a strong participatory component.

15   Eun Jeung Kim, "The Entire Nation In Protest ... Counterattack of the Masses, or the Era of Mob Rule?," *Chosun Ilbo*, August 18, 2018. http://news.chosun.com/site/data/html_dir/2018/08/17/2018081701710.html (accessed June 25, 2019).

Military Tribunal over crimes committed by US troops on Korean soil. This SOFA was modified through a series of revisions in 1967, 1991, and 2001 in order to put South Korea and the US on a more equal footing. While South Korea had jurisdiction over most crimes committed by American soldiers while off duty, crimes committed while on duty were handed over to the US military for adjudication.

On June 13, 2002, two schoolgirls were killed by a US armored mine-clearing vehicle driven by American soldiers on duty. After separate trials of the driver and commander of the armored vehicle, the soldiers were found not guilty of charges of negligent homicide. Following these rulings, on November 20 and 23 mass rallies protesting their acquittals began immediately and lasted into the early months of 2003. The candlelight protests started with anger over the perceived injustice and evolved into a popular demand to revise SOFA to be more equal. These six-month candlelight protests can be considered the first case of the South Korean model of popular protest.[16] Many believe that the previous months of massive street cheering for the Korean national team that reached the semi-finals in the 2002 World Cup games created a sort of collective mentality. The protests intertwined with the presidential election campaign as people demanded the US concede jurisdiction of on-duty crimes to South Korean authorities.

This round of candlelight protests was quelled in December 2002 after American President George W. Bush apologized directly and negotiated a shortening of the timeline to release charged American GIs to the Korean authorities. Concerned with rising anti-American sentiment in South Korea, the US Ambassador to South Korea, Thomas Hubbard, and the State Department Deputy Secretary, Richard Armitage had apologized before President Bush made a telephone call to Korean President Kim Dae-jung. The "powerful" US government's protection of American soldiers against the young victims of a "weaker" South Korea led to a public perception that South Korea's national sovereignty had been encroached upon. This case can be characterized as populism mixed with nationalism where the outsider was a powerful foreign country. The bottom-up popular movement was between the Korean people and the US government, while the Korean government was in the difficult position of having to manage its relations with both. The anti-American protests of 2002 took the US government by surprise, and they spurred the US Forces in Korea (USFK) to emphasize outreach efforts to local communities near its military bases.

---

16   Sook Jong Lee, "The Rise of Korean Youth," 15–30.

4.2 The Mad Cow Disease Candlelight Protests

The so-called mad cow disease candlelight protests bear more populist features than the SOFA protests described above.[17] On April 18, 2008, the Lee Myung-bak government struck a deal with the US to lower the inspection criteria for imported American beef. It was agreed that nearly all parts of American beef from cows aged less than 30 months would be imported without inspections, while the import of specified risky portions of beef from cows aged 30 months and over would be inspected. Students, mothers with young babies, consumers, and people from all walks of life took to the streets to voice their opposition to this decision. Candlelight protests continued for more than two months, and subdued only after the government renegotiated the beef import deal with the American government. The presidential aids in the Blue House were reshuffled after taking the blame for the unpopular policy. The media report broadcast by MBC on the program *PD Diary*, which discussed the potential dangers of American cows with this disease, contributed to ignite public fear. Rumors and unscientific claims went viral. Public officials and some doctors tried to assuage the baseless fears of the public, but were no match for those who believed the fake news.

Angry protestors attacked the Lee administration for compromising public health in order to speed up a free trade deal with the US. Conservative commentators maintained that the whole event was manipulated by leftists who could not accept the win of conservative President Lee in the previous year's election. Protestors clashed with police when they tried to march toward the Blue House. This time, the candlelight protests that had started peacefully turned into violent riots and left a controversy over who was more responsible for the ugly confrontations. Subsequently, in 2011, the Supreme Court ruled that MBC had to make an apology for airing fake news, but the producers who made the program were firmly opposed to the broadcasting company making any sort of apology.

This case is structured between the potential consumer victims and the elite technocrats inside the government. It was a clash between the masses and elites where an import policy transformed into a public health issue. The whole episode remains populistic and played out in terms of domestic politics.

4.3 The Choi Soon-Sil Gate and Park Impeachment Candlelight Protests

The so-called Choi Soon-sil Gate was unique among South Korean government corruption cases. Its impact was huge, leading to the unprecedented

---

17   Bovine Spongiform Encephalopathy (BSE).

impeachment of incumbent President Park Geun-hye. The candlelight protests lasted from October 2016 to March 2017, drawing large number of people onto the streets. The protests were able to avoid descending into violence despite their massive scale and long duration. The story began in late in July 2016 when *TV Chosun* reported suspicious Blue House involvement in the raising of funds to establish the Mir and K Sports Foundations. *The Hankyoreh* newspaper revealed Choi Soon-sil as President Park's close confidante and exposed her involvement in the fundraising process for these two foundations. The report quickly drew public attention to this previously unknown woman, attention which exploded as media outlets competed to bring to light stories about the relationship between Choi and President Park. Whether the stories were true or not, a significant number of people who used to support Park began to turn their backs on her. How could Choi, a private citizen, intervene in government affairs using her close ties with the aloof President? The very idea was enough to anger the public. When it was exposed that Choi had used her money to gain admission for her daughter to a prestigious university, Choi became the embodiment of the corrupt rich in the public eye. Cable TV outlet JTBC reported on October 24 that they had discovered Choi's tablet PC, which became the smoking gun of her involvement in the fundraising scandal. This prompted people to hold candles on streets in an expression of their anger over the injustice. The first protest on October 29 drew several thousand people, and later protests grew to a crowd of more than a million. One estimate stated that about 16 million people participated in the total of 20 candlelight protests. The protests soon developed into a movement calling for Park's impeachment. Faced with this popular pressure, the legislature voted to impeach on December 9, 2016, a parliamentary decision that was upheld by the Constitutional Court on March 10, 2017. Progressive civil society organizations and labor unions provided leadership, but spontaneous grassroots participation was the key to sustaining the peaceful popular protests.

The candlelight protests of 2016 started with public outcry over the illegitimate involvement of Choi in public affairs and evolved into the impeachment movement. Naturally, opposition party leaders, including now President Moon and other progressive leaders, participated in the rallies. However, the candlelight movement remained a festive expression of civil society activism without being tied to any particular political party. This time, the candlelight protests defied the negative characteristics of populism in the following ways. First, people were aware of the limited role of mass rallies as a channel to show the public will, and retained the belief that official decisions should be made by both the legislature and the courts, which are pivotal democratic institutions. Simply put, popular passion was tamed by respect for constitutional order. People restrained their behavior to keep the protests peaceful. Second, personal attacks and moralistic accusations were integrated into constructive discourses about how to restore justice and reform the nation. In this way, people felt connected as members of the republic. The massive rallies unified rather than divided civil society, although a small number of Park loyalists revolted against the majority and still do so even today. Third, the impeachment protests left a positive impact, especially upon younger Koreans. Today's Korean youth in their 20s and early 30s suffer from underemployment and unemployment and are not well represented in the world of politics. The successful candlelight impeachment movement enhanced their feelings of political efficacy and invited ongoing minority activism, with the #MeToo movement as one such example.

Outsider assessments did not always agree with this characterization. For example, Max Fisher, a reporter with the *New York Times*, compared the Korean impeachment movement with the French populist movement, pointing out that the Korean movement embraced institutions and sought to bridge social divides.[18] On the other hand, Nilsson-Wright characterized the late 2016 impeachment movement as populist, writing that Park Geun-hye "has been denied natural justice and the presumption of innocence until proven guilty."[19] This was written when the team headed by Special Prosecutor Park Young-soo had started a three-month investigation into the Park and Choi scandal. Nilsson-Wright argued that this movement reflected the long shadow of identity politics and unresolved disagreements about the achievements of Park Geun-hye's father, the late President Park Chung-hee, and the country's other postwar historical narrative. This assessment holds some truth since the anti-impeachment rallies, dubbed "*Taekeukki* (national flag)" rallies, were largely filled with older people who took pride in the country's successful modernization under Park Chung-hee. At the same time, one should note that this social divide did not accompany the typical populist tendency of each group labelling the other as illegitimate. Rather, both groups called themselves patriotic nationalists and the essence of their social divide was whether the existing system should be honored or needed radical transformation.

---

18 Max Fisher, "When a Political Movement is Populist, or Isn't," *New York Times,* May 10, 2017.

19 John Nilsson-Wright, "Populism Comes to South Korea," Chatham House, December 20, 2016, https://www.chathamhouse.org/expert/comment/populism-comes-south-korea (accessed June 25, 2019).

5 Populist Politics from the Top

5.1 The Politics of Eradicating "accumulated evils"

The Moon Jae-in administration was established in May 2017 after presidential elections were held seven months early following the impeachment of former President Park. After winning the election as an extension of the reform-driven candlelight movement, the Moon administration launched a political drive to eradicate the wrongdoings of previous governments. Dubbing them "accumulated evils," public investigations were initiated in a number of cases involving former high-ranking public officials. A series of prosecutorial investigations have been widely criticized by conservative media as political reprisals, while progressive outlets have praised them as long overdue. Following her impeachment, Park was imprisoned on March 31, 2017, and sentenced to 25 years in prison and a fine of 20 billion KRW (approximately 18 million US$) by the higher court on August 24, 2018. The majority of the public did not view the ruling as unfair, although legal controversy has remained over the bribery of a third party, namely Choi, by conglomerates under Park's influence. The drive to "root out accumulated evils" also reopened the bribery case of another former president. On September 6, 2017, the court sentenced former President Lee Myungbak to 20 years in prison and a fine of 15 billion KRW (approximately 14 million US$) for taking bribes, taking money from a company he had denied ownership of, and other similar crimes. He was imprisoned for about a year and released with conditions in March 2019. But he was jailed once more in February 2020 and as of June 2020 is waiting to hear the decision of the Supreme Court. The unfortunate imprisonments did not stop with these two presidents. Former public officials who had been involved in several controversial policies were also investigated and charged. Some deserved this, but others did not.

From the fall of 2018, the drive to eradicate "accumulated evils" went to the judicial body. An investigation of former Supreme Court judges and the top officials of the Office of Court Administration was initiated. It was alleged that judges who belonged to the court administration under former Supreme Court Chief Justice Yang Seung-tae had discussed trials with government officials working under President Park Geun-hye and had conveyed their opinions to trial judges. After warrants for the arrests of the judges involved were dismissed several times, two Supreme Court judges were jailed. The judiciary was divided. For the first time in the history of the South Korean constitution, judges representing courts across the nation announced on November 21 that impeachment needed to be considered for judges alleged to have abused their authority during the tenure of former President Park Geun-hye. The prosecutor's office started investigating Chief Justice Yang on January 11, 2019, indicting him a week later. It was the first time in Korean history that a Supreme Court Chief Justice was charged and indicted. He was imprisoned for 179 days and trials are ongoing as of April 2020. The whole episode undermined the authority of courts that used to have more trust than legislature and government. Prosecutors were often criticized for being tied to Blue House in the past. But this was the first time that the courts were charged with illicit political dealings.

The Moon administration has pushed for judicial reform since it seized power. The reform centers on breaking the monopolistic indictment rights of the powerful prosecutor's office. The "political" prosecutors are regarded as "accumulated evils" that either condone the corruption of top government officials and politicians, or target them unfairly to benefit their political desires. Following the walkout of the opposition party, the ruling party and its coalition passed a law on December 31, 2019 to establish an agency for investigating high-ranking public officials. The agency has the capacity to investigate around 7,000 public officials including the president, and nearly 5,000 judges and prosecutors. This law has been a subject of controversial debate, with both public support and concerns. On the one hand, people hope the agency will bring "political" prosecutors to justice and enable quick investigations on potential criminal activities by top government officials, even the president. On the other hand, people are also concerned that the judiciary branch may fall victim to government influence since the agency is still considered to be an administrative body.

Law Minister Cho Kuk, who served President Moon as the Senior Secretary for Civil Affairs, pushed the law forward. But Cho, once deemed a man of justice, was soon criticized as a hypocrite due to a scandal that erupted surrounding his family's suspicious financial transactions and his daughter's forged educational credentials. This scandal has been under investigation since August 2020 by Attorney General Yoon Seok-ryul, who was handpicked by President Moon for his impartial dealings of former president Park Geun-hye's bribery cases. After Minister Cho's scandal was publicized by the media, domestic politics in South Korea divided into two different camps—one defending Minister Cho, and the other in support of Attorney General Yoon's investigations into his case. Beginning with campus protests by university students criticizing Minister Cho in August 2019, the conservative political force organized massive street protests against the Moon government. Even after Minister Cho stepped down from his position in early September amid mounting criticisms, rallies criticizing the Moon government continued. To counter these rallies, the progressive force began organizing its own rallies from early October to support Minister Cho and President Moon. The Cho Kuk scandal has sharply divided the South Korean political environment with the two political camps pointing fingers at each other for being the "accumulated evils."

Corruption needs to be rooted out. But demonizing former public officials and weakening the authority of the Supreme Court is neither a fair nor reasonable method. Outsiders have also observed that the vilification and demonization of political opponents under the "accumulated evils" reform wave is harming functional democracy.[20] If accumulated evils are to be effectively rooted out, the country needs to embark on institutional reforms rather than simply focusing on persecuting former officials. Korean politics is riddled with this negative cycle of populist correction driven by new power which is followed by the same populist revenge after the loss of power. The correction drive is usually pushed during the first two years of a new presidency, losing momentum as presidential power declines under the single-term presidency system. People cheer the initial correction drive but lose interest in favor of more pragmatic economic matters. The worst form of political correction is for a new government to interfere in ideologically divisive issues such as the official interpretation of modern history. When the governing system is repeatedly subject to corrective measures after power is handed over to a new administration, this discredits institutions. If the correction drive attempted by both progressive and conservative governments has been viewed as a way of gaining political advantage, it will only serve to intensify the divisions in Korean political society. A system prone to power abuse and corruption can be fixed only through bipartisan consensus for more transparent and accountable institutional reform.

6   Conclusion

In this chapter, I argue that it is difficult to categorize South Korean politics as the type of populism typically found in Latin America or Europe. There have been no signs of charismatic populist leaders or parties. There is no such conspicuous horizontal populism wherein the majority rules over the minority within society. Radical rightists and leftists alike treat each other as enemies and achieving political compromise between them is nearly impossible. Nevertheless, this chasm does not form a horizontal structure of populism since both groups are part of mainstream society. On the other hand, South Korea shares the essential element of anti-elite populism where the decisions of the plebiscite have more legitimacy than decisions made by the elite, and political

---

20   Bernard Rowan "Of Accumulated Evils and Foolishness," *The Korea Times,* January 16, 2018, https://www.koreatimes.co.kr/www/opinion/2018/01/625_242467.html (accessed June 20, 2019).

discourse is centered on moral debates of right and wrong. Major public decisions need to be legitimized by popular support, which causes political leaders to seek more direct ties and emotional rapport with their supporters. Korean populism is primarily vertical, flowing in both directions between the government and the people.

South Korea's vertical populism has been enacted by ordinary people who opposed incumbent presidents and administrations for failing to adequately respond to issues of social justice or national sovereignty. Korean society shows the symptoms of public anxiety and discontent that result largely from economic difficulties and rising inequality. But these economic factors remain in the background and are insufficient to mobilize the masses on their own. Most of the issues that have sparked protests have been primarily political, ranging from a corruption scandal to seemingly illegitimate policy decisions, as shown in the several cases illustrated in this chapter. This oppositional form of popular protest from below has had a greater impact than the oppositional protests of other countries. Government policies have changed and a president was impeached. Some of these popular protests resembled fear-driven irrational populism, but most cases addressed problems of democratic deficit. Therefore, one can argue that the popular protests of South Korea have served the positive function of correcting flaws in Korean democracy. At the same time, incumbent power can mobilize public support to carry out a political campaign, which is populism from the top. Those in power have continually exploited the popularity of persecuting corrupt politicians and officials, often compromising due process and levying judgments via the court of public opinion. With this pattern repeated after each administration change, populist correction drives have discredited public institutions and so undermined the ability of any administration to govern effectively. This type of populist politics from ruling power is a threat to effective democracy based on collaborative governance. Nevertheless, the intense competition for power embodied in bids to win elections serves as an antidote against the emergence of the authoritarian type of populism that is a real threat to democracy. With these features, the vertical populism of South Korea can be characterized as "tamed populism," with more positive than negative results.

CHAPTER 2

Populism in Taiwan: A Bottom-Up Model

Chin-en Wu and Yun-han Chu

1 Introduction

During President Ma's terms of office between 2008 and 2016, a series of social protests took place in Taiwan. These movements disapproved of the way the Kuomintang (KMT, often referred to as the Nationalist Party) was handling cross-strait relations, economic development, social justice, and environmental management. It is widely conceived among civil society organizations that the KMT, domestic big business, and multinational companies constitute a power bloc that rigs the economy and weakens Taiwan's democracy. The direct political results of these anti-establishment social movements were the creation of the White Force (WF) and the New Power Party (NPP). The leaders of both forces are political novices and opinion leaders of the social movements. These two political forces tend to assert a Manichean dualism between the corrupt elite and the pure masses.

Taiwan's populism movement features a bottom-up model in which autonomous civil society organizations cooperate to voice their opposition to the ruling elite. Over time it has given rise to new political forces. In addition, the movement helps push forward several political reforms to level the playing field of political competition and increase civil participation in public policies. However, some observers consider that it is interfering with the function of representative democracy and technocratic governance. How this bottom-up model of populism affects the function of democracy is our main research question in this chapter. Another unique feature of Taiwan's populism is that in large part it stems from the fear of a close economic relationship between Taiwan and China and from concern about the authoritarian legacy of KMT rule, such as its party assets. Protecting and strengthening democracy appear to be important goals for the movement. We will ask how the nature of the movement affects the functioning of democracy.

In what follows, we first identify who the populists in Taiwan are. We then discuss their issues and agendas, the demographics and socioeconomic backgrounds of the populists, including their leaders, and how these new parties fared in elections. Finally, we examine the positive and negative impacts of the populist movement on the functioning of democracy. In terms of research

© CHIN-EN WU AND YUN-HAN CHU, 2021 | DOI:10.1163/9789004444461_004

approaches, in addition to a detailed account of the movement, we will employ two surveys, the 2015 Democratic Governance survey conducted by the Taiwan Foundation for Democracy and the Fourth Wave Asian Barometer survey (hereafter ABS) conducted in 2015 to help us to understand people's attitudes toward the movement. The first survey examines who is more likely to support the populist movement. The second examines how democratic values affect people's image of China and how this factor plays an important role in affecting popular views of the populist movement.

2   Definition of Populism

Following Mudde, Mudde and Kaltwasser, Woods, and many others, we define populism as political movements that clearly make the distinction between a pure people and a corrupt elite and that claim to represent the interests of the ordinary people.[1] Moreover, because populism condemns the corruption and ineffectiveness of representative systems, the populist leaders emphasize the importance of a direct interaction between leaders and the people. Thus, populists endorse many forms of direct democracy.[2] Yet it is important to consider who organizes the populist movements in Taiwan.[3] The top-down model is often mentioned, in which politicians mobilize people to help them win an election.[4] Less frequently mentioned is the bottom-up model in which autonomous civil society organizations cooperate to form a populist movement which may, after a period of time, generate populist politicians. As a bottom-up example, Taiwan differs from the top-down model. The two models are likely to have different implications for democratic development. We will explore this aspect throughout this article.

---

1   Cas Mudde, "The Populist Zeitgeist," *Government and Opposition* 39, no. 4 (2004): 541–563; Cas Mudde and Cristóbal Rovira Kaltwasser, "Populism," in *The Oxford Handbook of Political Ideologies*, ed. Michael Freeden, Lyman Tower Sargent, and Marc Stears (Oxford, UK: Oxford University Press, 2013), 493–512; Dwayne Woods. "The Many Faces of Populism: Diverse but Not Disparate," in *The Many Faces of Populism: Current perspectives* (Bingley: Emerald Group Publishing Limited, 2014), 1–25.

2   Mudde and Kaltwasser, "Populism."

3   Paris Aslanidis, "Populism and Social Movements," in *The Oxford Handbook of Populism*, ed. Cristóbal Rovira Kaltwasser, Paul A. Taggart, Paulina Ochoa Espejo, and Pierre Ostiguy (Oxford, UK: Oxford University Press, 2017), 306–325.

4   For example, the cases discussed in Steven Levitsky and Kenneth M. Roberts, eds., *The Resurgence of the Latin American Left* (Baltimore, MD: Johns Hopkins University Press, 2011).

3 Populists and Their Demands

3.1 *Who Are the Populists?*

During President Ma's terms in office, a series of social protests took place in Taiwan.[5] Civil society organizations (csos) disapproved of the ruling KMT elites and their policies. These social movements railed against the coalition of the KMT, big business, and the importance of economic development. The KMT government denoted an old regime that is politically, socially, and economically conservative. csos and the young generation tend to embrace progressive values and perceive the KMT's policies as putting too much emphasis on economic growth and paying too little attention to distributive justice and environmental protection. Besides, they disapprove of the KMT's authoritarian legacy, such as huge party assets and its close relationship with local factions. In addition, csos demand open government and greater civic participation in the government decision-making processes. Moreover, they are uneasy with the close economic relationship between Taiwan and China and official interactions between the two sides. It is perceived that the KMT's economic policies rely too heavily on the Chinese market. It is also widely conceived in civil society that the KMT and big business groups, which invest heavily in China, form a coalition that rigs the economy and even tries to weaken Taiwan's vibrant democracy. The csos care about freedom and democracy and have a low level of trust in the KMT government, meaning they worry about the political implications of Taiwan's economy increasingly relying on the Chinese market. A typical observation is that the big conglomerates monopolize local and cross-strait business, depriving ordinary people and the young generation of economic opportunities.[6]

Taiwan is now a high-income economy. In the wake of globalization, manufacturing companies have moved to developing countries with abundant sources of labor, cheap land, and poor environmental regulations. Given this situation, some politicians have begun to blame China for causing their economic problems. Along with rising globalization and advances in production automation, income inequality and unemployment rates in Taiwan have increased. The income ratio of the 5th to 95th percentile was 1:33 in 1998, but

---

5   These protests were all launched by civil society groups. In some cases, the main opposition party – the Democratic Progress Party (DPP) – also took part, but DPP did not orchestrate these protests.

6   Another example is that many people think that the country's fourth nuclear power plant is the product of old KMT authoritarian rule. Stopping the nuclear plant equals eliminating the KMT's rule and advancing democracy.

rose to an alarming 1:99 in 2014.[7] Compared with other major industrialized countries, Taiwan's tax rates are relatively low, making it difficult to correct the unequal distribution of wealth and opportunity.

Moreover, Taiwan's young generation faces a shrinking economic outlook. Expanding college enrollment rates and shrinking job opportunities have created bleak employment prospects for young people. At the same time, many of the high-level, white-collar jobs are already occupied by older people. Although the youth unemployment rate in Taiwan is still lower than in other parts of the world, it remains much higher than the adult unemployment rate. The youth unemployment rate (defined as aged 18 to 24 years) in Taiwan hit 13 percent in 2014, 2.8 times higher than the rest of the population.[8] In addition to rising youth unemployment, the young generation also faces the problem of underemployment. Many young adults are forced into accepting jobs below their level of education with little chance of upward mobility. This situation has intensified the youth's discontent with the existing political and economic regimes.

All these economic factors provide fertile ground for the anti-establishment movement. The 2015 Democratic Governance Survey, conducted by the Taiwan Foundation for Democracy, found that 15.8 percent of people who do not endorse the Sunflower Movement are satisfied with the way the government deals with income inequality, while only 3.2 percent of people who endorse the movement are satisfied. Moreover, 66.5 percent of people who do not endorse the Sunflower Movement believe that the central government is corrupt, while 86 percent of its supporters think so.[9] As we can see, even those who do not endorse the movement tend to be dissatisfied with the state of income distribution and corruption. There were strong feelings of discontent in society during that period. It is likely that even those who did not approve of the protests also want to see some change. Many people perceive that the representative institutions controlled by the main political parties, especially the KMT, fail to respond to the needs and discontent of the public.

The Blue–Green divide has been the main theme of Taiwan's political development since 2000. Both camps fiercely compete for control of the state apparatus so that they can decide on the pace and direction of the cross-strait

---

7 Directorate General of Budget, Accounting and Statistics, *Statistical Yearbook* (Taipei: Executive Yuan, 2015).

8 Directorate General of Budget, Accounting and Statistics, *Statistical Yearbook*.

9 Chen-hua Yu, *Evaluation of Democratic Governance in Taiwan Survey Report* (Taiwan: Taiwan Foundation for Democracy, 2015), http://www.tfd.org.tw/opencms/english/ (accessed June 20, 2020).

economic and political relationship. After 2008, President Ma's administration sought a closer economic relationship with China. His government sequentially introduced direct air, sea, and postal links with mainland China, opened the door to mainland Chinese tourists, lifted the ban on inbound investment by mainland Chinese firms, and loosened the 40 percent cap on mainland-bound investment by listed companies. The opposition is anxious that cross-strait economic integration may eventually aggravate Taiwan's economic vulnerability, facilitate Beijing's political infiltration into Taiwanese society, and lead to the erosion of Taiwan's autonomy. On the political side, President Ma embraced the "One China, Two Interpretations" policy, or the so-called 1992 Consensus. The Pan-Green camp believes the one-China policy constrains Taiwan's international space and hurts Taiwan's sovereignty.

Using the Fourth Wave Asian Barometer survey of 2015, we found that people of different party identifications have starkly different opinions about the negative influence of China on the region and on Taiwan.[10] Figure 2.1 shows that the Pan-Blue identifiers hold a more favorable view of China's impact, while the Pan-Green identifiers tend to hold an unfavorable view. Some 26 percent of Pan-Blue leaners say the influence of China on the region is negative, while 64 percent of Pan-Green leaners say so. Some 33 percent of Pan-Blue leaners say the influence of China on Taiwan is negative, while 72 percent of Pan-Green leaners think this is the case.

Liberal democratic values also play an important role in shaping Taiwanese attitudes toward China and the KMT's political economic policies. A standard battery of questions on liberal values in the 2015 ABS demonstrated that Taiwanese tend to hold more liberal-leaning views than the rest of the East Asian region. This situation is particularly pronounced among young people.[11] It is interesting to compare the attitude of liberal value holders and non-liberal value holders toward China. Liberal value holders are less likely than non-liberals to have a positive image of China. ABS data shows that 56.7 percent of liberal respondents perceive that China has a negative influence on Taiwan, while only

---

10   Asian Barometer Survey Fourth Wave, 2015, http://www.asianbarometer.org/ (accessed June 10, 2020).

11   A great majority of Taiwanese respondents disagreed with the following statements: the government should consult the religious authorities when interpreting the laws; if we have political leaders who are morally upright, we can let them decide everything; government leaders are like the head of a family and we should all follow their decisions; if the government is constantly monitored and supervised by the legislature, it cannot possibly accomplish great things; the harmony of the community will be disrupted if people organize lots of groups; and when judges decide important cases, they should accept the view of the executive branch.

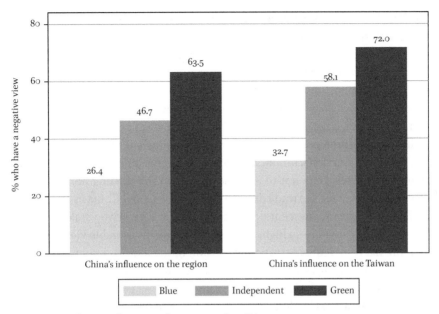

FIGURE 2.1 China's influence on the region and on Taiwan
SOURCE: ASIAN BAROMETER SURVEY FOURTH WAVE, 2015, HTTP://WWW.ASIANBAROMETER.ORG/ (ACCESSED JUNE 10, 2020)

43.1 percent of non-liberal respondents hold an unfavorable view of China. In the 2015 Democratic Governance Survey, conducted by the Taiwan Foundation for Democracy in 2015, 72.9 percent of people who do not endorse the Sunflower Movement agree that democracy is the best form of government, while 85.5 percent of those who endorse the movement agree with this statement.[12] These attitude patterns suggest that people who endorse democratic principles or democracy are more likely to see the expansion of China's influence as a threat and thereby tend to support anti-China political forces.

Such attitudes toward China and the establishment also reveal a generational gap. The fourth wave ABS shows that 36 percent of the young generation and 44 percent of adult respondents think that China's influence on Taiwan is positive.[13] The young generation has less of a shared cultural identity and fewer familial ties with people in China. Related to this, as the young generation did not experience rapid economic development under authoritarian rule, they are less likely to view authoritarian rule as a viable option to promote

12 Yu, *Evaluation of Democratic Governance in Taiwan.*
13 Asian Barometer Survey Fourth Wave, 2015.

development. Instead, they see authoritarian rule as a threat to their freedom. Along with the bleak economic outlook they face, attitudes toward China are the main reasons that the young generation disapproves of President Ma's approach in managing the cross-strait relationship. This factor contributes to the anti-establishment voices among the youth.[14]

Thus, when witnessing the patronage and vote-buying practices of many KMT candidates, large KMT party assets, the primacy of economic growth over environmental protection, rising income inequality, and the pension system that favors civil servants, military, and education personnel, liberal value holders are more likely than not to endorse change in the existing policies. More importantly, they see the trade deals between Taiwan and China as an existential threat to Taiwan's nascent democracy. Since the perceived stakes and the threat of China are both so high, those who hold an unfavorable view of China are more likely to demand strong supervision of the KMT government. We can also use the Fourth Wave ABS to examine this pattern. This battery of questions includes whether the legislature is capable of keeping government leaders in check, and, between elections, whether the people have a way of holding the government responsible for its actions. As shown in Figure 2.2, across different parties, people who hold an unfavorable view of China are not satisfied with the state of supervision of the government.[15]

In using the ABS we find that those who hold an unfavorable view of China are more likely to perceive that the government abuses its power. Specifically, they tend to believe that the government blocks information from ordinary people, it does not respond to what people want, and that government leaders break the law or abuse their power. In addition, in another question, people who hold an unfavorable view of China are less satisfied with the overall functioning of democracy.

During this period, civil society organizations staged several large-scale protests and were able to successfully block several government policies.[16] In each

---

14   After 2010, there is a pronounced generational gap in party support. For example, in the 2016 presidential election, 73 percent of voters under the age of 30 voted for the opposition candidate, Tsai Ing-wen. Only 15 percent of young voters voted for the KMT candidate. In contrast, 59 percent of adult voters supported Tsai Ing-wen and 29 percent of this age cohort voted for the KMT candidate.

15   Moreover, this group is likely to be less satisfied with the overall functioning of democracy.

16   Ming-sho Ho, "The Resurgence of Social Movements under the Ma Ying-jeou Government: A Political Opportunity Structure Perspective," in *Political Changes in Taiwan under Ma Ying-jeou: Partisan conflict, policy choices, external constraints and security challenges*, ed. Jean-Pierre Cabestan and Jacques deLisle (Abingdon and New York: Routledge, 2014), 100–119.

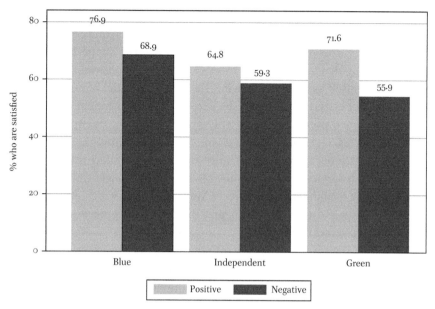

Unit: percentage; Data Source: Asian Barometer Wave 4

FIGURE 2.2   Views of China and perceived democratic supervision
SOURCE: ASIAN BAROMETER SURVEY FOURTH WAVE, 2015, HTTP://WWW.ASIANBAROMETER.ORG/ (ACCESSED JUNE 10, 2020)

protest, hundreds and sometimes thousands of people participated. Among such events were protests over the death of Hung Chung-chiu, a young enlisted soldier who was mistreated while serving in the army; the Miaoli Dapu land case about the expropriation of farmland for use by an industrial park; stopping the fourth nuclear power plant project; the Sunflower Student Movement that opposed the ratification of the service trade agreement with China; preservation of the Losheng Sanatorium; and the Wenlin-Yuan urban renewal project. Anti-KMT sentiment piled up during President Ma's second term, which eventually brought down the ruling party in the 2016 election.[17]

In addition to the election victory of the Democratic Progress Party (DPP), the direct political products of these anti-establishment movements were the rise of the White Force (WF) and the New Power Party (NPP).[18] The leaders of

---

17   Although in these movements "elite" mainly refers to the KMT, for some people there is disappointment toward both the KMT and the DPP.

18   The Internet and the popularity of social media have enabled people to disseminate news and ideas faster. This development also strengthens the power of civil society in checking the discretion and encroachment of the state. With the rising popularity of Internet forums and social media and the decline of traditional media, which tend to be more

both forces are political novices and the opinion leaders of the social protest movements. The WF is led by Ko Wen-je, previously a surgeon at National Taiwan University Hospital. Ko originally was a deep Green supporter, but later on strategically distanced himself from conventional politicians and began identifying himself as a political novice. He is not the leader of any particular movement, but he rode the crest of the strong anti-establishment wave of this period. He gained popularity amid widespread distrust of the main political parties and elites. The NPP is the direct result of the Sunflower Student Movement in 2014 that occupied the legislature for 24 days and successfully blocked the Cross-Strait Service Trade Agreement between Taiwan and China. The NPP was formed by leaders of the Sunflower Movement. It is widely described by the participants and the opposition that these free trade negotiations were conducted in a secret manner.[19]

Because of their anti-establishment views, the Sunflower Student movements, the WF and NPP assert a clear dichotomy between the corrupt elites and the people. They argue that the existing political and economic system is corrupt and ineffective. They use this argument to summarize the source of Taiwan's political and economic problems. This rhetoric serves as an effective tool to raise awareness and mobilize people. The DPP uses much the same campaign rhetoric, but they are more moderate and pragmatic.[20] From 2008 to 2016, the DPP rode on the bandwagon of the anti-establishment movement, which helped it defeat the KMT in the 2016 presidential election. Although the focus here is mainly on the KMT, on many occasions people feel frustrated with both major political parties. Some people argue that they are both are working against the will of the people.

3.2 The Populist Issues and Agendas

The social movements focus on a wide variety of social issues, ranging from ecology, distributive justice, human rights protection, judicial reform, and China's encroachment. They are based on progressive social values or so-called post-material values, and tend to embrace liberal democratic values.

---

conservative, Taiwan's ordinary people now have more channels through which to get information, express their discontents, and discuss issues. This new media profile helps the two new political forces gain popularity and mobilize people.

19 Actually, discussions surrounding this trade agreement were technically no less transparent than the trade talks with other countries, such as New Zealand.

20 After the DPP took office in 2016, the KMT also from time to time has used the same elite–common people rhetoric. But it delivers fewer anti-establishment messages.

All these movements disapprove of the way the KMT has handled cross-strait management, economic development, distributive justice, and environmental management. They focus individually on one particular social issue while in many cases expressing support for each other. These CSOs are independent and are not officially affiliated with any political party. They undertake a variety of direct actions such as marching, sit-ins, petitions, boycotts, and staging protests against the government and, in some cases, companies. As the direct political results of the social movements, WF and the NPP clearly declare a Manichean dualism of corrupt elites and pure masses and consider representative democracy to have failed. Although the Taiwan case is a bottom-up model, not all groups that oppose the government can be labeled as populist. It is only when the social and political forces uphold a Manichean dualism of corrupt elite versus pure people and thus in some cases demonize the political enemy and oversimplify the underlying problems that will we label them as populists. As the direct products the string of social movements, WF and NPP exhibit clearer characteristics of populism than prior social movements.

During the 2015 elections, Ko Wen-je took advantage of popular discontent and the portrayal of the existing political and economic systems as corrupt. Once elected, he declared five main build-operate-transfer (BOT) projects in Taipei to be scandals and set up committees to investigate each one. In some cases, the Taipei City government unilaterally ended the contracts. The investigations, however, eventually went nowhere and his government seldom mentions them two years later. These actions hurt the stability of rule of law and scared off many would-be investors. Business investment in Taipei has declined dramatically since Mayor Ko took office. In addition, because he spent so much time dealing with the accusations against the former administration and BOT, he did not have much time left to see to other tasks. This phenomenon largely explains the difference in approval ratings between Ko and Taoyuan Mayor Cheng, a DPP member, who avoids such rhetorical language and is much more pragmatic. Besides these large-scale, prominent cases, once elected, Mayor Ko's policy stances on several issues shifted to being very close to those of the former government. In the latter half of Mayor Ko's first term, he scaled back the corrupt elite and pure people rhetoric and shifted his policy stance to be more moderate on both economic issues and the cross-strait issue spectrum. For example, before he was elected, he complained that many urban renewal projects favored the developers. However, Mayor Ko adopted an even tougher stance toward tearing down the buildings whose owners did not want to be part of urban renewal projects. He also criticized the BOT developers for caring only about money while at the same time his government endeavored to develop public land by soliciting business investment, including in the form of BOT. In many interviews, his answers were quite vague regarding many public policy issues.

Mayor Ko believes that the representative institutions fail to be responsive to people's needs and discontent, so he promotes people's direct participation in the decision-making process. With the popularity of the Internet in general and social media in particular, online participation methods such as e-voting (proposed by the government) and online policy initiatives (proposed by individuals) have become possible. Mayor Ko thinks that politicians should respond more directly to the people. He has introduced i-voting, participatory budgets, and open data schemes. In 2015, the Taipei City government introduced the i-voting online polling platform, which allows citizens to express their preferences on certain important public policy issues. I-voting was even used to decide who would be the city commissioners of many units such as education and transportation and is being used to evaluate the performance of the commissioners. Using i-voting to decide on city officials, however, has not been a great success.[21] Moreover, some issues are highly complicated and technical, such as the public works BOT projects, so i-voting may not always be the best way to decide such policies. In 2017, Ko even proposed allowing civic participation to decide the bidding on a US$25 billion BOT project, including the qualifications of the bidders, bidding procedure, technology requirements, and the bid price. Here, tension inevitably emerges between civil participation and technocratic governance regarding such technical and complicated issues.

Because of the alleged failure of representative democracy to address the needs of the people, the NPP also promotes direct democracy. In 2018, the DPP government amended the Referendum Act, lowering the threshold of eligible voters to initiate a referendum proposal (from 0.5 percent to 0.01 percent) and the threshold to put a referendum proposal to a vote (from 5 percent to 1.5 percent). The amendments also reduced the quorum to pass a proposal. Before the amendment, the law required that at least 50 percent of the electorate cast ballots and an absolute relative majority of valid votes. Now it only requires that at least 25 percent of the electorate cast ballots and a relative majority of valid votes. This new law also did away with the need for the review committee,

---

21   Two years later, the system allows citizens to submit proposals on issues to be voted on by the public, upon approval by city officials and a public participatory committee. But in practice, government in most cases rejected the i-voting results. For participatory budgeting, many proposals were raised but most are not mature and nearly all were later rejected by the Taipei City government. Many forms of citizen participation in decision-making are still experimental.

which could reject a referendum proposal.[22] The direct result of the change in the quorum was the mushrooming of the number of citizen initiatives. There were ten referendum proposals to be voted on in the municipal and county elections in 2018, ranging from gay marriage, nuclear power, and air pollution, to changing the name used for Olympic and international competitions from Chinese Taipei to Taiwan.

In reviewing the referendum law, the NPP proposed extending it so that constitutional clauses could be decided by referendum. One of the most important issues is the nation's official title and territory, both of which are very sensitive given Taiwan's unique position in the international power structure. The NPP also proposed amending the law to require that any cross-strait political negotiations be voted on in a referendum before the negotiations begin. The term "political negotiations" is vague. Following the Sunflower Movement, trade agreements have also taken on important political and national security implications. These two proposals were eventually struck down by other major parties.

To promote direct democracy, the NPP also rejected the right of party leaders to control how individual party members vote in legislative reviews. Strong party discipline, however, is important for party leaders in democracies to command loyalty from fellow party members during legislative voting. In 2015, the founding members of the party launched a campaign to recall several KMT legislators for strictly following the party line, a common practice in Western parliamentary systems. In 2016, the NPP and the DPP jointly passed a law that lowered the popular vote threshold that is required to recall an elected official. Previously, it was a requirement that more than half of total voters in a district actually vote and that there be an absolute majority of valid votes. The NPP favored requiring a simple majority and no electorate restrictions. The final version adopted a simple majority and one-fourth of the electorate cast ballots as the threshold. The low quorum for a recall vote may induce legislators not to follow party discipline to pass some tough reform bills. In democracies, strong party discipline is an important foundation enabling ruling parties to govern effectively.[23]

---

22   Sean Lin, "Referendum Act Amendments Approved," *Taipei Times*, December 13, 2017, http://www.taipeitimes.com/News/front/archives/2017/12/13/2003683881 (accessed June 20, 2020).

23   One year later, the chairman of the NPP almost became a victim of the new rule. Because of his stance in supporting the Same-Sex Marriage Act, anti-equality organizations launched a campaign to recall him. The requirement that 25 percent of the electorate cast ballots saved him.

3.3 *Absorbed into the Existing Political System*

Both the NPP and the WF participate in elections and remain independent from the main political parties. The discontent against the ruling elites during President Ma's second term contributed to the victory of the DPP, and the growth of the NPP and the WF. The DPP did not nominate candidates in those districts where the NPP nominated candidates, allowing them to win several seats. The NPP gained 6.11 percent of the votes and five seats from the total of 113 in the 2016 parliamentary elections, quickly becoming the third largest party in the legislature. The main supporters of the two political forces tended to be young people, liberal-minded people, and people who favored Taiwan's independence or maintain the status quo. Mayor Ko enjoyed quite high approval ratings in the first half of his term, especially among younger voters, although his approval ratings declined in the second half. Ko received 57 percent of the vote in the 2014 Taipei mayoral elections, but only received 41 percent in the 2018 elections. Meanwhile, the NPP's approval rating dropped from 14 percent in 2016 to 6 percent in late 2017.

There are several reasons for the general decline in approval ratings. First, in the three years after the DPP assumed power, the basic economic conditions for ordinary Taiwanese people have changed little. Young people still face a bleak economic outlook. China still uses every means available to weaken Taiwan's de facto sovereign status, so Taiwan's international space has not improved. Second, the DPP and the WF have shifted their economic policies to be more pro-market. There is virtually no difference between the DPP, the KMT, and the WF in terms of economic policy other than the cross-strait economic relationship. Next, since the DPP assumed office, there have been no trade agreements between Taiwan and China under review. The NPP is largely a protest party focusing mainly on the China issue. No negotiations between the two sides of the strait means no protests. Moreover, former President Ma Ying-jeou, whom some allege sold out Taiwan, does not show any signs of rushing to promote unification.

Even though Mayor Ko's approval rating declined in the four years since his inauguration, he remains quite popular among some people. Many people think that since the KMT cannot address Taiwan's economic problems, the DPP should be given the chance. Now that it appears that the DPP is not doing a good job either, Ko is the sole remaining hope for many. As mayor, he is not responsible for managing Taiwan's economic growth, distribution, and social justice, so people do not attribute Taiwan's sluggish economy to him. Moreover, some people agree that he has not done well in terms of managing the city, but Mayor Ko speaks in a way that connects with them.

4 The Influence of Populism upon Democracy

Populism can bring good or bad to a society and is not necessarily incompatible with democracy. Ernesto Laclau argues that many populist movements advocate progressive agendas and demand large-scale changes in the political system.[24] Populist movements in many countries contribute to furthering democratization, such as extending franchise to working-class men and women, and inducing governments to address neglected social issues.[25] By encouraging the political participation of disfranchised groups, populism can enhance democracy.[26] Michael Kazin, who examined the populist movement at the turn of the 20th century in the United States, argues that populist movements may rebalance the distribution of political power between the established powers and social groups.[27] It becomes the tool for marginal groups to protest against economic and political inequality. The function of checks and balances in existing democratic institutions may only serve to protect the interests of the elite, and do not represent the true will of the common people.[28]

Populism also has its downsides. Since populist leaders believe they represent the will of people, and therefore nothing should stand between them and enacting their agenda, they have problems with checks and balances and minority rights.[29] By emphasizing direct engagement and plebiscites, populism may also undermine "the legitimacy and power of political institutions (e.g. parties and parliaments) and unelected bodies."[30] Contemporary populism

---

24 Ernesto Laclau, *Politics and Ideology in Marxist Theory* (London: New Left Books 1977); Ernesto Laclau, *On Populist Reason* (London: Verso, 2005).

25 Aslanidis, "Populism and Social Movements."

26 Cristóbal Rovira Kaltwasser, "The Ambivalence of Populism: Threat and Corrective for Democracy," *Democratization* 19, no. 2 (2012): 184–208; Cristóbal Rovira Kaltwasser, Paul A. Taggart, Paulina Ochoa Espejo, and Pierre Ostiguy, "Populism: An Overview of the Concept and the State of the Art," in *The Oxford Handbook of Populism*, ed. Cristóbal Rovira Kaltwasser, Paul A. Taggart, Paulina Ochoa Espejo, and Pierre Ostiguy (Oxford, UK: Oxford University Press, 2017), 1–24.

27 Michael Kazin, *The Populist Persuasion: An American history* (Ithaca, NY: Cornell University Press, 1998).

28 The movement in the 19th century advocated greater voter participation that included secret ballots, direct primaries, and direct election of senators. On the economic side, it included fewer working hours, increased social welfare, and consumer protection. Many of these ideas were later adopted during the progressive movement in the earlier 20th century.

29 Mudde and Kaltwasser, "Populism"; Bart Bonikowski, "Ethno-nationalist Populism and the Mobilization of Collective Resentment," *The British Journal of Sociology* 68 (2017): S181–S213.

30 Mudde and Kaltwasser, "Populism."

accepts the idea of democracy as majority rule and elections but is less enthusiastic about checks and balances, freedom of the press, and procedural fairness.[31] Other scholars instead argue that the influence of populism on democracy is more complicated as it is context-dependent.[32] Steven Levitsky and James Loxton argue that populism in nascent democracies could pose a serious threat to the functioning of democracy.[33] Populism in general has a stronger effect on unconsolidated democracies. In addition, populism in government tends to exert a greater adverse effect on democracy than populism in opposition.[34] Thus, in consolidated democracies, populism launched by the opposition is expected to have a positive effect on the functioning of democracy. In contrast, in unconsolidated democracies, populism launched by the government is expected to have a negative effect on democracy. Populism in Taiwan is a bottom-up model, namely in opposition, and since Taiwan is a consolidated democracy, it seems natural to suggest that the populist movement will have a positive effect on democratic development.

4.1 Contributions of the Populist Movement

Taiwan's populism is originally formed by autonomous civil society organizations that have launched several social movements. These movements have over time given rise to new political forces: the WF and the NPP. As a bottom-up model of populism, Taiwan's populism does not pose a threat to liberal democracy. All parties in Taiwan firmly believe in the superiority of democracy and embrace democratic principles. The KMT, the DPP, the WF, and the NPP have no intention of interrupting existing democratic norms. Both the NPP and the WF were absorbed into the existing political system by participating in elections and following democratic rules. At the individual level, as discussed above, popular support for liberal democracy in Taiwan is very high compared with other East Asian countries. Most populist supporters in Taiwan are liberal value holders and more likely to believe in the superiority of democracy. It is the threat from a closer KMT–Beijing relationship that sparks their fears. The Sunflower movement in part seeks to protect Taiwan's democracy by forcing the government not to make deals with the communist regime and to pass

---

31   Jan-Werner Müller, *What is Populism?* (London: Penguin UK, 2017).

32   Mudde and Kaltwasser, "Populism."

33   Steven Levitsky and James Loxton, "Populism and Competitive Authoritarianism: The Case of Fujimori's Peru," *Populism in Europe and the Americas: Threat or corrective for democracy?*, ed. Cas Mudde and Cristóbal Rovira Kaltwasser (Cambridge, UK: Cambridge University Press, 2012), 160–181.

34   As a bottom-up model, Taiwan is definitely a populism-in-opposition model.

the Supervision Act to regulate future trade negotiations. Those who strongly believe in liberal democratic values tend to feel the threat most forcibly. In addition, they advocate citizen initiatives, referendums, and recall voting to give people more of a voice in the political process. Such populist issues essentially are associated with protecting and deepening democracy.

In 2017, the ruling DPP tried to initiate the National Public Security Act to counter pressure from China.[35] Many DPP legislators think that China's penetration of Taiwan poses a serious threat to Taiwan's autonomy. This proposed act raised concerns about the control of civil society by the state. The government has proposed setting up many security units in various public and private organizations to report, question, and interview suspects who engage in activities that may threaten national security. In addition, the ruling party legislators have proposed an act to regulate fake news both related and unrelated to national security. If passed, this law would allow the government to regulate speech they do not like in the name of attacking fake news. These initiatives pose a potential threat to the freedom of speech. Many people, including civil society organizations, oppose the bill. Civil society organizations that endorsed the DPP in the 2016 presidential election have gone against the proposal. They worry that these laws give the government too much power to regulate ideas they do not like. In short, the bottom-up model clearly shows that civil society organizations that initiate populist movements are also firmly willing to prevent the government from abusing its power.

Moreover, the populist movement has made significant contributions to Taiwan's political and social development. First, it has expanded citizen political participation. Mayor Ko introduced i-voting, participatory budgets, and open data schemes to enhance civic participation in decision-making. The NPP has promoted direct democracy such as reducing the quorum for referendums and recalls, and encouraged youth political participation by reducing the voting age to 18. Second, the populist movement contributes to a level playing field for political competition. It led to the third peaceful transition of power in Taiwan that forced out the KMT government, which in turn led to a series of reforms that focused on tackling the KMT's huge party assets and addressing financial transparency for several types of civic organization such as religious groups. On the socioeconomic front, the populist movement advocates several progressive social issues such as raising public awareness of social justice, inequality, and human rights. This movement also contributes to environmental

---

35   "KMT: Users' Accounts Were Suspended for Criticizing the President. It Is Likely due to Malicious Reporting," *Apple Daily*, June 21, 2017, http://www.appledaily.com.tw/realtime-news/article/new/20170621/1144704/ (accessed June 20, 2020).

protection such as stopping the sprawl of industrial zones and protecting the natural habitats of endangered species. In addition, when the DPP took office, with the help of many CSOs, it began to address the issue of transitional justice associated with Taiwan's authoritarian past. The NPP is also a leading advocate of transitional justice and intergenerational justice. This advocacy is helping to push through several important and progressive policy initiatives.

4.2 Potential Negative Influence

This populist movement, however, also has some potential negative impacts on the functioning and governance of Taiwan's democracy. These impacts include interference with the functioning of representative democracy, constraints on the profession of technocrats, and the oversimplification of main socioeconomic problems, which we will discuss in turn. Because the newly revisited referendum law lowers the quorum requirement, ten referendum cases were voted upon in the 2018 local elections. This number is simply too high for people to understand, digest, and ultimately make decisions on. Moreover, such cases are proposed, deliberated, and voted upon within just two months, which does not allow thorough social deliberation as practiced in some matured democracies. Taiwan is a divided society with different national identities and views of the cross-strait political and economic relationship. Referendum questions often carry a dichotomous message and provide less room for compromise. For these identity-related issues, it might be better to deliberate and make compromises in representative institutions. Finally, the amended referendum law removes the power of the referendum reviewing committee, making it unable to check whether an initiative violates the constitution or confirm that its wording is understandable.[36] The current referendum practice is an interesting experiment, but the institution needs to be carefully modified.

Also associated with the functioning of representative democracy is the issue of majority rule in the legislature. The occupation of Parliament during the Sunflower Movement sought to stop China's political and economic infiltration into Taiwan. It did successfully stop the trade agreement about which many civil society organizations were deeply concerned. Representative democracy, however, relies on party discipline and majority control of the legislative agenda to ensure governability. In many Western parliaments, there are motions to end the debate on a matter, limit the amount of time that MPs can spend on a particular bill, and to timetable a bill's progress by setting out the

---

36   Among these cases, three were initiated by the KMT. It essentially became another battleground of partisan competition. The purpose was to boost the party's electoral performance.

time allowed for debate at each stage in advance.[37] Taiwan's nascent democracy survived the two transfers of power as both parties have demonstrated a willingness to hand over executive power to the opposition when they lose an election. However, neither the DPP nor the KMT were willing to respect the ruling party's legislative power, even in the case of unified government.[38] Despite a majority in the parliament, presidents were still unable to advance their party's policy agenda because of filibustering. During the review of the service trade agreement, without the presence of a filibuster launched by the opposition party, the so-called black box review or 32nd review surely would not have happened. The unstoppable filibuster and occupation of Parliament clearly damaged representative decision-making. The revised recall vote law has a similar problem in that it induces the legislators not to follow party discipline to pass some tough reform bills.

Weak control of legislative power by the ruling party in a united government hurts the governability of the democracy. As William Galston points out, gridlock is an important reason that people are losing their confidence in representative democracy as weak governance increases popular discontent with the existing political system.[39] This situation points to a dilemma that Taiwan faces. On the one hand, the country needs to ensure majority rule to enhance governability. When checks and balances are pushed to an extreme, they weaken democratic governability. On the other hand, the threat from China is looming and real, and civil society by and large is not comfortable with a closer economic relationship between Taiwan and China. Therefore, people demand greater supervision of the government. To be sure, Taiwan's electoral competition is not a level playing field. Vote-buying and huge party assets give the KMT a decided edge. Only when Taiwan reaches a politically level playing field will it be legitimate to demand majority rule. The majority rule in Parliament improved after the DPP gained control of both the executive and legislative branches after 2016 as they passed several laws with very limited debates simply by exerting its majority power. This may set a precedent for future governments.

Next, Mayor Ko's indictment of the former mayor compelled society to further investigate the existing BOT cases and to deliberate on a better bidding mechanism. However, Ko's investigation of the five BOT scandals did not turn

---

37   For example, the UK parliament has the Guillotine motion and the Program motion.
38   Yun-han Chu and Chin-en Wu, "State of Democracy in Asia: Taiwan," in *State of Democracy in Asia Report* (Seoul: Asian Democracy Research Network, 2017).
39   William A. Galston, "The Populist Challenge to Liberal Democracy," *Journal of Democracy* 29, no. 2 (2018): 5–19.

up enough evidence of corruption. This damaged the technocrat professionals and the city government's credibility to recruit investment. The expansion of the direct democracy initiatives proposed by Ko aims to expand civic participation in decision-making, breaking the monopoly of technocrats and elected politicians. However, the limits of their application need to be considered carefully. Some public projects are highly complicated and technical, such as the public works BOT projects, so i-voting may not always be the best way to decide such policies. Mayor Ko proposing to let citizens decide the bidding process of a US\$ 2.5 billion BOT project is probably not practical. Allowing citizens to decide the bidding process including the qualifications of the bidders, bid procedure, technology requirements, and the bid price no doubt creates tension between civil participation and technocratic governance regarding these technical and sophisticated issues.

Finally, as in other populist movements, populist politicians in Taiwan pinpoint the enemies of the people and oversimplify the substantive problems. By doing so, Taiwanese society risks omitting the structural problems it needs to address. After 2010, the populist movements argued that the failure of representative democracy, political elites, and big corporations, many of which invest heavily in China, have rigged the economy and weakened Taiwan's democracy. There was indeed rampant crony capitalism, bribe taking, party-controlled enterprises, and monopolies before the first party turnover in 2000. These conditions significantly improved after that. Concerns over rising income inequality and equality of opportunity are considered fair and important by the movement's supporters. But aside from these, one may not solely attribute the economic stagnation in Taiwan in recent years to the flaws of representative democracy and to the close economic relationship between Taiwan and China. As discussed above, representative democracy in Taiwan has its own problems with deep partisan antagonism, gridlock in parliament, and vote-buying in elections, but direct democracy also has its limitations. In some cases, it is the weak grasp on legislative power by the ruling party that hurts governability. Taiwan needs to address this aspect as well.

Next, the cross-strait economic relationship is just part of the global competition Taiwan faces. Taiwan's economy has for a long time relied on original equipment manufacturers that supply components and depended on the technology and machinery from more advanced countries. It faces competition from developing countries and has achieved only partial success in catching up and establishing its own brands. The manufacturing sector over the years has moved offshore to mainland China and other low-cost countries. Companies focus on expansion (for example, building new factories in China and Vietnam) rather than upgrading their own technology. Furthermore,

Taiwan's government overly regulates and intervenes in the market, for example by subsidizing energy fuel prices. In short, the populist movement proposes an easy answer by identifying and attacking enemies, but it fails to propose actual plausible solutions. By doing so it tends to overlook the more important structural factors that a country needs to address to boost the economy.

5   Conclusion

Taiwan features a bottom-up model of populism. Taiwan's populist movement is organized by autonomous civil society organizations. This movement has given rise to new political forces, the White Force and the New Power Party. The movement rejects the KMT's handling of cross-strait management, economic development, distributive justice, and environmental management. It portrayed that KMT, domestic big business, and Taiwanese companies that invest heavily in China form a coalition that has rigged the economy and is trying to weaken Taiwan's democracy. Civil society organizations have staged several large-scale protests and were able to successfully block several government policies. As a bottom-up model, the populist movement has helped introduce several political reforms to level the political playing field and increase civic participation in decision-making. In addition, a unique feature of Taiwan's populism is that this movement in large part stems from fears over a close economic relationship between a small democracy and a large authoritarian power. Some of those who feel the threat most strongly are those who are liberal-minded. They seek to protect Taiwan's democracy by forcing the government not to make any deals with a communist government. Popular support for liberal democracy is also high in Taiwan. The source of the populist movement and its bottom-up characteristics mean that it is unlikely to influence the stability of the country's democracy. Instead, this movement has made significant contributions to Taiwan's political and social development. This populist movement, however, also has some potential negative impacts on the functioning and governance of democracy. The related issues include the functioning of representative democracy, technocratic governance, and oversimplification of the substantive problems.

Threats related to the inflow of capital and emigration from China have triggered a populist movement. There is a fundamental dilemma facing Taiwan, namely that Taiwan's economy is inextricably intertwined with the Chinese economy. Taiwan exports strategic components to China where they are assembled to be consumed locally or exported to another part of the world. Without the huge trade surplus from China, Taiwan would have a trade deficit.

But on the other hand, China is not a democracy and it has not given up on the possibility of using military force to bring Taiwan into the fold. Hence, the rise of China poses a threat to democracy in Taiwan. Even though Taiwan's government wants to diversify its export market, it has not been very successful to date. The two sides have developed a "frenemy" (friend + enemy) relationship. The emergence of a more assertive China and the tightening of controls under President Xi are incompatible with the liberal democratic values of Taiwan. Any ruling parties who want to ease the relationship with Beijing government are likely to trigger populist movement again.

Finally, Taiwan is also a divided society. Views of cross-strait economic policies, filibusters in parliament, history textbook revisions, and several massive social protests have been highly divided along party lines. A broad and inclusive definition of "the people" is a better approach for the health of democracy. For example, political leaders should define and interpret the "Taiwanese people" broadly, including people with different national identities and unification–independence preferences. Since everyone is included under this definition, it may reduce confrontation and foster compromise and cooperation.

PART 2

Authoritarian Populism

∵

CHAPTER 3

Contemporary Populism and Democratic Challenges in the Philippines

Francisco A. Magno

1 Introduction

Populism is not a novel event but a periodic one. It is a type of direct democracy that emerges when people sense that they are pushed to the margins by mainstream politics. Riding on the back of political discontent, populism gains traction and thrives amid an atmosphere of divisiveness cultivated by identity-driven politics. It focuses blame on certain domestic groups, countries, and international organizations for the ills of the nation. Populism is defined as a thin-centered ideology that delineates society into two homogeneous and adversarial groups—the pure people versus the corrupt elite. It insists that politics should express *la volonté générale* or the general will of the people.[1]

Given that populism is a recurrent feature of Philippine society, this chapter seeks to find out how the persistence of weak institutions, contemporary globalization processes, and the expansion of social media heighten the speed of transmitting populist ideas among the citizenry. It defines the key themes that are used in populist discourse and describes the demographic and socio-economic backgrounds of populist leaders and supporters. This study examines the various social, economic, and political factors that have given rise to populism. It also considers the challenges posed by populism to the values and institutions of representative democracy.

2 Institutional Lens

An institutional theoretical lens is appropriate to assess the role of weak institutions in fostering the rise of a populist leadership that promises to make up for the ineffectual performance of previous regimes. In this regard, institutions

---

1 Cas Mudde and Cristóbal Rovira Kaltwasser, "Exclusionary vs. Inclusionary Populism: Comparing Contemporary Europe and Latin America," *Government and Opposition* 48, no. 2 (2013): 147–174.

© FRANCISCO A. MAGNO, 2021 | DOI:10.1163/9789004444461_005

are framed in terms of enduring rules and organized practices embedded in structures of meaning and resources. Such constitutive rules and practices stipulate appropriate behavior for specific actors under given circumstances. Structures of meaning provide the explanation and justification for behavioral codes while structures of resources foster capabilities for action.[2]

Populism castigates elites and formal institutions as inept and untrustworthy. It appeals to extravagant emotions and insists on extreme measures to address collective action problems. During the 2016 presidential elections in the Philippines, administration candidate Manuel Roxas II vowed to continue the reforms of the previous Aquino government. On the other hand, candidate Rodrigo Duterte blazed the campaign trail with the promise to shake up the political establishment if elected to office. In a national survey conducted prior to the elections, Filipinos were asked to identify the top five urgent national issues that distressed them. Among these were controlling inflation, increasing worker pay, reducing poverty, creating jobs, and fighting graft and corruption. Duterte's signature campaign to wage war against criminality came only sixth spot among voters' concerns.[3] Yet Duterte was able to frame criminality as the key topic in the presidential contest.

3 From Mayor to President

Unlike the other presidential candidates who made their marks on the national scene before seeking the highest office of the land, Duterte spent most of his political career as a local government official. As mayor, Duterte dramatically transformed Davao, which is the biggest city in the world and located in the southern island of Mindanao, from being a cradle of insurgency during the martial law years from 1972 to 1986 into a progressive urban center starting in the late 1980s He installed security outposts surrounding the city where militias had to surrender their weapons. He imposed a smoking ban in public places, ordained curfew hours, and enforced road speed limits. The Davao City Investment Code was passed and business processes and licensing systems were streamlined to ease the regulatory cost of doing business. The influx of

---

2 Rod A. W. Rhodes, Sarah A. Binder, and Bert A. Rockman, eds., *The Oxford Handbook of Political Institutions* (Oxford, UK: Oxford University Press, 2008).

3 "Pulse Asia Research's September 2015 Nationwide Survey on Urgent National Concerns and the Performance Ratings of the National Administration on Selected Issues," *Pulse Asia*, https://drive.google.com/file/d/oB3b9qPFV1cRDdlAzdmx2Vo5QeXc/view (accessed October 5, 2015).

investment was accompanied by the proliferation of high-rise condominiums and shopping malls in the city. In 2014, Davao's economy grew by 9.4 percent, outpacing the growth rate of other urban hubs.[4]

Duterte was certainly not the first city mayor to become president of the Philippines. Before notching a landslide victory in the 1998 elections, Joseph Estrada was a long-time mayor of San Juan City. However, the similarity ends there as Estrada had a more conventional climb to the presidency having been elected in national elections as a senator and vice president before occupying the highest office of the land. Duterte, on the other hand, had no prior experience in vying for an elective post with a national constituency prior to the 2016 elections. He had been mayor and vice-mayor and served briefly as congressman of the first district of Davao City from 1998 to 2001.

The route to national prominence though local politics that Duterte took is comparable to that of President Joko Widodo of Indonesia. Before Jokowi captured the presidency in 2014, he won the position of mayor of Solo in 2005 and governor of Jakarta in 2012. As local chief executives, both Duterte and Jokowi sought to enhance economic growth through reforms such as removing bureaucratic red tape to improve public performance.[5] They barged onto the national scene with the political narrative that the success of competitive cities governed by strong leaders could be brought up to scale and replicated throughout the entire nation.

4 The Populist Appeal

A survey of 38 nations conducted by the Pew Research Center in 2017 indicates that unrestricted executive power is not uncommon: in 20 countries, a quarter or more of those polled preferred an arrangement in which a strong leader can make decisions without interference from the legislature and judiciary. This political trajectory is evident in countries where executives have extended or consolidated their power since 2016 such as the Philippines. The overpowering executive demonstrates a weakening of the system of checks and balances that is inherent in representative democracy. In the case of the

---

4 Ehito Kimura and Erik Martinez Kuhonta, "Jokowi and Duterte: Do Local Politics Apply?" *East–West Wire*, February 12, 2018, https://www.eastwestcenter.org/news-center/east-west-wire/jokowi-and-duterte-do-local-politics-apply (accessed June 10, 2020).

5 Edward Aspinall and Marcus Mietzner, "Indonesian Politics in 2014: Democracy's Close Call," *Bulletin of Indonesian Economic Studies* 50, no. 3 (2014): 347–369.

Philippines, the survey finds that half the population is favorably inclined toward strongman rule.[6]

Populist politicians bolt into power with the support of voters who feel left behind in the globalization game. Anti-elitism and xenophobia paint a conjoined picture of elites and outsiders as enemies of the people. Xenophobia brings together anti-globalization and anti-immigrant sentiments in Europe and the Americas that enhances the visibility of strongman rule. Some form of Putinism may be at play in these unfolding events. In the Philippines, even President Duterte expressed strong admiration for the long-serving Russian president. Nevertheless, the rising stock of populist authoritarian leaders should not be attributed loosely to Russian influence. The reason behind this phenomenon can be traced to the fragility of democratic institutions in many countries, and solutions must be found at home.[7]

The growth of populism is anchored in the belief that the political system of representative democracy has failed the masses. It feeds on the notion that elites orchestrated an elaborate system to accumulate private gain at the expense of the people. In this context, presidential candidate Duterte projected himself in 2016 as a crusader and an outsider who would battle the oligarchy and carry a cudgel for the people. While this form of populist rhetoric is fairly common, what differentiated Duterte was that he looked and sounded the part as an outsider who refused to follow the modalities of formal presidential bearing.[8]

Populism is characterized by a leadership style that deviates from the standards of high politics anchored on formal behavior. Adept at delivering informal speeches using rough language and laced with hometown jokes before an adoring audience, populist politicians seek to project sincerity shorn of hypocrisy. Through such actions, a political base is cultivated that galvanizes a stable following for a non-conventional leader. The massive appeal generated by populist leaders comes from their ability to open the gates to certain sectors that were disregarded in the past and felt abandoned by the elite-controlled political establishment. Such people languished, their resentment kept under

---

6   Richard Wike, Katie Simmons, Bruce Stokes, and Janell Fetterolf, "Globally, Broad Support for Representative and Direct Democracy," *Pew Research Center* 16 (2017), https://www.pewresearch.org/global/wp-content/uploads/sites/2/2017/10/Pew-Research-Center_Democracy-Report_2017.10.16.pdf (accessed June 10, 2020).

7   Olga Oliker, "Putinism, Populism and the Defence of Liberal Democracy," *Survival* 59, no. 1 (2017): 7–24.

8   Randy David, "Duterte, Trump, and Populism," *Philippine Daily Inquirer*, March 5, 2017, https://opinion.inquirer.net/102168/duterte-trump-populism (accessed November 13, 2018).

wraps. Silenced for a long time, the muted citizens found their voice through populism.[9]

Nicole Curato provides a good example of the neglected constituencies, especially the victims of the 2013 super typhoon Haiyan in Tacloban City. The high public approval rating for President Benigno Simeon Aquino III at that time suffered a reversal with the seeming absence of empathy by the national leadership for the survivors of the disaster. A key example cited was that of a business owner who appealed to the chief executive to declare a state of emergency and deploy security personnel since mayhem had erupted in Tacloban City after the storm. However, he was rebuffed in no uncertain terms. This was strikingly different from then Davao City Mayor Duterte's response. With no fanfare, Duterte deployed his city's emergency responders. While other politicians distributed relief goods with stickers that displayed their names and faces, Duterte's aid packages were generically stamped "from the People of Davao City." Three years later during the 2016 presidential campaign, banners with Duterte's image were displayed throughout Tacloban City, inscribed with a simple statement: "It's our turn to help him."[10]

5   Duterte and Populism

President Duterte's political rhetoric and action are consistent with the conceptualization of populism provided in this chapter. There is a determined effort to portray his leadership as championing the people against the elite. Ronald Mendoza and Leonardo Jamisola points out that "the uber-rich are an attractive target for populists who often brand them as oligarchs." Duterte promised to vanquish the oligarchs within weeks of taking over the reins of power.[11] In populism, there is a penchant to blame certain groups, countries, and international organizations. In response to criticisms related to extrajudicial killings, Duterte condemned the United Nations, Western countries, and human rights organizations.[12]

---

9   Nicole Curato, "Flirting with Authoritarian Fantasies? Rodrigo Duterte and the New Terms of Philippine Populism," *Journal of Contemporary Asia* 47, no. 1 (2017): 142–153.

10   Nicole Curato, "The Power and Limits of Populism in the Philippines," *Current History* 117, no. 800 (September 2018): 209–214.

11   Ronald Mendoza and Leonardo Jamisola III, "Is Duterte a Populist?: Rhetoric or Reality," *Horizons: Journal of International Relations and Sustainable Development* 15 (Winter 2020): 266–279.

12   Mark Thompson, "Bloodied Democracy: Duterte and the Death of Liberal Reformism in the Philippines," *Journal of Current Southeast Asian Affairs* 35, no. 3 (2016): 39–68.

The genteel politics of old is shattered in contemporary populism. At the September 2016 Association of Southeast Asian Nations (ASEAN) Conference held in Laos, Duterte responded profanely to US president Barack Obama's criticism of the drug war. This led to the cancellation of the bilateral meeting between the two leaders.[13] Like other populist leaders, Duterte ascended to power as an outsider with historical grievances. Julio Teehankee emphasizes that "not only does he represent Mindanao's resentment towards imperial Manila but also a historical blowback against US imperialism."[14]

6   The Drug War

After being elected president of the Philippines in May 2016, Duterte delivered on his campaign promise to wage a drug war. He offered bounties for the bodies of drug dealers and guaranteed the police that they would be shielded from prosecution. From 2016 to 2018, around 4,500 people were killed either in police operations or suspected vigilantism. The killings sparked widespread condemnation from the United Nations and other international human rights organizations. Chris Beyrer, Professor of Public Health and Human Rights at the Johns Hopkins Bloomberg School of Public Health and an expert on the health implications of drug policy, registered his protest that "this is not the rule of law. People are being killed on the accusation or presumption that they are involved in the drug trade: that is a recipe for vigilante violence." In 2003, a similar policy action was pursued in Thailand through Prime Minister Thaksin Shinawatra's war on drugs where more than 2,400 extra-judicial deaths were registered.[15]

In 2015, the Philippine Dangerous Drugs Board estimated the number of illegal drug users at 1.8 million out of a total population of 100 million. When Duterte assumed the presidency a year later, he declared that the country had more than three million drug users. Like other countries in the region, the Philippines has experienced a rise in the consumption of methamphetamines, locally known as shabu. The UN Office on Drugs and Crime identified

---

13   Alfred McCoy, "Global Populism: A Lineage of Filipino Strongmen from Quezon to Marcos to Duterte," *Kasarinlan: Philippine Journal of Third World Studies* 32, nos. 1–2 (2017): 7–54.

14   Julio Teehankee, "The Early Duterte Presidency in the Philippines," *Journal of Current Southeast Asian Affairs* 35, no. 3 (2016): 69–89.

15   Sophie Cousins, "Five Thousand Dead and Counting: The Philippines' Bloody War on Drugs," *BMJ: British Medical Journal (Online)* 355 (2016), https://www.bmj.com/content/355/bmj.i6177 (accessed June 10, 2020).

shabu as the top illicit drug threat in East and Southeast Asia. The seizure of amphetamine-type stimulants in the region quadrupled from 11 tons in 2008 to 42 tons in 2013.[16]

In the first few months of the Duterte presidency, the anti-drug campaign led to the surrender of 800,000 drug users. They registered with the *barangay* (village government) and police authorities with the hope of receiving immunity from the killings and getting treatment for drug addiction. The number of people who surrendered caught the government by surprise because it lacked the infrastructure to assist so many people suffering from drug dependency. In 2002, the government repealed the Dangerous Drugs Act of 1972 and passed the Comprehensive Dangerous Drugs Act, which focused less on law and order and more on preventing drug use and rehabilitating people with drug dependency, in line with globally accepted standards. However, while government officials maintain that drug use will be treated as a health problem, the country appears unprepared and unwilling to pursue that direction.[17] The death toll from the initial two years of the anti-drug campaign has already reached more than 4,500 based on estimates made by the Philippine National Police (PNP). In comparison, the martial law regime of President Ferdinand Marcos resulted in the death of 3,257 over a much longer period of 14 years from 1972 to 1986.[18]

According to PNP data, the nationwide crime rate from July 2016 to June 2018 dropped by 21.48 percent compared to the same period from 2014 to 2016. A total of 1,040,987 crimes were reported from July 2016 to June 2018, lower than the 1,325,789 cases reported during the same period in 2014 to 2016. Crimes against persons like homicide, physical injuries, and rape also declined, except for murder which saw an increase of 19,210 or 1.5 percent from 2016 to 2018. The murder rate in Metro Manila soared by around 112 percent, or 3,444, from July 2016 to June 2018, which is significantly higher than the 1,621 murder cases reported between July 2014 and June 2016. This could be due to the vigilantism that emerged with the onset of the drug war. On the other hand, crimes against property like robbery, car theft, and theft went down by around 50 percent during the same period.[19]

---

16   Cousins, "Five Thousand Dead and Counting."

17   Cousins, "Five Thousand Dead and Counting."

18   Rambo Talabong, "PNP's Drug War Death Toll Tops 4,500 before SONA 2018," *Rappler*, July 23, 2018, https://www.untvweb.com/news/sc-upholds-quo-warranto-ruling-voids-serenos-appointment-as-chief-justice/ (accessed November 19, 2018).

19   Maan Macapagal, "PNP: Crime Rate Drops, but Murder Rate up in 2 Years," *ABS-CBN News*, July 20, 2018, https://news.abs-cbn.com/news/07/19/18/pnp-crime-rate-drops-but-murder-rate-up-in-2-years (accessed November 19, 2018).

7   Social Media as a Battlefield

Cyberspace has evolved into a battlefield for political engagement and contestation. Aside from official government sites, many cyber-troop teams manage fictitious accounts to cloak their identities and interests. This phenomenon is also depicted as a form of astroturfing where the identity of a sponsor or organization is depicted in terms of grassroots activism. In many cases, these fake accounts are bots that refer to bits of code that are programmed to connect with and imitate human users. Media reports indicate that bots have been widely utilized by state actors around the world. These include Argentina, Azerbaijan, Iran, Mexico, Russia, Saudi Arabia, South Korea, Syria, Turkey, Venezuela, and the Philippines. These bots are usually deployed to inundate social media networks with spam and fake news. However, not all governments make use of this type of automation.[20]

Social media is used by political actors to mislead the public through the use of fake accounts and artificially bloat the number of followers, likes, shares or re-tweets a candidate receives, fostering a false sense of popularity, momentum, or relevance. This was a tactic that the Australian Coalition Party used during the 2013 electoral campaign. Sometimes, when political parties or candidates use social media platforms as part of their campaign arsenal, these operations are sustained even after they assume the reins of government. In various countries, many of the keyboard trolls employed to spread propaganda during the election campaign are extended to continue distributing and amplifying messages to support the policies of the victorious coalition.[21]

The mob-like tendency of social media, and the way in which it makes certain information content and leader profiles acquire disproportionate visibility, can lend itself to this type of unifying mission of populist politics. This was exhibited in the viral results obtained by populist memes that celebrated the personality of candidates, especially in the political campaigns of Donald Trump and Bernie Sanders during the 2016 United States presidential elections. The personality and celebrity element of social media supplies a reference point around which a crowd can congregate. Social media provides a platform where millions of disaffected individuals, otherwise deprived of common

---

20   Samantha Bradshaw and Philip Howard, "Troops, Trolls and Troublemakers: A Global Inventory of Organized Social Media Manipulation," Working Paper 2017.12 (Oxford, UK: Project on Computational Propaganda, Oxford Internet Institute, Oxford University, https://comprop.oii.ox.ac.uk/wp-content/uploads/sites/89/2017/07/Troops-Trolls-and-Troublemakers.pdf.

21   Bradshaw and Howard, "Troops, Trolls and Troublemakers."

organizational ties, can meet up as an online crowd and multiply the power of each of its members.[22]

8 The Rising Tide of Populism

Globalization has had mixed effects, producing winners and losers. It has been pointed out that globalization benefited exporters, transnational corporations, international banks, and the professional sectors that thrive in bigger markets. In China, millions of farmers made the transition from farmers to workers in the export-led manufacturing industry. On the other hand, globalization also deepened the rifts that divide capital and labor, urban and rural areas, sunrise and sunset industries, mobile professionals and local producers, and elites and ordinary people.[23]

Globalization allowed people to fall into the cracks. This provided an opening for critics to blame liberalism on both the domestic and international fronts, including rules-based and rights-based governance, as the culprit. If there is an ideological anchor in the wide varieties of democracies in the world, it is more social democratic and solidarity-based rather than neo-liberal. In this regard, democratic systems become sustainable when combined with inclusive development and social protection. Democracy and the rule of law could be seen as fostering both freedom and development.[24]

Who would be the bearers of the general will of the people in terms of the capacity to wield a vision that transcends particular wills and sectional interests? Trends indicate the diminishing influence of political parties in social and political life. Membership and trust in political parties have plunged. The role of parties as formal institutions for interest representation and aggregation has weakened in the face of personality-based politics. What is occurring is a process of individualization where political leaders become more receptive to appeals to the people that bypass established parties and other intermediary institutions.[25]

---

22   Paolo Gerbaudo, "Social Media and Populism: An Elective Affinity?," *Media, Culture & Society* 40, no. 5 (2018): 745–753.

23   Dani Rodrik, "Populism and the Economics of Globalization," *Journal of International Business Policy* 1, nos. 1–2 (2018): 12–33.

24   John G. Ikenberry, "The End of Liberal International Order?," *International Affairs* 94, no. 1 (2018): 7–23.

25   Rogers Brubaker, "Why Populism?," *Theory and Society* 46, no. 5 (2017): 357–385.

Populism thrives in economies featuring high levels of inequality and sufficiently weak political institutions. These enable the rich elite, or segments of the elite, to have a disproportionate influence on politics. Voters often distrust politicians and believe that they may adopt the rhetoric of redistribution, leveling the playing field, and defending the interests of the common citizen. However, they end up pursuing policies that are skewed towards the interests of the elite. This makes it valuable for politicians to signal to voters that they are not captives of narrow elite concerns. Given the high levels of inequality in many societies, political platforms built on redistribution are not surprising. Nonetheless, populist rhetoric and policies may cause harm rather than help the majority of the population.[26]

An example of a populist policy in the Philippines is the Universal Access to Quality Tertiary Education Act (Republic Act No. 10932) that was passed in 2017. The law mandates the state to draw from the public coffers to cover the tuition fees of students enrolled in 112 state universities and colleges (sucs), 78 local universities and colleges, and all technical vocation education and training programs registered under the Technical Education and Skills Development Authority (tesda) starting in the 2018–2019 school year. In addition to the provision of free school fees, there are also affirmative action programs for indigenous people, persons with disabilities, and students from public high schools and depressed areas. It also allows students who have financial capacity to opt out of the free higher education provision or even contribute a specific amount to their higher education institution of choice.

The provision of tuition subsidies for everyone enrolled in sucs harbors negative effects. The subsidy will be financed through general taxes. In this regard, all taxpayers, whether or not they have family members who take advantage of free tertiary education will have an obligation to pay for those who study in sucs. This would also discourage efficiency because those who were not considering tertiary education previously may now find tertiary education appealing and be more likely consume this good to a greater extent than they would if they were required to pay. Moreover, those who are willing and capable of paying for tertiary education will begin transferring the resources intended for tertiary education to other expenses. This constitutes an unnecessary loss

---

26   Daron Acemoglu, Georgy Egorov, and Konstantin Sonin, "A Political Theory of Populism," *Quarterly Journal of Economics* 128, no. 2 (2013): 771–805.

CONTEMPORARY POPULISM AND DEMOCRATIC CHALLENGES

of private investments at a crucial time when the country needs resources to fund strategic expansion in tertiary education.[27]

Subsidized college education would deepen income inequality. If it is not targeted to serve the poor, who usually have lesser qualifications, they will lose out to students with better backgrounds who often come from more affluent households. In the context of other equally important policy priorities, the additional budget to implement the free college tuition program will undoubtedly take away resources from the K-12 basic education program, infrastructure, agriculture, drug rehabilitation, national security, and other high-priority and pro-poor development programs. It would be unwise to just ignore this effect given present initiatives to further increase taxes to prevent the deficit from further escalation. There is a need to recover some of the cost of public service provision and to choose carefully and exercise caution in the deployment of subsidies as a policy tool. Populist expenditure policies are worrisome because of how the value of targeting is downgraded, and consequently how they neglect the legitimate needs of the poor.[28]

Another populist policy is the Free Irrigation Service Act of 2017 (Republic Act No. 10969). The law exempts all farmers from paying irrigation fees for landholdings of eight hectares and below. The measure also nullifies all unpaid irrigation service fees and corresponding penalties, as well as loans and past due accounts and corresponding interests and penalties of the irrigator associations from the records of the National Irrigation Administration. President Duterte raised the salary of the police during his first year in office. Rather than legislate the pay increase through the General Appropriations Act, an Executive Order was issued that increased the combat duty pay of the police from PhP 340 to PhP 3,000 a month and the combat duty pay of soldiers from PhP 500 to PhP 3,000 a month. On top of this, the police and soldiers will benefit from a big increase in combative incentive pay from PhP 150 a day or a maximum of PhP 1,500 a month to PhP 300 a day or a maximum of PhP 3,000 a month.[29]

---

27   Aniceto Orbeta Jr. and Vicente Paqueo, "Who Benefits and Loses from an Untargeted Tuition Subsidy for Students in SUCs?," *PIDS Policy Notes* No. 2017-03 (Quezon City: Philippine Institute for Development Studies, 2017).

28   Orbeta Jr. and Paqueo. "Who Benefits and Loses?"

29   Filomeno Sta. Ana, Jr. "Populism, the Bad and the Good," *Yellow Pad*, Action for Economic Reforms, December 20, 2016, http://aer.ph/populism-the-bad-and-the-good/ (accessed November 19, 2018).

9 Erosion of Independent Institutions

Populism can use an electoral mandate to decimate independent institutions that are considered bedrocks of liberal democracies like the courts and the free media. Populism might lead to political tribalism, which derails civil discourse and prevents political consensus.[30] The substitution of global democratic norms with authoritarian practices would mean more elections in which the incumbent's success is a matter of course. It would lead to more media spaces that are flooded by propaganda mouthpieces that sideline the opposition while presenting the ruler as omnipotent, tough, and committed to the welfare of the nation. It would mean state control over the Internet and social media through both censorship and active manipulation that promotes pro-regime messages.[31]

The free press is faced with tremendous challenges in the age of populism. In 2018, the government barred online news platform Rappler from covering Palace press briefings and other presidential events, citing the ruling of the Securities and Exchange Commission (SEC). The regulatory agency revoked Rappler's registration papers for violating foreign ownership rules. However, the SEC said the online news site may still continue with its operations pending its appeal to the courts.[32] The government also threatened to block the renewal of the franchise to operate of the media outfit ABS-CBN. The franchise is set to expire in 2020. House of Representatives Bill No. 4349 seeking to renew the franchise granted to ABS-CBN for 25 years is still at the committee level.[33]

President Duterte also threatened to abolish the Commission on Human Rights (CHR) during a press conference that followed his second State of the Nation Address in 2017 as he continued to defend the police and armed forces amid allegations of human rights violations. The CHR is an independent office created under the 1987 Constitution of the Republic of the Philippines that is

---

30 Claes H. De Vreese, Frank Esser, Toril Aalberg, Carsten Reinemann, and James Stanyer, "Populism as an Expression of Political Communication Content and Style: A New Perspective," *The International Journal of Press/Politics* 23, no. 4 (2018): 423–438.

31 Michael J. Abramowitz and Sarah Repucci, "Democracy /Beleaguered," *Journal of Democracy* 29, no. 2 (2018): 128–142.

32 Dharel Placido, "Duterte Says He Merely Followed SEC Ruling in Blocking Rappler," *ABS-CBN News*, February 22, 2018, https://news.abs-cbn.com/news/02/22/18/duterte-says-he-merely-followed-sec-ruling-in-blocking-rappler (accessed November 19, 2018).

33 Pia Ranada, "Duterte: If It Were Up to Me, No ABS-CBN Franchise Renewal," *Rappler*, August 3, 2018, https://www.rappler.com/nation/208802-duterte-threatens-again-block-abs-cbn-franchise-renewal-august-3-2018 (accessed November 19, 2018).

CONTEMPORARY POPULISM AND DEMOCRATIC CHALLENGES

tasked with investigating all forms of human rights violations involving civil and political rights.[34]

The House of Representatives voted to give a budget of PhP 1,000 to the Commission on Human Rights (CHR) for 2018. During the House budget plenary debates in September 2017, at least 119 lawmakers voted to approve the P1,000 budget for the CHR. Only 32 lawmakers voted against it. The decision of the House to erase the agency's budget from the proposed PhP 649.484 million down to PhP 1,000 was the result of House Speaker Pantaleon Alvarez making good on his word to give the Commission, which has long been critical of the administration's war on drugs, a measly budget which would render it ineffective in its operations in 2018.[35] Lawmakers from the lower House later decided to give the agency a budget of PhP 537 million following a meeting with CHR Chair Jose Luis Martin Gascon during the third and final reading of the proposed 2018 national budget. On the other hand, the Senate approved a budget of PhP 693 million for the agency in October 2017. The Senate version was higher than the house version by PhP 156 million. It includes a PhP 28.5 million allocation for the Human Rights Victim's Memorial Commission.[36]

The Office of the Ombudsman is another independent agency that earned the ire of the presidency. It is a constitutional body with the mandate to investigate and prosecute public officials accused of crimes, especially graft and corruption.[37] In July 2018, the Office of the President ordered the dismissal of Overall Deputy Ombudsman Melchor Arthur Carandang over his partisanship in investigating the presidential family's wealth. Aside from his separation from public service, Carandang was also slapped with the forfeiture of retirement benefits and perpetual disqualification from holding public office. The ruling, signed by Executive Secretary Salvador Medialdea, said Carandang was accused of violating the Code of Conduct and Ethical Standards for Public Officials and Employees (Republic Act No. 6713) when he disclosed or misused

---

34   Tricia Macas, "Duterte to CHR: You Are Better Abolished," *GMA News*, July 25, 2017, http://www.gmanetwork.com/news/news/nation/619330/duterte-to-chr-you-are-better-abolished/story/ (accessed November 19, 2018).

35   Marc Jayson Cayabyab, "House Gives Commission on Human Rights P1,000 Budget for 2018," *Philippine Daily Inquirer*, September 12, 2017, https://newsinfo.inquirer.net/930106/house-budget-deliberations-chr-p1000-budget-speaker-alvarez (accessed November 19, 2018).

36   Abner Mercado, "Senate Approves 2018 Budgets for CHR, DPWH," *ABS-CBN News*, October 10, 2017, https://news.abs-cbn.com/news/10/10/17/senate-approves-2018-budgets-for-chr-dpwh (accessed November 19, 2018).

37   Macas, "Duterte to CHR."

confidential information in order to give an undue advantage to Senator Antonio Trillanes IV who filed a plunder complaint against the president.[38]

10 Silencing Critics

Critics of the Duterte presidency have been silenced either through detention, removal from office, or the use of public derision. In September 2018, President Duterte said in a speech before the Filipino community in Jordan that detained Senator Leila de Lima is not a prisoner of conscience. He maintained that De Lima is involved in the illegal drug trade and is not politically persecuted. The senator has been detained in the PNP Custodial Center since February 2017 on charges that she benefited from the drug trade in the New Bilibid Prison during her tenure as Justice Secretary under the Aquino administration. De Lima is a staunch critic of Duterte of the president's anti-drug war.[39] She has petitioned a Muntinlupa City court to disqualify 13 convicts as witnesses in the drug charges she is facing. The inmates do not qualify as witnesses since they have been convicted of drug trafficking, murder, homicide, kidnapping and robbery. De Lima argued that witnesses who are convicted of crimes with moral turpitude violate the law on state witnesses.[40]

In a special en banc session, the Supreme Court voted eight to six in May 2018 to declare Maria Lourdes Sereno's appointment as Chief Justice invalid. The case against Sereno stemmed from a number of allegations, including her failure to file her Statement of Assets, Liabilities and Net Worth (SALN) for certain years as a public officer, that were originally consolidated in impeachment charges brought before Congress. However, even before Sereno could be tried by the Senate in impeachment proceedings, Solicitor General Jose Calida lodged a petition for *quo warranto* with the Supreme Court. The petitioner argued that *quo warranto* is available as a remedy even against impeachable officers. The Supreme Court denied with finality in June 2018 Sereno's motion for reconsideration.[41]

---

38 Eimor Santos, "Palace Sacks, Penalizes Overall Deputy Ombudsman Carandang," *CNN Philippines*, August 1, 2018, http://cnnphilippines.com/news/2018/08/01/Palace-dismisses-Overall-Deputy-Ombudsman-Carandang.html (accessed November 19, 2018).

39 Llanesca Panti, "Duterte: De Lima deserves to be in prison," *GMA News*, September 7, 2018.

40 Robertzon Ramirez, "De Lima Wants 13 Convicts Disqualified as DOJ Witnesses," *The Philippine Star*, September 20, 2018, http://www.gmanetwork.com/news/news/nation/667005/duterte-de-lima-deserves-to-be-in-prison/story/ (accessed November 19, 2018).

41 "SC Upholds Quo Warranto Ruling, Voids Sereno's Appointment as Chief Justice," *UNTV News*, June 29, 2018, https://www.untvweb.com/news/sc-upholds-quo-warranto-ruling-voids-serenos-appointment-as-chief-justice/ (accessed November 19, 2018).

President Duterte described Vice-President Leni Robredo as weak when it comes to strategy. In the face of health issues, Duterte stressed that he will not hand the presidency to Robredo during a speech before members of the Philippine Military Academy Alumni Association in October 2018. Under the Constitution, the vice-president shall become the president to serve the unexpired term in case of death, permanent disability, resignation, or removal from the Office of the President. On previous occasions, Duterte claimed Robredo was not suitable to be the next head of state. Instead, he declared his preference for losing vice-presidential candidate Ferdinand Marcos Jr. as his successor.[42]

11   Marginalizing the Opposition

Using an institutional theoretical lens, this study considered how weak institutions aided the rise of contemporary populism. Institutions are conceived as enduring rules and organized practices located in structures of meaning and resources. Political parties play a crucial role in fostering democratic linkage. They are the agents of representation in contemporary democratic systems.[43] Substantive representation requires consistency between the policy preferences of voters and the policy positions that political parties adopt. In addition, it is also important that political parties listen to their voters with regard to the policy issues they emphasize in democratic societies.[44]

In Philippine politics, it is common for elected officials to join the mass exodus to the party of the new Chief Executive after every presidential election. Given the absence of strong policies on political turncoatism, many elected legislators jumped to the party of President Duterte and allied parties after the 2016 elections. This changed the complexion of the leadership structure and the assignment of legislators to powerful Committee positions in the House of Representatives. For instance, the opposition Liberal Party was seriously depleted when members jumped to join the administration camp. Even the lone LP seat on the Commission on Appointments (CA) became precarious

---

42   Nathaniel Mariano and Rio Araja, "Duterte: Leni Weak; VP: No Need to Hit Me," *Manila Standard*, October 6, 2018, http://manilastandard.net/news/top-stories/277270/duterte-leni-weak-vp-no-need-to-hit-me.html (accessed November 29, 2018).

43   Russell J. Dalton, "Party Representation across Multiple Issue Dimensions," *Party Politics* 23, no. 6 (2017): 609–622.

44   Jae-Jae Spoon and Heike Klüver, "Do Parties Respond? How Electoral Context Influences Party Responsiveness," *Electoral Studies* 35 (2014): 48–60.

following the transfer of five House Members from the LP to the ruling Partido Demokratiko Pilipino-Lakas ng Bayan (PDP-Laban) in May 2017. This reduced the number of LP lawmakers in the House from 32 to 27. The House leadership gives a slot in the House contingent to the CA for every party that consists of at least 24 legislators.[45]

The existence of an opposition ensures the existence of a functioning democracy as it serves to restrain the ruling coalition in the exercise of power. In the long run, the active competition between the administration and opposition parties contributes towards forging democratic norms and rules.[46] Hence, it is a cause for alarm when the administration coalition sought to control even the selection of the Minority Leader in Congress. In August 2018, a majority of the 292-member House of Representatives voted to retain Rep. Danilo Suarez as leader of the minority bloc to end the fierce rivalry for the post. Administration lawmakers from the majority coalition expressed their support for Suarez through a voice vote after House Majority Leader Rolando Andaya Jr. moved to recognize him as the Minority Leader. However, the victory of Suarez was questioned by Rep. Romero Quimbo of the Liberal Party and Rep. Eugene de Vera of the ABS Party-list, both of whom vied for the post. They argued that Suarez properly belongs to the administration coalition having voted for Rep. Gloria Macapagal-Arroyo to unseat Rep. Pantaleon Alvarez as Speaker of the House of Representatives in July 2018.[47]

12 Conclusion

Populism has always been around in the Philippines. Its presence is heightened or muted based on the confluence of actors and events that affect the political system. The framers of the 1987 Philippine Constitution sought to establish the foundations of a representative democracy that would bar the return of authoritarianism. Hence, the fundamental law is replete with features to ensure a system of competitive elections; checks and balances among the executive,

---

45   Mara Cepeda, "If LP Exodus Continues, Party Loses Commission on Appointments Seat," *Rappler,* May 21, 2017, https://www.rappler.com/nation/170122-liberal-party-seat-commission-appointments (accessed November 19, 2018).

46   Seymour Martin Lipset, "The Indispensability of Political Parties," *Journal of Democracy* 11, no. 1 (2000): 48–55.

47   Delon Porcalla, "It's Final: Danilo Suarez is House Minority Leader," *The Philippine Star,* August 8, 2018, https://www.philstar.com/headlines/2018/08/08/1840687/its-final-danilo-suarez-house-minority-leader (accessed November 19, 2018).

legislature, and judiciary; respect for civil and political rights; and independent oversight agencies that promote accountability. However, there is a wide disparity between what is envisioned under the democratic Constitution and the actual exercise of democracy. The democratic gap lies in the failure to set up strong institutions to make representation work for the people.

Using an institutional lens, the study considered how weak institutions aided the rise of contemporary populism. The absence of strong political parties carrying well-defined platforms of governance prevents the institutionalization of political contestation based on policy differentiation. In this regard, political parties become mere vehicles for the election of candidates into office instead of being substantive agents of representation. When parties underinvest in policy research and political education, personality-oriented elections are routinized and become the norm. Citizens become less meticulous in scrutinizing the plans and programs of the leaders they choose to run the affairs of the state. Democratic systems are marked by the compatibility between the policy preferences of voters and the policy positions taken by leaders. For example, in a survey conducted by Pulse Asia a few months before the 2016 elections, fighting criminality ranked only sixth in the list of most urgent national concerns. Yet, then-candidate Duterte was able to frame criminality as the key topic in the presidential contest.[48]

Populism thrives where citizens look at strong leaders more favorably than strong institutions. The Philippines belong to the group of countries identified in a 2017 survey done by the Pew Research Center where a quarter or more of those polled preferred an arrangement in which a strong leader can make decisions without interference from the legislature and judiciary. The overpowering executive demonstrates a weakening of the system of checks and balance that is inherent in representative democracy. In Philippine politics, it is common for elected officials to jump onto the presidential bandwagon after national elections. In the post-2016 election period, a mass exodus to the party of the new President ensued. Given the absence of strong policies on political turncoatism, many elected legislators transferred to the party of President Duterte and allied parties to avail themselves of choice congressional committee positions. The authoritarian tendencies of populism are reinforced when the ranks of opposition parties are decimated through party switching. This results in the diminished independence of the legislature from the executive.

Populism rides on the crest of strong electoral support to erode independent institutions that are important in a functioning representative democracy. The

---

48   "Pulse Asia Research's September 2015 Nationwide Survey."

Chief Justice of the Supreme Court was removed without going through the impeachment procedures stipulated by the Constitution. Independent agencies such as the Commission on Human Rights and the Office of the Ombudsman that monitor the behavior of state officials were threatened with budget cuts and dismissal of their key officers. Media outfits that ran critical stories of the government were met with lawsuits and risked losing their franchises to operate.

Rather than political parties, media has become the main platform for generating political support in the age of populism. This explains the sensitivity of populist leaders to media criticism. Modern populism is occurring in the context of the mediatization of politics where public support is cultivated through both mainstream media and social media. The populist manner of political communication is marked by simplification, dramatization, confrontation, and negativity. Given their autonomy from the disciplinary norms, representative mechanisms, and policy discipline provided by political parties as intermediary institutions, populist leaders usually exercise immense discretion in going directly to the people in addressing their concerns.

While democratic norms and principles may be written in the Constitution, the case for democracy has to be demonstrated by providing avenues and mechanisms for citizen voices and participation in policy development and monitoring. Aside from improving democratic processes and practices, the case for democracy has to be made in the minds of the broader public. Citizens may have to be convinced that deficits in performance and accountability can be remedied through democracy and the rule of law rather than banishing rules-based governance away.[49] The threat to democracy has intensified amid the crisis of public knowledge. The enormity of this crisis is exhibited in the proliferation of fake news and alternative facts in media spaces. In a highly connected digital world, the spread of misinformation either for profit or propaganda has diminished the authority of the mediating institutions that generate and share knowledge, including universities, science, and the press.[50]

The role of knowledge institutions, including universities, research organizations, and policy think tanks in developing new content to educate the new generation of citizens for democracy and rules-based governance is valuable. Media is tasked with performing the critical task of ensuring integrity,

---

49   Francisco Magno, "Fostering Rules-Based Governance at Home or Abroad," *Philippine Star*, August 24, 2018, https://www.philstar.com/other-sections/news feature/2018/08/24/1845476/commentary-fostering-rules-based-governance-home-or-abroad (accessed August 24, 2018).

50   Brubaker, "Why Populism?."

credibility, and comprehensiveness in providing mechanisms for information and knowledge dissemination. On the other hand, political parties should be strengthened as representative institutions to aggregate interests, produce evidence-based policies, and foster adherence to rules-based governance. Support for a rules-based system is nurtured through interdependent civic and knowledge practices and institutions.

CHAPTER 4

Judicial Populism and Its Impact on the Quality of Democracy in Pakistan

Aasiya Riaz

1   Introduction

In December 2017, the Chief Justice of Pakistan, Saqib Nisar, likened the role of the judiciary to a *baba* (a village elder), and said that "this judiciary is your *baba*, do not doubt its integrity." The Chief Justice made these remarks in response to a mounting public perception that the judiciary had become part of a larger plan or design.[1] However, these remarks were only the beginning of what is now known Judicial Populism 2.0 under Chief Justice Nisar, who seems to have gone beyond the previous Chief Justice, Iftikhar Muhammad Chaudhry, in his quest for populism.

In an article published in the *New York Times* on March 1, 2018, titled "Pakistan's Judges Are on a Mission. But What Is It?,"[2] writer and journalist Mohammad Hanif refers to Nisar as a "man on a mission," quoting him as saying "the aim of my struggle is clean air, clean water, pure milk." *The Economist* wrote on the issue under the headline "Justice on the Loose, Pakistan's Top Court Is Eager to Take on Any Brief Just as Long as it Doesn't Have to Say 'Boo!' to the Army."[3] It also tweeted on April 1, 2018, "as the judiciary groans under a backlog of 3 million pending cases, one judge investigates the quality of chicken feed."[4]

---

1   Wajih Ahmed Sheikh, "Judiciary Won't Become Part of Any Plan: CJ," *Dawn*, December 17, 2017, https://www.dawn.com/news/1377119/judiciary-wont-become-part-of-any-plan-cj (accessed June 5, 2018).

2   Mohammad Hanif, "Pakistan's Judges Are on a Mission. But What Is It?," *The New York Times*, March 1, 2018, https://www.nytimes.com/2018/03/01/opinion/pakistan-judges-mission-corruption.html (accessed June 5, 2018).

3   "Pakistan's Top Court Is Eager to Take on Any Brief," *The Economist*, March 28, 2018, https://www.economist.com/asia/2018/03/28/pakistans-top-court-is-eager-to-take-on-any-brief (accessed June 5, 2018).

4   *The Economist* (@theEconomist), "As the Judiciary Groans under a Backlog of 3 Million Pending Cases, One Judge Investigates the Quality of Chicken Feed," Twitter, April 1, 2018, 6:46pm, https://twitter.com/theeconomist/status/980380938180923393 (accessed June 5, 2018).

© AASIYA RIAZ, 2021 | DOI:10.1163/9789004444461_006

JUDICIAL POPULISM AND ITS IMPACT ON THE QUALITY OF DEMOCRACY   81

The quest for populism has continued, even as the number of cases pending with the higher judiciary reached a record high of 38,913 as of April 2018. The rate of pendency rose by almost 100 percent between 2010 and 2018. In 2001, the number of cases in the Supreme Court backlog was recorded at 13,070, which has since multiplied several times.[5]

This chapter examines judicial populism in Pakistan and its impact on the quality of democracy during the period of one year, from May 2017 to April 2018. The chapter will analyze the causes and effects of judicial activism and how it has impacted democracy in Pakistan.

2   Background

In December 2013, when Chief Justice Chaudhry retired, he claimed the judiciary had strengthened democracy in Pakistan under his leadership. Thanking judges, lawyers, and activists who had "stood up to defend the independence of the judiciary and the rule of law," he also mentioned cases of missing persons in Balochistan, the Hajj scam, and cases regarding the law and order situation in Karachi, adding that through such cases, the courts had played their role in strengthening democracy in Pakistan.

In 2007, General Pervez Musharraf had asked Chief Justice Chaudhry to resign, as he was resisting being pushed out. He had to be dismissed, after which he and other senior judges were placed under house arrest. Lawyers rallied to support him through what is now known as the Lawyers Movement, joined by citizens across the country, which finally forced Musharraf out of power and resulted in the reinstatement of Chaudhry and his colleagues.

The former Chief Justice was correct to mention the proactiveness that saw an unprecedented increase in cases taken *suo motu*, or on the court's own authority, during his tenure. The world also saw a Supreme Court that grew increasingly populist under his leadership. As he recounted the unprecedented autonomy of the courts from the government—both during the tenures of elected government and the earlier tenure of Musharraf—he did not mention the growing criticism of what began to be described as "overreach" by the superior judiciary in matters of governance constitutionally under the domain

---

5 Hasnat Malik, "SC Annual Report: Pendency of Cases Reaches 15-Year High," *The Express Tribune*, May 21, 2018, https://tribune.com.pk/story/1715028/1-sc-annual-report-pendency-cases-reaches-15-year-high/ (accessed June 5, 2018).

of the executive. Chaudhry lavished praise on superior courts for enforcing fundamental rights and scrutinizing the executive's "far from perfect" public administration while decrying the "ever-growing cancer of corruption" in politics.

While successive Chief Justices since Chaudhry have painted themselves as Messiah-like figures who are able to resolve every issue in the country, the courts have continued to ignore the severity of the problems facing the lower courts, which essentially means the issues encountered by ordinary Pakistani citizens and the increasing pendency of cases both at superior and lower courts.

3 Constitutional Domain

As one of the three pillars of the state, which also comprises the executive and the legislature, the powers and roles of the judiciary are defined under part VII of the Constitution of Pakistan, the judicature (Articles 175–212).

Pakistan has a hierarchical judiciary system with two classes of courts: the superior (or higher) judiciary and the subordinate (or lower) judiciary. Subordinate or lower courts consist of civil and criminal district courts, and numerous specialized courts. The superior judiciary is composed of the Supreme Court and High Courts and is charged with the responsibility to preserve, protect, and defend the Constitution of Pakistan. It has a number of *de jure* powers outlined in the Constitution including appellate and constitutional jurisdiction, and *suo motu* power to try human rights matters.

Under the Constitution, the Supreme Court has various jurisdictions.

- The first is an appellate jurisdiction; it is the court of appeals from the four provincial High Courts and the Islamabad High Court.
- The Supreme Court has an appellate jurisdiction on appeals from service tribunals.
- It also has an advisory jurisdiction, wherein the President of Pakistan refers questions on matters of public importance on which the federation requires an answer to the Supreme Court.
- The Supreme Court also has a review jurisdiction, which gives it the power to review its past decisions made by a different bench.
- The Supreme Court additionally has an original jurisdiction, which is invoked under Article 184(3) of the Constitution, when it relates to matters of public importance and the enforcement of fundamental rights guaranteed under the Constitution to every citizen of Pakistan.

JUDICIAL POPULISM AND ITS IMPACT ON THE QUALITY OF DEMOCRACY 83

The original jurisdiction of the Supreme Court is the area known as judicial populism.[6]

4 Military Dictatorship and Democracy

Pakistan was ruled directly by the military for more than 30 years between the country's independence in 1947 and 2017. Not a single elected prime minister of Pakistan has been able to complete the constitutional tenure of given years in office as of 2017. In addition to four direct interventions by the military since Pakistan's independence in 1947, successive military commanders have exercised de facto authority on crucial aspects of national security management, including regional and international affairs.

Instead of serving as bulwarks against the bulldozing of democracy, the courts served to legitimize these coups. The country has seen constitutions abrogated and martial law imposed in 1958, 1969, 1977, and 1999. After each imposition of martial law, the Supreme Court granted validation to the orders under what has been infamously termed the "Doctrine of Necessity," giving itself the dubious honor of playing handmaiden to military dictators.

In the military intervention under General Musharraf (1999–2008), the Supreme Court re-invoked the Doctrine of State Necessity in a constitutional case entitled *Zafar Ali Shah v. General Pervez Musharraf, Chief Executive of Pakistan*, allowing the military dictator to amend the Constitution at will. However, restrictions were also imposed, such that general elections should be held within three years and that the salient features of the Constitution of 1973 would not be changed.

The preambles of all regular constitutions of Pakistan (1956, 1962, and 1973) assign sovereignty over all the universe to God Almighty. The people exercise this authority as a sacred trust within the limits prescribed by Him. This exercise of power and authority is to be undertaken through their chosen representatives.[7] This means that the authority and power of the state is located in the elected Parliament, making it the salient institution as compared with the bureaucracy, the military, and the judiciary, although these institutions also have their own domains of authority under the Constitution and law.[8] Political

---

6 Interview with Shahid Hamid by PILDAT on the topic of judicial populism, see A. Tarar, S. Hamid, and I. Qadir, "On Judicial Populism," August 11, 2018, https://www.youtube.com/watch?v=6uidaCXDlVQ (accessed June 10, 2020).

7 Iram Khalid, "Role of Judiciary in the Evolvement of Democracy in Pakistan," *Journal of Political Studies* 19, no. 2 (2012): 125–142.

8 Khalid, "Role of Judiciary."

stability is an essential ingredient for democratization. Unfortunately, political institutions in Pakistan have been unable to flourish due to the repeated dissolution of Assemblies at the behest of military interventions. Constitutional petitions were filed before the Supreme Court of Pakistan at the time of every dissolution of an Assembly in the hopes that they would be restored. However, the court verdicts by and large upheld these dissolutions.[9]

Furthermore, the Supreme Court did not just sanction the dissolution of elected Assemblies. It was also party to the hanging of elected Prime Minister Zulfikar Ali Bhutto in 1979 and the ousting of Premier Yousaf Raza Gilani.

In 2017, the Supreme Court disqualified yet another prime minister, Nawaz Sharif, who was elected to office on June 1, 2013, in the tenth general election in Pakistan. The reason given for his disqualification was his "dishonesty" under Article 62(1)(f) of the Constitution, as he failed to disclose his receivable salary from the company he was employed with in the United Arab Emirates in his nomination papers for the general election of 2013.

5   Cases of Judicial Populism in Pakistan

Legal experts believe that the rise of social and electronic media has contributed to the rise of judicial populism. Judges are part of society, and are tempted by the need to project, and see depicted, a positive, larger-than-life self-image in the media and, through that, among the public. This also explains the rise in immediate notices issued by courts on issues or incidents widely covered in the media, as judges seem to desire a constant, positive, and public media spotlight on their role. Some experts are of the opinion that the judges are trying to reframe the institution as "The People's Supreme Court" in order to gain popularity, which, needless to say, is a poor stance to take. It is the Parliament to which citizen representatives are elected to represent the people, to legislate, and to hold the executive to account. This increase in *suo motu* notices, as well as attempts by Chief Justice Nisar to take the lead in the initiative to build dams and to visit schools and hospitals, is not in the domain of judges and is a blatant violation of the code of conduct to be observed by all Supreme Court judges.[10]

---

9   Khalid, "Role of Judiciary."

10   Christine Fair, "The Only Enemy Pakistan's Army Can Beat Is Its Own Democracy," *Foreign Policy.* August 9, 2017, http://foreignpolicy.com/2017/08/09/the-only-enemy-pakistans-army-can-beat-is-its-own-democracy/ (accessed June 18, 2018). See also https://www.supremecourt.gov.pk/downloads_judgements/all_downloads/supreme_judicial_council/CODE_OF_CONDUCT_FOR_JUDGES.pdf.

While the judiciary is swift in taking *suo motu* notices, some blame also lies with the executive in its failure to resolve matters of public importance, which, some argue, creates a vacuum that is then filled by the judiciary.[11] Experts believe that the "Supreme Court has felt that in various areas the executive authority has perhaps not been discharging its responsibilities to the full extent." Alleged corruption in the services sector and in society involving high-level personalities, where "the Supreme Court has felt that its interference or its control is required because the concerned agencies have not been acting for extraneous considerations," is another factor temping the judiciary to overstep into the executive domain.[12] However, in raising its own profile, the judiciary has failed to ensure that the image and standing of other stakeholders, including elected governments, the executive, political parties, and even lower courts, are elevated in the public opinion.

From visiting hospitals unannounced and making remarks in court to the effect that simple surgical instruments were unavailable and that the provision of healthcare is the Supreme Court's responsibility, to openly calling elected provincial governments inept and total failures, the list of incidents of judicial overstepping into the executive domain is rather long. While the Supreme Court regularly pronounced that the judiciary did not want to interfere in executive matters but was "compelled" to do so due to the poor state of affairs, it continued to make populist remarks and issue orders. For instance, the Supreme Court ordered the entire city of Karachi, with a population of nearly 15 million, to be cleaned up within one week; the provision of clean drinking water in hospitals across Punjab; and the closure of illegal clinics run by quacks across Punjab within one month. The judiciary continued to make populist remarks, from threatening to shut down all mega projects if the state of public hospitals and educational institutions didn't improve in provinces, to slapping fines on senior officials and harshly admonishing them in court, directing the federal government to seek the apex court's approval before proceeding with the privatization of the flag carrier Pakistan International Airlines (PIA), and ordering authorities to place the names of all former managing directors of the PIA on the Exit Control List, to calling them "oppressors, enemies, and traitors of the State"—the list of populist actions and pronouncements goes on.

It is often said that judges should only speak through their verdicts. This, however, has become an exception, rather than the norm, among Pakistan's senior judges. The state of affairs has regressed to a level where remarks made

---

11   Tarar, Hamid, and Qadir, "On Judicial Populism."
12   Tarar, Hamid, and Qadir, "On Judicial Populism."

by judges while hearing cases become instant headlines in the media. More often than not, judges seem to give their personal views instead of waiting to arrive at a judgment in hearing cases. In his opinion in a corruption case against Sharif, part of a scandal broadly known as Panamagate, Justice Asif Saeed Khan Khosa quoted Mario Puzo quoting Balzac in the novel *The Godfather*: "Behind every great fortune there is a crime." He called the mafia novel's epigraph "fascinating" before saying that the case before the court revolved around the same notion.

The Supreme Court's agenda increasingly seems to be set by what's on television. Major news stories have spurred the court to start proceedings *suo motu*.[13] The hearings that follow then feed the news cycle again, with the justices making headline-worthy comments and cracking jokes. Last year, one of them told the attorney general that the government was like "the Sicilian mafia."[14]

In keeping with its previous role in negatively impacting democracy, the judiciary's actions have influenced democracy by stepping into the political arena, as in the Panama Papers scandal, which involved the family of former Prime Minister Sharif. While the Supreme Court initially declined the government's request to form a judicial commission to probe the revelations that surfaced in the Panama Papers data leaks, its decision to take up a political case was rightly criticized by many legal experts as a likely cause of a larger future national calamity.

In April 2017, a five-member bench of the Supreme Court gave the verdict in the Panama Papers case that the Premier would not be disqualified and that a Joint Investigation Team would be formed to probe the money trail of the Sharif family. The Team would report to the court every two weeks and would complete its proceedings in 60 days. The six-member Team, which submitted a report to the Supreme Court based on which the Court made its decision to disqualify Sharif for being "not honest" under Article 62(1)(f) of the Constitution,[15] included two serving military officers from Inter-Services Intelligence and Military Intelligence. Legitimate concerns were raised not only about the fact that military institutions such as the Inter-Services Intelligence and the Military Intelligence do not have a professional role to investigate white collar

---

13   Khurram Hashimi, "The Power of *Suo Moto*," *The Express Tribune*, May 1, 2012, https:// tribune.com.pk/story/372164/the-power-of-suo-motu/ (accessed June 10, 2020).

14   Haseeb Bhatti, "Supreme Court Rages at Nehal Hashmi's Threats, Likens Govt to Sicilian Mafia," *Dawn*, June 1, 2017, https://www.dawn.com/news/1336729/supreme-court-rages-at-nehal-hashmis-threats-likens-govt-to-sicilian-mafia (accessed June 10, 2020).

15   "Nawaz Sharif steps down as PM after SC's Disqualification Verdict," *Dawn*, July 28, 2017.

JUDICIAL POPULISM AND ITS IMPACT ON THE QUALITY OF DEMOCRACY 87

crime, but also about the Supreme Court involving military agencies in the highly politicized Panama Papers enquiry.[16]

It was later reported in the media that the Registrar of the Supreme Court allegedly used a WhatsApp call to tell the top bosses of the State Bank of Pakistan and the Securities and Exchange Commission of Pakistan to include specific names in the panel to be forwarded to the Supreme Court's special bench for the constitution of the Joint Investigation Team. Initially, as per the Supreme Court decision on the Panama Papers case, all the concerned institutions including the Federal Investigation Agency, the Inter-Services Intelligence, Military Intelligence, the State Bank of Pakistan, the Securities and Exchange Commission of Pakistan, and the National Accountability Bureau had sent their respective panels of officers to the Supreme Court for the setting up of the Joint Investigation Team.

Prominent lawyers argued that the *suo motu* notice against Sharif issued by the Supreme Court resulted in the loss of the fundamental right of appeal and was therefore wrong. "Every time we looked for support from the judiciary, it supported dictatorship instead, leaving us weak," said ousted Prime Minister Sharif.[17]

After the disqualification, widespread local and international media reports indicated that instead of being received as a Supreme Court verdict, the disqualification was seen by many people as having been orchestrated by the army in what appeared to be a "Get-Nawaz" agenda. While some resorted to whispers and innuendo in the media, others, including the international media, described the disqualification as an outcome of sour civil–military relations and questioned the future of democracy in Pakistan.

The national media offered analyses, stating that "elected governments in Pakistan have less to fear from the Indian army than from their own," and that "[Pakistan's] security establishment regularly betrays contempt for civilians. There is a view that elected governments are regarded as unwanted pregnancies, to be aborted whenever need be, to save the motherland. The latest stillbirth is the ouster of a third-time prime minister Nawaz Sharif."[18]

---

16   PILDAT Monitor on Civil–Military Relations in Pakistan, June 2017, https://pildat.org/civil-military-relations1/monitor-on-civil-military-relations-in-pakistan-jun-2017 (accessed June 20, 2020).

17   "Factions of Army, Judiciary Sabotage Democracy in Pakistan: Nawaz," *Pakistan Today*, February 3, 2018, https://www.pakistantoday.com.pk/2018/02/02/factions-in-army-judiciary-sabotage-democracy-says-nawaz/ (accessed June 20, 2020).

18   F.S. Aijazuddin. "An Unburied Lion," *Dawn*, August 10, 2017, https://www.dawn.com/news/1350643/an-unburied-lion (accessed June 18, 2018).

The criticism of the disqualification was even more scathing in the international media, which said that "the judicial farce that resulted in Sharif's most recent ouster demonstrates that the courts remain tools for the generals to clip democracy's wings."[19]

The same Supreme Court that first disqualified Sharif from holding elected office later also disqualified him from holding party office, and all his actions and notifications as head of the party were termed null and void in February 2018.[20] The Court ordered the Election Commission of Pakistan to remove Sharif as president of the Pakistan Muslim League-Nawaz (PML-N). It further ruled that "all steps taken, orders passed, directions given and documents issued" by Sharif since his disqualification "will be deemed to have been nullified." Following the Supreme Court verdict, the Election Commission ruled that the nominees fielded by the PML-N could only take part in the Senate polls, scheduled for March 2018, as independent candidates.

In April 2018, the Supreme Court also ruled that disqualification handed down under Article 62 (1)(f) of the Constitution is for life, which resulted in the lifetime disqualification of Sharif.[21]

In a continuing probe based on National Accountability Bureau references filed against Sharif, many legal experts have anonymously quoted NAB officials saying that while apparently NAB has to work under the Supreme Court's appointed Supervisory Judge, NAB is really answering to the military (Inter-Services Intelligence and Military Intelligence) in these proceedings.[22]

Some experts believe the judiciary is just like any other organ of the state and that the person heading it at any point in time reflects its behavior. For others, the problem is more structural than behavioral; they believe the issue arose with the reinstatement of Justice Chaudhry through an Executive Order, which went against the judgment in the Tikka Khan case and was therefore illegal. The perception is that Provisional Constitutional Order (PCO) judges

---

19   Fair, "The Only Enemy."

20   Haseeb Bhatti, "Nawaz Sharif Removed as PML-N Head after SC Rules Disqualified Person Cannot Lead a Party," *Dawn*, February 21, 2018, https://www.dawn.com/news/1390816/nawaz-sharif-removed-as-pml-n-head-after-sc-rules-disqualified-person-cannot-lead-a-party (accessed June 10, 2020).

21   Haseeb Bhatti, "Disqualification Under Article 62 (1)(F) Is For Life, SC Rules In Historic Verdict," *Dawn*, April 13, 2018, https://www.dawn.com/news/1401362/disqualification-under-article-62-1f-is-for-life-sc-rules-in-historic-verdict (accessed June 10, 2020).

22   "PILDAT Study on the Future of Democracy and Civil–Military Relations in Pakistan, Developments in 2017," http://pildat.ipower.com/publications/Publication/CMR/futureofdemocracyandcivil-militaryrelationsinpakistan_developmentsin2017_astudybypildat.pdf (accessed June 10, 2020).

JUDICIAL POPULISM AND ITS IMPACT ON THE QUALITY OF DEMOCRACY   89

removed non-PCO judges to do away with any opposition among the benches, and pursued self-preservation through subjugation of the elected government via excessive use of Article 184(3) of the Constitution.[23]

6   *Suo Motu* and Judicial Populism

In their quest for populism, the courts have employed *suo motu* powers as their key arsenal, but have been criticized for an inconsistent application of these powers.

By and large, court decisions have reinforced the politician-bashing that military leaders have used to delegitimize civilian democratic rule. While on the one hand the Court has validated military takeovers, its general commentary and decisions have lamented governance, criticized Parliament, and excoriated Pakistan's civilian politicians for corruption and lack of morality.

It has therefore rightly been argued that:

> In a country shifting away from authoritarian military rule, these are hazardous roads to follow, since they risk further delegitimizing representative institutions that are not yet fully consolidated. In fashioning this role as the ultimate arbiter of political integrity and morality, the Court also has frequently invoked "independence of the judiciary"—but has often seemed to neglect that judicial independence is not an end in itself. Rather, it exists to serve other goals, including democracy, constitutionalism, fundamental rights, the rule of law. Advancing those goals requires not unconstrained judicial autonomy, but rather an appropriate balance between judicial autonomy and constraint, along with empowered representative institutions with strengthened governance capacities, democratic legitimacy, and sufficient power to resist the military and affiliated interests. A Supreme Court that genuinely understands itself as legitimized by the Pakistani people also has an interest in stronger representative institutions and stronger lines of accountability to those institutions.[24]

Following the lead of former Chief Justice Chaudhry, Pakistan's Supreme Court has largely used *suo motu* on fundamental rights and constitutionalism to

---

23   Tarar, Hamid, and Qadir, "On Judicial Populism."

24   Anil Kalhan, "Beyond Judicial Populism," *The Express Tribune*, December 24, 2013, https://tribune.com.pk/story/649601/beyond-judicial-populism/ (accessed June 5, 2018).

TABLE 4.1   Trust in institutions

Institutions	A lot	Somewhat	A little	Not at all	DK	NR	Approval Rating
National Assembly	20%	38%	30%	10%	1%	0%	58%
Provincial Assembly	10%	33%	35%	19%	2%	0%	43%
Political Parties	8%	28%	37%	23%	3%	1%	35%
Supreme Court/ High Court	30%	31%	19%	15%	3%	1%	62%
Election Commission	10%	29%	32%	24%	4%	1%	39%
Civil Courts	10%	32%	34%	19%	3%	2%	43%
National Accountability Bureau	12%	27%	28%	24%	6%	2%	39%
Electronic Media	15%	39%	26%	16%	3%	1%	54%
Print Media	12%	36%	28%	18%	4%	1%	48%
Government Officials	5%	24%	33%	33%	4%	1%	29%
Armed Forces	54%	21%	12%	10%	2%	1%	76%
Police	3%	15%	32%	47%	3%	1%	18%

SOURCE: PILDAT REPORT ON PUBLIC OPINION ON THE QUALITY OF GOVERNANCE IN PAKISTAN: OCTOBER 2016

define its identity. In the process, it has improved its public standing. In 2016, it became the second most trusted institution according to public opinion after the first-ranked Pakistan Army, receiving a 62 percent approval rating.

The populism of the judiciary has increased to such an extent that it seems to have become a factor in weakening the basic requirement of democracy, that is, elections. In 2018, the PILDAT Score Card on Perception of Pre-Poll Fairness (May 2018)[25] deemed the role of the judiciary an "unfair" factor in the run-up to the 2018 general election.

---

25   PILDAT, "Score Card on Pre-Poll Fairness," PILDAT, May 2018, https://pildat.org/wp-content/uploads/2018/05/PILDATScorecardonPerceptionofPre-PollFairness_May-2018.pdf (accessed June 10, 2020).

The conduct of the 2018 general election, which resulted in the formation of the federal government by Imran Khan's Pakistan Tehreek-i-Insaf (PTI), as well as governments in three out of four provinces including Punjab, Khyber Pakhtunkhwa, and a coalition government in Balochistan, was questioned widely both nationally and internationally by the media, which cried foul over the alleged interference to subvert the mandate of the people.

Some analysts were of the opinion that "the military persuaded politicians from other parties to defect to [the] PTI along with their voters … The army bullied the press into providing [the] PTI with positive coverage while attacking the PML-N. The security apparatus rounded up, detained, and otherwise harassed [the] PML-N party workers, and the army worked behind the scenes to disqualify [the] PML-N candidates from running."[26] The international media believed that "they appear determined to keep former Prime Minister Nawaz Sharif out of politics"[27] using the judiciary. "In this election, the court was instrumental to the army's scheme to elect Khan."[28]

7 Conclusion

This chapter has argued that in its quest for populism, the higher judiciary in Pakistan appears to be increasingly and openly partisan and, in an apparent joining of hands with the military, it is serving to weaken the course of democracy in Pakistan.

The disqualification of the Prime Minister in 2017 is seen by analysts and the media to have occurred through what is termed "a military–judiciary nexus" that has been created to manage and undermine a popularly elected party.

An overview of developments preceding the 2018 general election also shows that instead of utilizing its power and popularity to strengthen democracy and democratic institutions, the judiciary used it to criticize, pick at, and practically desecrate other state institutions, including the executive and the legislature. Senior judges continued to publicly lash out at elected leadership and political parties and humiliate the civil bureaucracy. The judiciary in

---

26 Christine Fair, "Pakistan's Sham Election," *Foreign Affairs*, July 27, 2018, https://www.foreignaffairs.com/articles/pakistan/2018-07-27/pakistans-sham-election (accessed August 10, 2018).

27 Shashank Bengali and Aoun Sahi, "As Pakistan Prepares for Elections, Its Powerful Military Appears to Be Meddling," *LA Times*, July 20, 2018, http://www.latimes.com/world/asia/la-fg-pakistan-elections-20180720-story.html (accessed August 9, 2018).

28 Bengali and Sahi, "As Pakistan Prepares."

Pakistan appears to fail to appreciate that its own popularity and independence cannot be long-lasting unless its powers are also used to empower representative institutions with strengthened governance capacities, democratic legitimacy, and sufficient power to resist the military and affiliated interests. A Supreme Court that genuinely understands itself as legitimized by the Pakistani people must also have an interest in promoting stronger representative institutions.

Despite resorting to populism, the judiciary has chosen not to put its own house in order. It has given surprisingly little attention to the problems facing the lower courts, where ordinary Pakistani citizens are much more likely to encounter the judicial system.

In going forward, experts agree that the judiciary should be reconstituted entirely. The Parliament needs to amend the laws to provide the right of appeal under Article 184(3), while its contours must be defined. Article 175(a) must be reconstructed. The powers of *suo motu* need to be limited. The Parliament must also undertake a constitutional amendment on the method of appointment of judges and bring reforms to the powers of the Chief Justice in the formation of benches.

8 Recommendations

Where do we go from here? Experts believe that there are no easy or instant solutions available to instantly reverse judicial populism, especially as it continues to find public approval. However, in order to push for institutions to play their rightful role according to the Constitution, the following policy prescriptions are required:

i. The courts must exercise the principle of restraint and let all institutions, including the executive, function in their constitutional domains. Courts require introspection with regard to the fact that judicial populism and the over-involvement of the judiciary in adjudicating political issues is undermining the courts and making them controversial.

ii. A process of in-house review of cases being considered by the Supreme Court, both through *suo motu* and otherwise, needs to be provided to determine whether the cases and issues need to be taken up.

iii. There needs to be an appeal procedure for cases decided by the Supreme Court on a *suo motu* basis.

JUDICIAL POPULISM AND ITS IMPACT ON THE QUALITY OF DEMOCRACY   93

iv.   The Parliament and the provincial assemblies need to proactively take legislative and administrative measures in areas that have been the subject matter of *suo motu* jurisdiction.[29]

v.   There is a need to make constitutional amendments to Articles 184(3) and 175(a) of the Constitution of Pakistan.[30] The national and provincial assemblies elected in the 2018 general election must take a proactive approach in this regard.

vi.   Parliament must also legislate to nullify controversial judgments by PCO judges.

vii. There is a need to reconstitute the judiciary and empower the Parliament to appoint neutral judges. Political parties and leadership elected to the Parliament must come together to write constitutional and legal provisions in a non-partisan manner.

Instituting reforms in any society, on any subject, and in any area is often a long-drawn-out and painstaking process. More often than not, self-evaluation and introspection do not occur within those institutions and entities most in need of it. Reforms to address the dangerous trends of judicial populism may not originate from within the institution of the judiciary, but they need to be carefully and effectively instituted through the joining of hands of elected political parties, citizens, citizen groups, lawyers' associations, and bar councils. Despite the rise in public trust in the judiciary, the trend of judicial populism is hurting the basic architecture, functions, and powers of the institutions as laid out in the Constitution of Pakistan. Judicial populism may be bringing short-term popularity to the individuals at the helm of affairs in the judiciary, but it has become a leading source of harm to the required nonpartisan status of the judiciary. Courts that are seen to be acting in a partisan fashion and in a manner unbecoming to the code of conduct for judges are primarily responsible for weakening the role of the judiciary, which can have serious and disastrous consequences for a country grappling with a fledgling democracy and a long-drawn-out transition to democratic consolidation.

---

29   Tarar, Hamid, and Qadir, "On Judicial Populism."
30   Tarar, Hamid, and Qadir, "On Judicial Populism."

PART 3

Redistributive Populism

∴

CHAPTER 5

Populism in Contemporary Indian Politics

Kaustuv Chakrabarti and Kaustuv Kanti Bandyopadhyay

1 Introduction

Populism is all around us, but its precise definition remains elusive. From a democratic point of view, the ambivalence is apparent in the very term "populism." Its root is the Latin word *populus* (the people), which exhibits a clear link with the democratic idea. Where there is democracy, in other words, there is always populism.[1] On the other hand, the suffix "ism" signals an ideological potential in contrast to the moderate character of modern-day democracies. By exaggerating the democratic element and mobilizing it against the constraints introduced into democratic systems by constitutional principles, populism moves at least potentially into proximity to opponents of the system.[2]

According to Yascha Mounk,[3] the list of movements that have historically been called populist is strikingly long and varied. There are the *populares* of Ancient Rome, the agrarians of 19th-century Wisconsin, and the Peronists of 20th-century Argentina. Even in the early 21st century, the populist label has been applied to Turkey's Recep Tayyip Erdogan, to Venezuela's Nicolás Maduro, and to Italy's Beppe Grillo, as well as France's Marine Le Pen. Yet the movements they lead are not inspired by one single political ideology. Some favor state ownership of the means of production, while others want to privatize prisons; some seek to put politics under religious tutelage, while others are stridently secular. In global politics, the term populism is often used to signify a movement in which an "outsider" or anti-establishment figure tries to capture power by appealing directly to the masses. Some dictionaries define populism as a political philosophy that favors the rights of "the people" as opposed to

---

1 Margaret Canovan, "Trust the People! Populism and the Two Faces of Democracy," *Political Studies* 47, no. 1 (1999): 2–16.

2 Frank Decker, "The Populist Challenge to Liberal Democracy," *Internationale Politik und Gesellschaft* 3 (2003): 47–59.

3 Yascha Mounk, "Why Populism Is Sweeping Europe?" *The New Republic*, July 19, 2017, https://newrepublic.com/article/143604/european-disunion-rise-populist-movements-means-democracy (accessed February 11, 2019).

© CHAKRABARTI AND BANDYOPADHYAY, 2021 | DOI:10.1163/9789004444461_007

those of elites.[4] This seems to be the common political imagination shared by populist leaders the world over.

Populist leaders do not only promise good things to everybody—although to be a merchant of dreams is an important part of their politics—they also articulate a political style. Populists claim to represent the people and that this stance places them above any institution, including the judiciary, because they identify directly with the people's sentiments, sense of justice, and morality. Jan-Werner Müller names this as a "moral monopoly of representation."[5] According to Müller, it is this posture that makes populists inherently dangerous. Because they see themselves as the only legitimate political actors, they seek to take over the judiciary, to gain control of the media, and to co-opt other institutions. While other political forces may, to varying degrees, engage in similar practices, only populists can "undertake such colonization openly." The openness of the populist challenge to pluralism makes it much more dangerous than more covert enemies of democracy.[6]

Populism, however, is not an ideology. It is not, for instance, either right or left wing. It is not simply demagoguery either. Populism invokes an idea of the masses of common people who are either excluded from or have limited access to privilege, as distinguished from the elite, who do have access to privilege and embody alternative cultural traditions. John Harriss quotes Arun Ranga Swamy and defines populism as a doctrine claiming that ordinary people have been robbed of their due through no fault of their own.[7] This idea further holds the elite sections of society responsible for simply seizing avenues for advancement and forgetting their moral obligations to protect the poor and underprivileged. Nevertheless, the ambiguity and ambivalence of populism as a philosophy make it impossible to arrive at a single definition of this phenomenon.

In contrast, populism in popular parlance in India is used to refer to virtually any policy that is redistributive in nature instead of being purely growth-oriented. This is particularly true when such a policy is announced before impending elections.[8] Given this background, this chapter seeks to understand

---

4   Bhaskar Dutta, "What is Populism?—Voters Have not Booted Out Re-distributive Schemes in India," *Telegraph India*, January 14, 2014, https://www.telegraphindia.com/opinion/what-is-populism-voters-have-not-booted-out-redistributive-schemes-in-india/cid/226319 (accessed October 9, 2018).

5   Jan-Werner Müller, *What Is Populism?* (London: Penguin UK, 2017).

6   Müller, *What Is Populism?*.

7   John Harriss, "Populism, Tamil Style: Is it really a success?," *Development Studies Institute Working Paper Series* 01-15 (2001), https://www.files.ethz.ch/isn/138126/WP15.pdf (accessed October 23, 2018).

8   In accordance with this idea, employment guarantee schemes, a food security bill (guaranteeing some amount of food grains at highly subsidized prices), and old-age pension

POPULISM IN CONTEMPORARY INDIAN POLITICS

the context (socioeconomic and political) in which populism is practiced in Indian politics. Subsequently, the chapter will also analyze populism's impact on Indian democracy and its democratic institutions. The second section will situate the rise of populism in India and the world while highlighting the causes contributing to its rise and significance. It will also elaborate upon popular perceptions of populism in the national and sub-national contexts. The third section will discuss the factors that incentivize the practice of populism in the national and sub-national contexts using case studies to exemplify how populism is employed in practice. In this section, the chapter will also examine the impacts of such populist policies on the Indian democratic system. In the concluding section the chapter will try to identify the role of civil society vis-à-vis populism.

2 History and the Rise of Populism in India

Since the late 19th century, populism has played a vital role in different phases of Indian history, particularly in mobilizing emergent groups and bringing about different movements and civil society initiatives. Populism has co-existed with several different ideological strands, and yet it has influenced a range of policies with its discourses and mobilization.

Contemporary politics is awash with populist developments surrounding elections, political parties, and leaders. These trends have significant implications for how we look at modern democracies and their institutions. Most significantly, they signal widespread distrust in conventional democratic institutions, an increasing disconnect between citizens and elected representatives, and a growing dislike of "politics as usual."

The term populism is generally used by the press in India to refer to the indiscriminate use of public resources to give away goods to voters. With these connotations of crowd-pleasing politics, populism has become a pejorative term. Populist politicians are criticized for giving away "freebies" or "sops" and pandering to the baser instincts of voters.[9] It is assumed that populists

---

schemes that are in place in several states are all "populist" measures. So too are the loan-waiver schemes for farmers that are implemented from time to time, and indeed all the various subsidies that are announced intermittently. All of these can be subsumed under the umbrella of "populism."

9 "Freebies Galore in AIADMK Poll Manifesto." *The Hindu*, March 25, 2011, http://www.hindu.com/2011/03/25/stories/2011032559560100.htm (accessed October 23, 2018).

govern in irrational and irresponsible ways,[10] and threaten fiscal chaos with their largesse.

In this context, it becomes imperative to understand contemporary populism within the realm of Indian history by tracing its roots and the reasons for its development. Politically, populist appeals were deployed extensively in the late colonial period, with Mahatma Gandhi's agro-artisanal romanticism, an imagined pre-colonial social economy based on self-sufficient villages.[11] Populist forces emerged in the 1960s to increase emergent group representation and enhance the quality of India's democracy. The most popular example of left-wing populism remains Prime Minister Indira Gandhi, who in the 1970s concentrated power in her own hands, pledging to work for the people and end poverty in the country.[12] Indira Gandhi's populism on the national stage vividly employed a strategy of anti-elitism. Paradoxically, the daughter of India's first prime minister, Jawaharlal Nehru, managed to portray herself as anti-elitist by delegitimizing the establishment of her own party and claiming not only to represent the people but even to personify the Indian nation itself.[13] Her brand of populism promoted clientelism and personal loyalty over party structure in order to expand her electoral base. Indira Gandhi's leadership is widely regarded as contributing to the rise of a politics based on caste, tribal ethnicity, and religion in the 1980s.[14] At the same time, while the Indian National Congress (INC) engaged with populism associated with the common people, the Bharatiya Janata Party (BJP) offered an indigenous populist alternative to India's secularist and multicultural institutions, believing it to be a Western import helping a narrow elite retain their dominance.

The Indian subcontinent has also seen popular struggles in the form of caste movements, environmental struggles, and farmer mobilizations. Lower and middle caste movements to oppose caste inequalities and exclusions have had a deep presence in western and southern India from the time of the Satya Shodhak Samaj (Truth Seeker Society) led by Jyotirao Phule in regions that now constitute Maharashtra. Similarly, in the state of Tamil Nadu, the Self-Respect Association has mobilized middle castes in an attempt to reclaim the

---

10   Francisco Panizza, "Introduction," in *Populism and the Mirror of Democracy*, ed. Francisco Panizza (London: Verso, 2005), 1–31.

11   Narendra Subramanian, "Populism in India," *SAIS Review of International Affairs* 27, no. 1 (2007): 81–91.

12   Subramanian, "Populism in India."

13   Ramachandra Guha, *India after Gandhi: The history of the world's largest democracy* (London: Pan Macmillan, 2017).

14   Thomas Blom Hansen, *The Saffron Wave: Democracy and Hindu nationalism in modern India* (Princeton, NJ: Princeton University Press, 1999).

POPULISM IN CONTEMPORARY INDIAN POLITICS

autonomy this group previously enjoyed. These organizations have pressed larger organizations to promote caste mobility. Environmental movements that resisted logging in the Himalayas in the 1970s and protested the construction of the Narmada dam from the 1990s have also been viewed through the lens of populist markers. The rise and fall of peasant movements in India between the 1980s and 2014 has been explored by eminent sociologist D. N. Dhanagare from the perspective of populist movements.[15] A steady popular wave began in 2011 when Anna Hazare and Arvind Kejriwal led the India Against Corruption movement, and it has been on the rise ever since.

The roots of post-2014 populism lie in the economic system. The reforms of the 1990s produced modest liberalization of the Indian economy, greater internal deregulation, and continued growth in the services sector but stagnation in agriculture and unstable growth in industry.[16] This economic growth has been unevenly experienced across different states.[17] Domestically, the service sector produced relatively few jobs, and the vast bulk of those that were generated were in lower-productivity activities.[18] The global competitiveness of services and manufacturing relies on informal production arrangements, the low wages and insecure informal contracts of those in supporting services such as logistics, security, and transport, and the ability to pay skilled professionals lower salaries than the global average.[19] This has negatively impacted employment, income, and the standard of living for the masses and prompted support for populism, which promises to change the status quo, propagating political and economic ideas that run counter to the established system. Thus, populist leaders often come to power in sustained weak economic conditions where they channel the rage of the people and garner support brought about by wealth gaps. Populist leaders promote the goal of working for the people and claim to represent the voice of the people, espousing formulas such as "India is Indira and Indira is India."

---

15   D.N. Dhanagare, *Populism and Power: Farmers' movement in western India, 1980–2014* (London: Routledge India, 2015).

16   Atul Kohli, "Politics of Economic Growth in India, 1980–2005: Part I: The 1980s," *Economic and Political Weekly* 41, no. 13 (2006): 1251–1259.

17   Aseema Sinha, *The Regional Roots of Developmental Politics in India: A divided Leviathan* (Bloomington, IN: Indiana University Press, 2005). For example, states such as Gujarat, Karnataka, and Tamil Nadu, with strengths in science, technology, and infrastructure, benefited the most.

18   Jayati Ghosh, "Growth, Industrialisation and Inequality in India," *Journal of the Asia Pacific Economy* 20, no. 1 (2015): 42–56.

19   Priya Chacko, "The Right Turn in India: Authoritarianism, Populism and Neoliberalisation," *Journal of Contemporary Asia* 48, no. 4 (2018): 541–565.

According to Johannes Plagemann and Sandra Destradi,[20] although the two most recent Congress-led governments (2004–14) were sometimes dubbed "populist" in the Indian discourse, they did not reflect Indira Gandhi's centralization of leadership nor anti-pluralism. Quite to the contrary, the Nehru–Gandhi era at the helm of the Congress party was the embodiment of India's political elite. Moreover, the Congress rather consistently stuck to the long-held principles of secularism and pluralism. An example of this is the Mahatma Gandhi National Rural Employment Guarantee Act (MGNREGA). According to Plagemann and Destradi,[21] the Indian government under Prime Minister Narendra Modi could be considered populist as it clearly entails both constitutive dimensions of populism: anti-elitism and anti-pluralism. The electoral victory of the BJP in 2014 came after a series of corruption scandals that tainted the image of the INC. The desire to replace corrupt elites and to put an end to India's dynastic politics was a core element in Modi's electoral success. Modi himself—the son of a tea-seller—embodied such anti-elitism.[22] For instance, mocking the INC candidate Rahul Gandhi, the scion of the Gandhi–Nehru family, as a "prince" was a common feature during his campaign. In their analysis of the 2014 national election campaign, Paula Chakravartty and Srirupa Roy found that the BJP media team cultivated the party's role as an underdog against the hereditary and corrupt political establishment in the form of Congress by "spending unprecedented amounts on an 'advertising blitz' " and attacking the established media outlets, particularly the English language ones.[23] After the BJP came to power, the notion of fighting corrupt, impure, and spiritually malformed elites in politics, economics, and society became a key component of the ascetic celibate's rhetoric.

Populists that rise in the wake of a social or moral crisis often mobilize people based on the philosophy of "the other," which can be any group representing imminent danger and conflict. For example, in colonial times this was the colonial power or the "non-sons of the soil." In contemporary India, the Government of Gujarat countered the uneven development of the state of Gujarat through an appeal to sub-national populism, which worked to neutralize or assuage the dissatisfaction among the impoverished marginalized groups within the category of the Gujarati people. This sub-national populism drew

---

20   Johannes Plagemann and Sandra Destradi, "Populism and Foreign Policy: The Case of India," *Foreign Policy Analysis* 15, no. 2 (2018): 283–301.

21   Plagemann and Destradi, "Populism and Foreign Policy."

22   Plagemann and Destradi, "Populism and Foreign Policy."

23   Paula Chakravartty and Srirupa Roy, "Mr. Modi Goes to Delhi: Mediated Populism and the 2014 Indian Elections," *Television & New Media* 16, no. 4 (2015): 311–322.

on the notion of Gujarati identity and set "the people" of Gujarat against the ineffectual governing elite in New Delhi. Moreover, this sub-national identity was defined specifically in Hindu terms and positioned against religious minorities.[24] In the wake of such a movement, nationalism is promoted as the social glue that holds people together and one that is an essential component of the struggle. The theory of cultural backlash positions populism among those holding traditional cultural values in any social space, mostly comprising the less educated groups or older individuals in a population. Populism as a political style flourishes in democracies as it requires a public space conducive to the freedom of expression.

Essentially, what this sequence establishes is what Gino Germani terms "national populism,"[25] which has affinities with the nationalist right and an identifiable ideology. This brand of populism has been successful in most regions of the world in the 21st century, whether in phenomena such as Brexit or systems of government voted into power in the most powerful democracies in the world.

3   Populist Measures in India

India is an example that proves economic liberalization can co-exist with populist politics and that populism can be used as an ideological framework within which the political contradictions that follow from economic change can be managed. The capaciousness of populism allows for a range of interests, some of them conflicting, to be acknowledged in both symbolic and practical ways.

According to Nehmat Kaur,[26] Pavan Varma, at the Jaipur Literature festival, said: "Ultimately the route to power is through winning elections, which is about swaying people's emotions in your favor."[27] Politicians can't act on

---

24   Christophe Jaffrelot, "Narendra Modi between Hindutva and Subnationalism: The Gujarati Asmita of a Hindu Hriday Samrat," *India Review* 15, no. 2 (2016): 196–217.

25   Gino Germani, *Authoritarianism, Fascism, and National Populism* (New Brunswick, NJ: Transaction Publishers, 1979). National Populism is a political ideology associated with authoritarian nationalism involving a rejection of liberal democracy, syndicalism, and secularism in favor of a traditionalist, militaristic, and one-party state dominated by a single leader.

26   Nehmat Kaur, "Populism Threatens Democracy, but Is it also Essential to It?" *The Wire*, December 15, 2017, https://thewire.in/politics/populism-democracy-jlf (accessed October 5, 2018).

27   Pavan K. Varma was a Member of Parliament in the Rajya Sabha (Upper House) and earlier was Advisor to the Chief Minister of Bihar with the rank of Cabinet Minister. He has authored over a dozen bestselling books and served as ambassador in several countries.

their promises if they don't win elections—and winning votes requires public support. It is widely perceived by political parties that providing individual benefits is the surest way to win over voters, especially the poor. Hence it can be said that populist measures are the means for politicians to be voted into power.

This section presents four case studies analyzing two populist measures at the state level and two at the national level. These case studies are presented chronologically. Through the following case studies, this article seeks to understand their impact on socioeconomic development as well as on democratic institutions.

3.1 Case Study 1: Guaranteeing Wage Employment in Rural India

The Mahatma Gandhi National Rural Employment Guarantee Act is a social security measure that guarantees the "right to work" to Indian rural citizens. The scheme provides a legal guarantee for at least one hundred days of employment in every financial year to the adult members of any rural household willing to do public works-related unskilled manual labor at the statutory minimum wage.

The scale of the program is staggering, providing employment to a third of India's rural population at an annual cost of nearly 1 percent of the GDP. It has formed the backbone of the United Progressive Alliance's (UPA) anti-poverty and rural safety net program.[28]

According to Dilip Mookherjee,[29] estimates from studies using the methodology difference in differences (DID) show a rise of approximately 5 percent in daily wages that can be attributed to the program, a figure that increases to 9 percent in the "star"[30] states. Different studies using this methodology find corresponding positive effects on food and non-food consumption, calorie and protein intakes, and savings. Rural–urban migration rates have dropped, largely because of a fall in "distress migration"; urban unemployment rates fell by 7 percent while child labor fell by approximately 10 percent.

Other studies have shown that the scheme has contributed to lowering poverty rates and altering rural power relations in ways that benefit the most

---

As of 2020 he is the National General Secretary and National Spokesman of the Janata Dal (United).

28 Dilip Mookherjee, "The Other Side of Populism," *The Indian Express*, May 3, 2014, https://indianexpress.com/article/opinion/columns/the-other-side-of-populism/ (accessed October 9, 2018).

29 Mookherjee, "The Other Side of Populism."

30 The top-performing states.

vulnerable in rural India—women, Adivasis, and lower caste groups.[31] Providing employment to rural unskilled labor is the single most direct and effective way of reducing poverty. Mookherjee insists that "with regard to targeting success, it beats the other big-ticket subsidy items in government budgets: food, fertilizer, and petroleum subsidies, each of which accounts for 0.8 percent of the GDP and benefits mainly the middle class rather than the poor. A leakage rate of 30 percent or less seems a vast improvement on the 70 percent-plus leakage rates associated with the Public Distribution System (PDS). The MGN-REGA is far from perfect, but considerably more effective than any of these schemes in lowering poverty."[32]

The Act emphasizes that the nature of work will be determined in Palli-Sabha[33] through participatory people's plans, approved in Gram Sabha,[34] and accordingly the list of activities would be prepared. The Gram Sabha is further entrusted to take an active role in the approval and monitoring of work and conducting social audits.[35] Such measures promote citizen participation and stand to strengthen local institutions of democracy.

The Act not only guarantees wage employment as a right, but also promotes community participation in planning and monitoring through vigilance and monitoring committees, as well as social audit though Gram Sabha, and also makes provisions for complete transparency as mandated by the Right to Information Act of 2005.

With regard to the implementation of mandated provisions, the evidence shows myriad shortcomings and wide variations across states. Less than 50 percent of beneficiaries were aware of the work-on-demand feature, and just 20 percent were aware of their unemployment benefit entitlement. There is substantial rationing: in 2009–10, while 25 percent of rural households were provided work, 19 percent sought work but did not become employed.[36]

---

31 Tanya Jakimow, "'Breaking the Backbone of Farmers': Contestations in a Rural Employment Guarantee Scheme," *Journal of Peasant Studies* 41, no. 2 (2014): 263–281.

32 Mookherjee, "The Other Side of Populism."

33 All voters living in the ward-level electoral constituency are members of the Ward Sabha. In a state such as Odisha it comprises all voters of a revenue village and is called Palli Sabha.

34 Gram Sabha means a body consisting of all persons whose names are included in the electoral rolls for the Panchayat at the village level. The term is defined in the Constitution of India under Article 243(b).

35 Social audit is a process of reviewing official records and determining whether state-reported expenditures reflect the actual monies spent on the ground.

36 Mookherjee, "The Other Side of Populism."

Household surveys and social audits reveal numerous complaints, including delayed wage payments, non-issuance of dated receipts, non-payment of the unemployment allowance, and payment of less than full wages.[37] Salim Lakha and colleagues have found that implementation of the innovative social audit provisions of the MGNREGA, which were to promote accountability, transparency, and participation, has been hampered by the lack of training for the monitoring committees entrusted to carry out these audits; the reliance on state governments, which lack the ability and commitment to ensure the effective functioning of the scheme; and the lack of awareness among potential beneficiaries of their entitlements.[38]

According to Mookherjee, MGNREGA helped the UPA win for the second time in the 2009 general elections. There is regression discontinuity (RD)-based evidence showing that the Congress reaped electoral benefits from rolling out MGNREGA and that the budgetary allocations for the program across districts and blocks have been manipulated in certain states to increase these benefits.[39] However, there is also more recent evidence that the electoral benefits that arose for the Congress in the early stages of implementation turned into a liability in the later stages. With the passage of years, citizen expectations from the scheme have risen, while the problems of implementation have become more evident. Failure to implement the MGNREGA properly has thus become a political liability for the Congress in the medium to long run. Herein lies a cautionary tale for parties in power when they introduce populist schemes: failure to implement them properly will turn out to be a political liability later on.

3.2 *Case Study 2: Providing Subsidized Prepared Food in Tamil Nadu*

Tamil Nadu's political history since the 1960s has been characterized by a slew of populist measures. The laundry list of freebies handed out by the late Jayalalithaa, former Chief Minister of Tamil Nadu, included the waiver of all farm loans, free laptops for students in Classes 10 and 12, free cell phones for all ration card holders, and government reimbursement of education loans.[40]

---

37 Mookherjee, "The Other Side of Populism."
38 Salim Lakha, Rajasekhar Durgam, and Manjula Ramachandra, "Collusion, Co-option and Capture: Social Accountability and Social Audits in Karnataka, India," *Oxford Development Studies* 43, no. 3 (2015): 330–348.
39 Mookherjee, "The Other Side of Populism."
40 "Why Tamil Nadu's Freebie Culture Works. It has Combined the Cult of Personality Politics with Real Economic Growth," *Live Mint*, May 12, 2016, https://www.livemint.com/Opinion/GGMQFv1iFGJiKMzPZWWVLN/Why-Tamil-Nadus-freebie-culture-works.html (accessed June 8, 2018).

POPULISM IN CONTEMPORARY INDIAN POLITICS

One of her flagship schemes was the Amma Unavagam (mother's canteen), launched with much fanfare in 2013. Meant to provide nutritious food at heavily subsidized rates, the canteens, run by the government but staffed by women from self-help groups (SHGs), were a runaway success as a measure to tackle urban hunger.[41] Following a positive public response, these canteens were set up at all 200 wards in Chennai city. The state government has taken these canteens to nine other cities.[42] NoIn 2019 Chennai alone had more than 400 Amma canteens; other cities and towns had 247 more.[43]

The clockwork precision with which Amma Unavagams are run is a testament to how ostensibly "populist" government schemes end up having a positive impact on the common person's life. The hallmark of Amma Unavagam lies in its innovative design of co-opting SHGs from local slum settlements to run and manage the canteens. In the process of ensuring food security through subsidized prepared food, these community kitchens have generated regular employment and remunerative wages for SHG members. The outcome of the Amma Unavagam scheme is not just limited to the mitigation of food insecurity; it has also created livelihood security for deprived urban women, thus enabling their inclusion into formal sector employment. These canteens are located at sites that are frequented by the poor and the vulnerable, such as opposite government hospitals or next to bus stops. "They are a boon for the urban poor and migrant workers, for whom one of the major issues is food security."[44] Such has been the success of these canteens that states such as Rajasthan, Madhya Pradesh, Odisha, Andhra Pradesh, Karnataka, and Delhi have also started their own versions of subsidized canteens.[45]

According to Vinita Govindarajan, "there is a huge opportunity cost in going ahead with this scheme."[46] The fiscal impact of distribution and subsidy

---

41   N. Doval, "Tamil Nadu's Amma Canteen Concept Catches on in Other States," *Live Mint*, March 7, 2017, https://www.livemint.com/Politics/pHvjY4PHykVOy7irb8H2cO/Tamil-Nadus-Amma-canteen-concept-catches-on-in-other-states.html (accessed June 8, 2018).

42   J. Sam Daniel Stalin, "What Makes Jayalalithaa's 'Amma' Canteens So Successful," *NDTV*, June 4, 2013, https://www.ndtv.com/south/what-makes-jayalalithaas-amma-canteens-so-successful-524236 (accessed June 8, 2018). Coimbatore, Madurai, Trichy, Tirunelvelli, Tuticorin, Salem, Erode, Vellore, and Tirupur are the cities.

43   "Popular Leader, Populist Schemes," *The Hindu*, December 6, 2016, http://www.thehindu.com/news/national/tamil-nadu/Popular-leader-populist-schemes/article15422328.ece (accessed June 8, 2018).

44   Vinita Govindarajan, "Indira Canteens Are Strikingly Similar to Amma Canteens, but Will They Work Equally Well?" *The Scroll*, April 27, 2017, https://scroll.in/article/847626/indira-canteens-are-strikingly-similar-to-amma-canteens-but-will-they-work-equally-well (accessed June 8, 2018).

45   Doval, "Tamil Nadu's Amma Canteen Concept."

46   Govindarajan, "Indira Canteens are Strikingly Similar to Amma Canteens."

programs leaves little for the state to spend in productive and long-lasting investment that could transform the economy. While acknowledging that the objective of the scheme was laudable, the Comptroller and Auditor General of India (CAG) pointed to the lack of surveys to identify beneficiaries such as wage laborers in each area of the city. The CAG said the food was "provided to all people" at subsidized rates in Amma canteens. Even as the state government claimed that the scheme was a social welfare measure, the CAG said the reply was not acceptable as the expenditure was incurred without providing funds for such a scheme in the budget passed by the municipal corporations such as Chennai. The deficit of Chennai Corporation increased from Rs. 303.1 crore in 2013–14 to Rs. 471 crore in 2014–15.[47] The percentage of deficit in Amma canteens in relation to the overall deficit of Chennai Corporation also increased, from 8.26 percent in 2013–14 to 13.44 percent in 2014–15.[48]

Although the canteens address some food-related issues and generate employment for some women in the state, they simultaneously promote political patronage. Lack of intervention by the state to address social and economic inequities cannot simply be wished away by patronage. Patronage and personality-driven politics also bring along with them the problem of corruption. The electorate are reduced to passive recipients of welfare, and politicians use elections as sites of transactions, or "social bribes."[49]

3.3 Case Study 3: Free Laptops for the Students of Uttar Pradesh

With nearly 200 million people, Uttar Pradesh (UP) remains the most populous Indian state. It ranks 16th among the 17 Indian states in the 2015 Human Development report.[50] According to Sunny Sen and Suchetana Ray,[51] UP continues to be counted among the "BIMARU" states while others, such as

---

47   1 crore is equivalent to 10 million rupees.

48   Aloysius Xavier Lopez. "Amma Canteens Eating into Civic Body Funds: CAG." *The Hindu*, September 22, 2016, https://www.thehindu.com/news/cities/chennai/Amma-Canteens-eating-into-civic-body-funds-CAG/article14621798.ece (accessed June 8, 2018).

49   Srinisvan Ramani and Deepu Sebastian, "The Price of Populism in Tamil Nadu," *The Hindu*, April 23, 2016, http://www.thehindu.com/opinion/op-ed/The-price-of-populism-in-Tamil-Nadu/article14253549.ece (accessed June 8, 2018).

50   Tadit Kundu, "Why Kerala Is like Maldives and Uttar Pradesh, Pakistan," *Live Mint*, December 17, 2015, https://www.livemint.com/Politics/3KhGMVXGxXcGYBRMsmDCFO/Why-Kerala-is-like-Maldives-and-Uttar-Pradesh-Pakistan.html (accessed June 8, 2018).

51   Sunny Sen and Suchetana Ray, "Uttar Pradesh Needs Lot More Than Political Will to Get Healthier." *Hindustan Times*, February 13, 2017, https://www.hindustantimes.com/assembly-elections/uttar-pradesh-needs-lot-more-than-political-will-to-get-healthier/story-snqR8Jrg5JkVcw9TforUTJ.html (accessed June 8, 2018).

POPULISM IN CONTEMPORARY INDIAN POLITICS   109

Rajasthan and Madhya Pradesh, are no longer considered as such.[52] The crisis in education is especially apparent in the four BIMARU states of Bihar, Madhya Pradesh, Rajasthan, and Uttar Pradesh—with 445.1 million of India's population of 1.2 billion and some of the lowest literacy rates in the country, according to the 2011 census.

The erstwhile Samajwadi Party (SP) government of the state deemed that distributing free laptops to students would provide the students some relief. The scheme, which would cost the state government Rs. 3,000 crore annually, was SP's election promise to 1.5 million students who had cleared higher secondary examinations and 2.6 million who had passed secondary examinations from the state government-run and -aided schools in 2013, making them eligible for laptops. In the 2012–13 budget, Rs. 96 billion was allocated for secondary education. Significantly, out of this total budget for secondary education, one-third was for the distribution of tablets and laptops to students. The money for laptops and unemployment allowance was arranged by diverting funds earmarked by the previous government for the construction and maintenance of Dalit memorials and parks.[53]

In December 2016, as election fever was rising, the previous UP state government seemed to suddenly wake up to its promise of free laptops, much to the delight of students in Ghaziabad and Noida. Days ahead of the Election Commission announcing the Assembly polls, 695 students in Noida and 631 in Ghaziabad, the two western UP districts adjoining the national capital, were gifted laptops— delivering on a promise made in 2012 that free laptops would be given to meritorious students in Classes 10 and 12.[54]

According to Piyush Shrivastava,[55] a minister in the state government said on the condition of anonymity that according to SP Supremo Mulayam Singh

---

52   BIMARU is an acronym formed from the first letters of the names of the India states of Bihar, Madhya Pradesh, Rajasthan, and Uttar Pradesh. It was coined by the Indian economist Ashish Bose in the mid-1980s. BIMARU has a resemblance to a Hindi word *Bimar*, which means "sick." This was used to refer to the poor economic conditions within those states.

53   Anirudha, "Uttar Pradesh 2012–2013 Budget: A Review," *Active India*, June 5, 2012, http://activeindiatv.com/national-news-and-views/245-uttar-pradesh-budget-2012-2013-a-review (accessed June 10, 2020).

54   Kritika Sharma, "UP Elections 2017: Ghaziabad, Noida Students Get Laptops in Poll Season," *DNA India*, January 26, 2017, https://www.dnaindia.com/india/report-up-elections-2017-ghaziabad-noida-students-get-laptops-in-poll-season-2296257 (accessed October 9, 2018).

55   Piyush Srivastava, "Laptops, Tablets Meant for UP Students to Have Pictures of Akhilesh and Mulayam," *India Today*, March 1, 2013, https://www.indiatoday.in/india/story/mulayam-singh-akhilesh-yadav-samajwadi-party-poll-promise-laptops-tablets-up-students-155158-2013-03-01 (accessed October 9, 2018).

Yadav, the distribution of laptops and tablets would instantly win over more than 4.1 million students and make them supporters of the party. "Some of them may be below eighteen years at the moment. However, the SP Supremo's analysis is that out of the 4.1 million new and young supporters of the SP, at least 3 million students would be first-time voters in 2014. Family members of the beneficiaries would also vote in their favor. If there are pictures of Mulayam Singh Yadava and Akhilesh Yadav on laptops and tablets, they would keep them in mind at the polling booths also. The SP leaders in the districts have already been asked to keep a record of the beneficiaries under these schemes to meet them during elections," he further added.

Before the 2017 state assembly elections, most politicians in the race were striving to deliver the most promising sops. Manifestos of political parties in UP promised to provide free laptops and smartphones. No party sought to specify where the finances to support such populist schemes would come from in a state already reeling under fiscal burdens from previous years. The then-ruling SP this time promised laptops to meritorious students and smartphones for all, while the BJP went a step further, promising a laptop to every student "without discrimination" along with 1 GB of internet data every month for a period of one year.

After being elected in 2017, the BJP government was criticized by the opposition for presenting a state budget for 2017 that was silent about the free laptops for the students of UP as promised before the elections. According to a right to information inquiry, it emerged that of the 1.5 million laptops purchased, only 600,000 were distributed by the SP government. The BJP government ordered a thorough investigation in response to the findings.

In April 2018, the BJP government proposed UP Free Laptop Yojana 2018, with a budget of Rs. 1800 crore. According to the proposal, the state government would provide free laptops along with 1 GB of data to students who have passed their standard 12 exams and are looking for admission to an undergraduate course. However, this time the proposal of around Rs. 1200 crore was less than the previous government had proposed during 2012–13.

According to Yogender Dutt,[56] the three central stakeholders—students, teachers, and educators—either remained silent or were excluded from the discussions. In the rush to provide a quick fix to the ailing education system by providing modern state-of-the-art technologies, the state government glossed

---

56   Yogender Dutt, "Missing the Power Point," *The Hindu,* June 13, 2016, http://www.thehindu.com/opinion/op-ed/missing-the-power-point/article5234483.ece (accessed October 9, 2018).

over the fact that most schools in UP do not have electricity, let alone desktop computers. Given the local context of UP, investing in building schools or buying books for the school library could benefit several successive batches of students and remain accessible to everyone in the school. However, when a government opts to gift laptops to individual students, it effectively turns public resources into private property.

3.4   *Case Study 4: Demonetization*

Corruption has long been a feature of the BJP's electoral mobilization against the Congress. An opinion poll of 19,000 respondents conducted in mid-2013 found that 69 percent of respondents thought the UPA government was corrupt and that corruption had increased under the UPA's rule, while only 23 percent thought corruption had increased under the NDA government.[57] Seeking to capitalize on these perceptions, a key theme in the BJP's election manifesto was a populist narrative on corruption, according to which a "lack of openness in government and lack of people's participation had led to concentration of power in a few hands and lack of transparency breeding corruption and nepotism on a massive scale." Corruption was also "a manifestation of poor governance" and "reflects the bad intentions of those sitting in power."[58]

After being elected, the BJP-led government tried to live up to its promise to address the issue of corruption with demonetization to invalidate and replace 500- and 1000-rupee notes (around 80 percent of the currency in circulation in November 2016). The government justified demonetization in populist terms as serving the interests of the "poor, neo-middle class and middle class" and as an attack on "black money" and the "anti-national elements" that support the shadow economy.

In a speech defending the policy, Modi claimed that over the previous ten to 12 years, 500- and 1000-rupee currency notes had been used less for legitimate transactions and more for a parallel economy. The excess of cash was fueling inflation and the black market and denying the poor their due. Invoking the neo-middle-class politics of aspiration, the Prime Minister noted that "according to information with the government, there are only 2.4 million people in

---

57   S. Rukmini, "Two Out of Three Say UPA is Corrupt," *The Hindu*, July 23, 2013, https://www.thehindu.com/news/national/two-out-of-three-say-upa-is-corrupt/article4945558.ece (accessed October 9, 2018).

58   "BJP Manifesto Pledges Good Governance, Talks of Constructing Ram Mandir, Abrogating Article 370," *The Indian Express*, April 7, 2014, https://indianexpress.com/article/india/politics/bjp-unveils-poll-manifesto-includes-contentious-issues-like-ram-temple-and-article-370/ (accessed October 23, 2018).

India who accept that their annual income is more than 10 lakh rupees. Can we digest this? Look at the big bungalows and big cars around you."[59]

In his speeches on demonetization, Prime Minster Modi repeatedly emphasized the benefits of "citizen sacrifice" and short-term pain for long-term gain. In this respect, Modi was following an established nationalist script of sacrifice for the nation.[60] The suffering caused by demonetization was depicted as a "historic rite of purification" and as an "ongoing *Yagna* (Hindu ritual sacrifice) against corruption, terrorism, and black money."[61] Both the BJP government and the Rashtriya Swayamsevak Sangh (RSS), whose support base of small traders and farmers were among the worst affected by demonetization, sought to justify the policy by drawing on key Hindu nationalist tropes on separatism and Islamic terrorism.

On the basis that secrecy was necessary for demonetization to proceed effectively, but also in a reflection of the centralization of power in the Prime Minister's office, only ten individuals in that office, the Finance Ministry, and the Reserve Bank were privy to the decision, which appears to have been ultimately made by the Prime Minister himself. Bypassing Parliament, Modi announced the decision in a televised public address and refused opposition calls for a parliamentary vote and formal debate. Instead, legislation related to demonetization was introduced through ordinances that allow the government to avoid the need for parliamentary approval. Such ordinances are a legacy of colonial governance.[62] In the post-independence period, however, the repeated re-promulgation of ordinances has been used by governments to circumvent parliamentary debate.[63]

While the Reserve Bank of India (RBI) has often tussled with the executive when it comes to the central bank's independence, it has maintained high standards of competence and professionalism. Unfortunately, the bank's

---

59 Siddharth Varadarajan, "Narendra Modi Just Dug Himself a Great Big Hole," *The Wire*, January 1, 2017, https://thewire.in/politics/modi-just-dug-great-big-hole-demonetisation-speech (accessed October 23, 2018).

60 Dilip M. Menon, "With Demonetisation, Modi Reiterates the Post-Colonial Indian Theme of Redemption Through Suffering," *The Scroll*, December 13, 2016, https://scroll.in/article/823759/demonetisation-brings-back-the-age-old-indian-theme-of-redemption-through-suffering (accessed December 13, 2016).

61 Chacko, "The Right Turn in India."

62 Ordinances, though objected to by the nationalist leadership during the colonial era, were incorporated into the constitution of independent India as a temporary emergency measure that allows governments to introduce policies when Parliament is not in session (Chacko, "The Right Turn in India").

63 Chacko, "The Right Turn in India."

credibility took a hit in the wake of demonetization. The ruling party maintained that demonetization was a call made by the RBI, although facts suggest an alternative narrative. On November 7, 2016, the government advised the RBI Central Board that it ought to consider withdrawing Rs. 500 and 1000 notes to mitigate the triple threat of counterfeiting, terrorism funding, and black money. The very next day, the RBI accepted the advice and that same evening Modi went on national television to announce the move. According to Milan Vaishnav,[64] either the RBI was used by the government or it genuinely backed the half-baked measure. Either way, the institution's stature was diminished—a position further reinforced by the foibles associated with the policy's sloppy implementation. To make matters worse, the RBI then prevaricated when it came to informing the public about how much of the old currency had come back into the system after November 8. It was finally forced to disclose in its August 2017 annual report that 99 percent of the notes that had ceased to be legal tender wound up in Indian banks—an embarrassment to the government.

4   Impact of Populist Measures on Democratic Governance

Democratic governance is the range of processes through which a society, in pursuit of justice, equality, welfare, and environmental protection, reaches a consensus on and implements regulations, human rights, laws, policies, and social structures. In this sense, democratic governance brings to the fore the question of how a society organizes itself to ensure equality of opportunity and equity (social and economic justice) for all citizens.

In light of the aforementioned case studies narrating specific measures of populist practices in contemporary Indian politics, this section examines populism's impact on India's democratic governance from the perspective of equality of opportunity and equity. This section also analyzes the positive and negative implications of the populist practices mentioned above.

4.1   *Positive Implications of Populist Measures*
One of the most important aspects of MGNREGA is that it gives villagers the right to demand employment. The authority is responsible for providing employment in response to demand or providing an employment allowance

---

64   Milan Vaishnav, "India's Elite Institutions Are Facing a Credibility Crisis," *Carnegie Endowment for International Peace*, February 20, 2018, http://carnegieendowment.org/2018/02/20/india-s-elite-institutions-are-facing-credibility-crisis-pub-75592 (accessed October 9, 2018).

in cases where it has failed to meet the employment demand. According to Shabir M. Alam and Mohammad Alam, it has made a dent in poverty by increasing employment opportunities.[65] During the first year of implementation (2006–07), in 200 districts, 21 million households were employed and 905 million person days were generated. In 2016–17, in 686 districts, 51 million households were provided employment and 2.35 billion person days were generated. In 2017–18, 51 million households were provided employment and 2.3 billion person days were generated across the country.

According to Swati Narayan, for recipient families, the 32 percent decline in their poverty stems from MGNREGA alone.[66] On a more positive front, 40 percent of households employed under the law are impoverished Dalits and Adivasi, even without any explicit targeting. The IHDS-II[67] attributes 38 percent and 28 percent of reduction in poverty in employed Dalit and Adivasi homes, respectively, to MGNREGA alone. As many as 55 percent of MGNREGA workers in 2014–15 were women, and their participation has soared to 38 percent since 2010. Tamil Nadu has employed 60,000 sanitation workers under MGNREGA across three-fourths of villages. The Act stipulates that wages will be equal for men and women. It is also committed to ensuring that at least 33 percent of the workers are women. By generating employment for women at fair wages in villages, MGNREGA has played a substantial role in economically empowering women. It has laid the foundation for greater independence and self-esteem by ensuring gender parity of wages and led to an increase in women's control over their earnings from MGNREGA.[68]

MGNREGA has been referred to as an "Act of the people, by the people, and for the people." From the perspective of social justice, the Act emphasizes that the nature of the work will be determined in Palli-Sabha through participatory people's plans, approved in Gram Sabha, and accordingly the list of activities will be prepared. The Act also empowers ordinary people to play an active

---

65   Shabir M. Alam and Mohammad Alam, "Good Governance and Employment Generation through MGNREGA," *International Journal of Economics Commerce and Management* 2, no. 9 (2014): 1–17.

66   Swati Narayan, "Half Full, Half Empty: 10 Years of NREGA," *IndiaSpend*, February 9, 2016, http://www.indiaspend.com/cover-story/half-full-half-empty-10-years-of-nrega-80147 (accessed July 24, 2018).

67   The India Human Development Survey-II (IHDS-II), 2011–2012, is a nationally representative, multi-topic survey of 42,152 households in 1,503 villages and 971 urban neighborhoods across India. See Sonalde Desai and Reeve Vanneman, *India Human Development Survey-II (IHDS-II), 2011–2012* (Ann Arbor, MI: Inter-university Consortium for Political and Social Research, 2018).

68   Desai and Vanneman, *India Human Development Survey-II.*

POPULISM IN CONTEMPORARY INDIAN POLITICS

role in the implementation of employment guarantee schemes through Gram Sabhas (village assemblies under Panchayati Raj Institutions), social audits, participatory planning, and other means.

Amma canteens are primarily run by SHG women, generating employment opportunities for them. All SHG members have been trained by the Chennai Corporation in catering, managing the different activities of the canteen, and serving customers. According to Mani Arul Nandhi,[69] many locally recruited SHGs and their members work as employees of the Chennai Municipal Corporation, and each woman earns a monthly remuneration of Rs. 9,000 (plus food).

Amma canteens can be seen as part of a truly social democratic tradition, because they are an important piece of the food security puzzle.[70] Along with the destitute—for whom they serve as a lifeline—they are crucial for working people, especially in the informal sector, in urban areas. In fact, such initiatives are equally important for working people in urban areas (from rickshaw pullers to delivery boys who are on the road the whole day) as a source of inexpensive and nutritious food.

The Amma canteens serve as a price stabilization measure at times of high inflation. According to Reetika Khera,[71] a survey by academics Hageman and M. Maragatham in Salem reported that private eateries had to reduce their prices in order to compete with the Amma canteens.[72]

Amma canteens have an important—if not immediately obvious—gender dimension. The canteens are primarily run by women, generating employment opportunities for them. The availability of inexpensive, hygienic, and nutritious options such as the Amma canteens relieves women of domestic drudgery. As Khera points out,[73] Amma canteens create democratic spaces that are surely needed in our deeply divided society. There is nothing like sharing a meal with people from diverse backgrounds to foster a spirit of togetherness.

---

69 Mani Arul Nandhi, "Cooperative Management, Food Security and Amma Unavagam—A case study from the Indian state of Tamil Nadu," November 16, 2015. International Co-operation Alliance, Asia Pacific.

70 Reetika Khera, "Community Kitchens: An Idea Whose Time Has Come," *The Scroll*, January 22, 2016, https://scroll.in/article/801742/community-kitchens-an-idea-whose-time-has-come (accessed July 24, 2018).

71 Khera, "Community Kitchens."

72 A 2013 survey by academics S. Thangamani and M. Maragatham on Amma canteens in Salem found that 75 percent of customers were satisfied with the food quality, 44 percent with the drinking water, and 58 percent with the cleanliness of the canteens.

73 Reetika Khera, "Why We Need to Open 'Amma Canteens' all over India," *The Wire*, December 8, 2016, https://thewire.in/government/jayalalithaa-amma-social-democracy (accessed July 24, 2018).

4.2 *Negative Implications of Populist Measures*

Despite many positive outcomes of the MGNREGA, it has been criticized for its poor implementation and leakages. Under the MGNREGA, which was promulgated in 2005, each household is guaranteed 100 days of work every year. On average, however, each household received only 45 days of work since 2010—less than half of what was guaranteed.[74] The India Human Development surveys report that up to 70 percent of interested poor households did not receive any MGNREGA work between 2004 and 2012. Unemployment allowance has rarely been paid.

It was argued not only that MGNREGA would increase the income of the poor, but also that the asset creation through the process of employment would generate a much-needed productive infrastructure for poverty alleviation and economic justice on a permanent basis.[75] However, there has been no significant increase in the number of assets created each year, with 2015–16 recording the worst statistics of a 23 percent drop from 2014–15. Doubts have also been raised about the durability of the assets. According to Shobit Mathur and Nomesh Bolia,[76] the law says that 60 percent of funds should be spent on wages and 40 percent on materials, which results in a preponderance of labor-intensive work rather than structures that require more and better material.

The budget outlay for the Amma canteens is a huge opportunity cost. The fiscal impact of distribution and subsidy programs leaves little for the state to spend in productive and long-lasting investments that could transform the economy. While acknowledging that the objective of the scheme was laudable, the Comptroller and Auditor General of India (CAG) pointed to a lack of surveys to identify beneficiaries such as wage laborers in each area of the city. The CAG said the food was "provided to all people" at subsidized rates in Amma Canteens. Even as the state government claimed that the scheme was a social welfare measure, the CAG said the reply was not acceptable as the expenditure was incurred without providing funds for such a scheme in the budget passed by the municipal corporations such as Chennai.

Amma canteens can simultaneously be seen to be promoting political patronage. Lack of intervention by the state to address social and economic inequities cannot simply be wished away by patronage. Patronage and

---

74   Narayan,. "Half Full, Half Empty."

75   Alam and Alam, "Good Governance."

76   Shobit Mathur and Nomesh Bolia, "Worst Year Ever for MGNREGA, 23% Drop in Assets Created," *The Wire*, April 30, 2016, https://thewire.in/economy/worst-year-ever-for-mgnrega-23-drop-in-assets-created (accessed October 23, 2018).

POPULISM IN CONTEMPORARY INDIAN POLITICS

personality-driven politics also bring along with them the problem of corruption. This reduces the electorate to passive recipients of welfare, who use elections as sites for transactions (social bribes).

The UP Free Laptop scheme cannot overcome the negative impact of a bad teacher or a poor school, nor can it make children smarter in the absence of electricity, water, toilets, or playgrounds. As mentioned earlier, there is no evidence that free laptops can provide equal opportunity to achieve a quality education. Yet the government persists in handing out laptops.

The original objectives of demonetization were to ensure economic justice and accountability by eliminating fake currency; inflict losses on those holding black money; and disrupt terror and criminal activities. According to Suyash Rai,[77] a study by the National Investigation Agency and the Indian Statistical Institute in 2016 estimated that fake Indian currency notes in circulation have a face value of Rs. 400 crore.

More than 90 percent of shops accept only cash or very short-term credit. Large numbers of laborers and small-value suppliers are paid in cash. The sudden ban led to disruptions in consumption and production. As reported by *Business Today*, barely six months after demonetization, India's GDP growth rate had slumped to 6.1 percent in the January–March period, the lowest in more than two years.[78] The cost of demonetization was disproportionately borne by the poor. According to a study by IFMR LEAD covering 2,200 households across six states, this episode had a severe adverse impact on the economic and financial lives of the poor.[79] Participants reported a 20 percent drop in their income immediately after demonetization and significant difficulty in finding employment. Many also reported delays in their wage payments due to the liquidity crunch caused by demonetization and heavy reliance on cash-based

---

77   Suyash Rai, "The Demonetization Decision: Event, Impact, Narrative and Meaning." *The Wire*, December 4, 2016, https://thewire.in/economy/demonetisation-costs-benefits-analysis (accessed July 25, 2018).

78   "PM Modi's Demonetisation Brings GDP Down to 6.1 Percent: Top Economists Stand Vindicated," *Business Today*, June 2, 2017, https://www.businesstoday.in/current/economy-politics/pm-modis-demonetisation-brings-gdp-down-to-61-per-cent-top-economists-stand-vindicated/story/253436.html (accessed July 25, 2018).

79   This study, conducted by IFMR LEAD, attempted to contribute to the ongoing debate on the short-term and long-term effects of demonetization on low-income households, which, although being formally financially included, are most prone to adverse effects of demonetization policy owing to their socioeconomic, demographic, and occupational profiles. The study is available at http://ifmrlead.org/wp-content/uploads/2018/08/IFMR-LEAD-Demonetization-Study-Final-Report.pdf (accessed June 10, 2020).

transactions in the informal sector.[80] In terms of welfare implications, these costs matter a lot more than the impact on GDP. Tax-paying working-class people, going about their lives, were suddenly asked to bear a burden associated with the project of imposing costs upon people with unaccounted wealth.

The credibility of the RBI took a hit in the wake of demonetization. The ruling party maintained that demonetization was a call made by the RBI, although facts suggest an alternative narrative. On November 7, 2016, the government advised the RBI Central Board that it ought to consider withdrawing Rs. 500 and Rs. 1000 notes to mitigate the triple threat of counterfeiting, terrorism funding, and black money. The very next day, RBI accepted the advice and that same evening Modi went on national television to announce the move. According to Vaishnav,[81] either the RBI was used by the government or it genuinely backed the half-baked measure. Either way, the institution's stature stood diminished—a position further supported by the foibles associated with the policy's sloppy implementation. To make matters worse, RBI then prevaricated when it came to informing the public how much old currency had come back into the system post November 8.

Demonetization reflected the centralization of power in the PMO. Bypassing Parliament, Prime Minster Modi announced the decision through a televised public address and refused opposition calls for a parliamentary vote and formal debate. Instead, legislation related to demonetization was introduced through ordinances that allow the government to avoid the need for parliamentary approval. Ordinances are a legacy of colonial governance.

5   Conclusion

Populism does not oppose the democratic system per se; on the contrary, the democratic system needs its support and tools (e.g., elections). As analyzed in this chapter, not all forms of populism are necessarily corrosive to democracy. In an unequal society where politics is governed by the interests of the political elite, populism plays an important role in balancing power by introducing citizen participation.

As quoted by Kaur, Varma notes that "populism is an essential part of democracy but also poses a threat to it. Political parties are incentivized to chase

---

80   Misha Sharma, Shambavi Shrivastava, and Anisha Singh, "Hitting the Bottom," *Businessline*, December 13, 2017, https://www.thehindubusinessline.com/opinion/hitting-the-bottom/article9992462.ece (accessed July 25, 2018).

81   Vaishnav, "India's Elite Institutions."

short-term goals in order to keep winning elections and to deflect from their unfulfilled long-term promises. This, in turn, leads to a devaluing of democracy. It reduces democracy to the lowest common denominator—who can tell the biggest lie."[82] Parties then are forced to continually deflect attention away from their old promises, which they do by appealing to people's emotions via their socioeconomic concerns.[83] Hence it can be said that populist measures that are redistributive in nature may be questioned from the perspective of political motives when they are introduced. Nevertheless, these measures need to be better implemented. Along with this, the aspect of good fiscal governance remains to be addressed through better targeting to avoid bad allocative consequences while initiating these measures. Populists, due to their plebiscitary view on democracy, inevitably end up being motivated by public opinion and mood, and therefore populist decisions can become more responsive and at the same time more irresponsible. In favoring quick decisions over patient negotiations, they diminish the quality of the decision-making process.[84] Some of the cases in this chapter have exemplified fiscal imprudence as the cost for short-term political gains and the creation of political patronage.

Such patronage is promoted by the populist leader through hostility towards intellectual economic and political elites. Populism as an anti-pluralistic ideology, if in power, can seriously threaten the fundamental rules of democratic systems. The same applies to the populist theory of voting, which can lead to the tyranny of the majority. Institutes of direct democracy can rarely capture the complexity of public opinion.

Populism thrives on splitting society along the lines of a majoritarian pure versus the minority of corrupt elites. Civil society needs to engage with the citizens, particularly with the youth, to create a counter-narrative that promotes the practice of liberal democratic values. Active citizenship can counter majoritarian populism. Adult education must play an important role in engaging citizens through popular media to sensitize them about active citizenship.

In order to counter populism effectively, civil society requires strategies that are well structured, long-term, and that transcend the current project logic that hinders decisive impacts. The key for civil society is learning how to communicate with the distinct social groups that hold populist ideals. In order to combat populism, particularly that which has a right-wing tilt, civil society needs a base for cooperation: right-wing populist groups have a strong common identity, yet communities often want to counter them from very different

---

82 Kaur, "Populism Threatens Democracy."
83 Kaur, "Populism Threatens Democracy."
84 Decker, "The Populist Challenge."

angles. Civil society therefore needs a common agenda and a common base from which to fight against populism.

Civil society groups are usually the first to witness happenings and patterns of action in societies, and hence they can effectively put forth propositions and protest. It is also in the best interests of politicians to engage with civil society, as they need popular support in order to survive elections.

CHAPTER 6

Populism in Thailand

*Thawilwadee Bureekul, Ratchawadee Sangmahamad, and
Nuchaprapar Moksart*

1   Introduction

Before the 1997 Asian financial crisis and the adoption of the 1997 Constitution, Thailand had endured a great number of fluctuations in its political development. The coming of the Thai Rak Thai (TRT) party and the Thaksin Shinawatra administration in 2001 paved the way for the establishment of a new form of politics in Thailand. The Thaksin administration created a new form of political campaign that included the implementation of populist policies to increase public trust in government and improve national well-being, such as the 30-baht healthcare scheme, community village funds, agrarian debt relief, the One Tambon One Product (OTOP) program, and others.

Following on from the Thaksin administration, which began in 2001, populist policies have been widely implemented by successive governments to provide benefits to the poor. Many policies were created following this administration; for example, the 15 years of free education program, elderly allowances in the Abhisit Vejjajiva period, and the rice pledging scheme and 300-baht minimum wage in the Yingluck Shinawatra period. Populist policies were used in 2017 by the National Council for Peace and Order (NCPO) in both political and economic ways, as in the *pracharat* ("Civil State Cooperation"), the "Public–Private–People Partnership," and the Thai Niyom Yangyuen, or "Sustainable Thainess," program.[1] This clearly shows that populism can be on the right, left, or in the middle of the political spectrum and can be adapted to any ideology by both elected and unelected governments. Populist policies and leadership also share a set of core values and a certain distinct rhetoric and discourse.[2]

From 2001, populist policies began to play a crucial role in Thailand and to create change in the political landscape. The functioning of populist policies

---

1   "Thai Niyom Yangyuen Program," Foreign Office, Government Public Relations Department, 2018, http://thainews.prd.go.th/th/website_th/news/news_detail/WNPOL6109210010003 (accessed June 10, 2020).

2   Pasuk Phongparchit and Kosuke Misuno, eds., *Populism in Asia* (Singapore: National University of Singapore Press, 2009).

© BUREEKUL, SANGMAHAMAD, AND MOKSART, 2021 | DOI:10.1163/9789004444461_008

under the Thaksin administration led to a greater public emphasis on policies than was the case under past political leaders. Populist policies therefore engender a competitive atmosphere between political parties during elections and can ensure a better quality of life for the people as well.

Hence, it is important to study the social, economic, and political impacts and challenges of populist policies in Thailand in order to gain an understanding of their positive and negative aspects. Recommendations to guide policy decision-making and prevent populist policies from having an adverse impact are also vital to ensure that fiscal mismanagement and public debt can be avoided in the future.

2   Context of Thailand

"Populism" has been employed in Thailand for many decades. The two broad types of populism discussed in this chapter are those defined by Jan-Werner Müller and by Cas Mudde.[3] Müller's "political populism" is a moral ideology that refers to a group of people united in opposition to the immorally corrupt elites. Such a group requires a leader to represent them and expand their voice. Müller argues that when populist leaders gain full control of state power, they govern harshly while claiming that they are doing so for the people. They also damage democratic norms in an attempt to consolidate power. Political leaders amend the constitution to facilitate policy implementation, and in the process block criticisms and reduce the power of others. President Donald Trump's "Make America Great Again" campaign is one such example. Trump, who designated himself as the voice of the American people who were dissatisfied with Barack Obama's neoliberal policies, promoted nationalism among white Americans.

The second type of populism is "economic populism." According to Mudde, economic populism is based on economic policies that convince people to support a particular political party. Such economic populism neglects the interests of people who are not included in the target groups of populist policy, and does not consider the future impacts such policies have on society.[4] An example of economic populism may be observed in the policies implemented in Thailand since the Thaksin Shinawatra period, which have been aimed

---

3   Jan-Werner Müller, *What Is Populism?* (London: Penguin UK, 2017); Cas Mudde, "The Populist Zeitgeist," *Government and Opposition* 39, no. 4 (2004): 542–563.

4   Cas Mudde and Cristóbal Rovira Kaltwasser, *Populism: A very short introduction* (Oxford: Oxford University Press, 2017).

at exchanging economic benefits for the political popularity of the country's leadership. In these instances, political leaders gained power by making populist promises to certain groups, and then once in power pursued neoliberal economic policies. As a result, the people who voted for these leaders benefitted less than was promised. This form and use of populism muddies the waters of the definition.

Apart from the Thaksin Shinawatra administration, Thailand's past politics shows limited adherence to populism and its political and economic aspects. For example, while monetary policy under Prime Minister Kukrit Pramoj in 1975 helped the people by providing a budget to develop livelihoods in local communities, such moves were not widely regarded at the time as populist. Only in 1997, more than 20 years later, did the Thai Constitution allow public participation in the policy decision-making process. Then, in 2001, the Thai Rak Thai party under Thaksin Shinawatra introduced a national populist agenda to attract Thai voters. The Thaksin political campaign promoted policies such as the 30-baht healthcare scheme, a community fund, an agrarian debt relief scheme, loans for education, and more. This political strategy helped him win the election and represented a new kind of politics in Thailand, changing the landscape of the policy-making process for all political parties. He used populist policies to alleviate poverty and help impoverished people gain access to social services. As a result of these policies, many people were satisfied with and supported the TRT and its leader, Thaksin.

Since Thaksin, populism has become a new means for all political parties to win elections. During the Abhisit Vejjajiva administration, the government formulated populist policies to gain popularity and solve national problems. The policies included free education for all, agrarian debt relief, agricultural price guarantees, political reconciliation, and social cohesion. The Yingluck administration provided free tablet computers to all primary school students in grade 1 across Thailand, improved the Thai education system, improved the pension retirement scheme, operated a rice pledging scheme, introduced a 300-baht minimum wage, and a first-car tax rebate policy to gain popular support. Populism has also played a role in the approaches of the National Council for Peace and Order (NCPO). In 2017 Prime Minister Prayut Chan-o-cha recently launched a national welfare scheme card as part of the implementation of the "Civil State" policy to carry out the national strategic plan by promoting the grass-roots economy and empowering a majority of Thais.

In this chapter we will analyze the role of populism in Thailand and discuss its social, economic, and political impacts. Then, we will look at how the adverse impacts of populist policies can be avoided in the future.

TABLE 6.1   Timeline of populist policies implemented by each government in the period between 2001 and 2018

2001–2006 Thaksin	2006–2007 Surayut	2008–2009 Samak	2009–2011 Abhisit	2011–2014 Yingluck	2014–2018 Prayut
1. 30-baht healthcare scheme	1. Reconciliation and social cohesion policies	1. OTOP	1. Pension retirement scheme	1. 30-baht healthcare scheme	1. Old age and disability pensions
2. Community fund	2. Political reform	2. Community fund	2. 15 years of free education for all	2. Community fund	2. Political reform
3. Overcoming poverty	3. Civil service reform	3. Free education for all	3. 2,000-baht aid check	3. Agrarian debt relief scheme	3. Reconciliation and social cohesion policies
4. Agrarian debt relief scheme	4. War against corruption	4. Reconciliation and social cohesion policies	4. Reconciliation and social cohesion policies	4. Civil service reform	4. "Civil State"
5. Loan for education		5. Agrarian debt relief scheme	5. Agricultural price guarantee	5. Pension retirement scheme	5. Thai Niyom Yangyuen Program
6. OTOP		6. Agricultural price guarantee	6. Loans for education	6. Rice pledging scheme	
7. War on drugs			7. Political reform	7. 300 baht per day minimum wage	
8. Civil service reform				8. 15,000 baht per month minimum wage for university graduates	
9. War against corruption				9. One laptop per child	
				10. First-time car buyer tax rebate policy	
				11. Thai Women Empowerment Fund	

POPULISM IN THAILAND   125

Table 6.1 shows the implementation of populist policies in each period of government. The following section will provide more detail on the populist policies of Thaksin, Abhisit, Yingluck, and Prayut, respectively.

2.1   *Populism in Four Periods of Government*
2.1.1   Populism in the Thaksin Shinawatra Period
Thaksin became the 23rd prime minister of Thailand on February 17, 2001, and was in power until September 19, 2006. In 2006, his government was overthrown by a military *coup d'état* following street demonstrations and political conflict. Before forming his government in 2001, Thaksin was a well-known, successful businessman. He used political marketing and policy strategy during his five years and 222 days in office, and together with his TRT party launched an array of policies to promote the rural economy and gain popular support from the people. Key examples include the 30-baht healthcare scheme, the agrarian debt relief scheme, and the 1 million-baht village fund.
– 30-Baht Health Care Scheme
   The 30-baht healthcare scheme was implemented in 2002. This policy gave 48 million Thais access to low-cost health services (less than one US$) and hospital visits. The scheme gained overwhelming support from ordinary Thais and made Thaksin the first prime minister to focus primarily on the poor.
– 1 Million-Baht Village Fund Program
   Thailand's Village Fund program was implemented by the TRT government in 2001 and is one of the biggest microcredit schemes in the world. This program saw the distribution of 1 million baht (US$ 24,000) to each of 78,000 villages. The objective of the village fund was to increase the incomes and asset accumulation of people in rural areas. Moreover, the village fund program decentralized government decision-making on rural projects by allowing local communities to create projects for themselves. In the process, it allowed local people to participate more fully in the decision-making process.[5]
– The One Tambon One Product Program (OTOP)
   The One Tambon One Product program, commonly known as OTOP, was implemented in May 2001 to generate employment and to increase income-earning opportunities, preserve local knowledge, and help overcome

---

5   Patana Tangpianpant, "A Study of Thaksin's Pro-Poor Populist Policies in Thailand," honors thesis, Wesleyan University, CT, https://wesscholar.wesleyan.edu/etd_hon_theses/528 (accessed June 10, 2020).

poverty in rural areas. The program encouraged citizens to produce original products with materials distinctive to their region, to be sold domestically and internationally.[6]

2.1.2 Populism in the Abhisit Vejjajiva Period

Abhisit Vejjajiva was Prime Minister of Thailand from 2008 to 2011, during the global economic crisis, and faced escalating domestic political tension. Therefore, his administration formulated many policies to help improve the quality of life for particular groups in society.

– Elderly Allowance

The elderly allowance was implemented under the Abhisit administration to promote income security for every elderly person in Thailand. People over the age of 60 receive an allowance starting at 600 per month for the rest of their lives, with the exception of civil servants, who benefit from a government pension. The allowance rises to a maximum of 1,000 baht a month according to age. In 2011, more than 3.5 million people registered for the elderly allowance, and approximately 6.75 million seniors have benefitted from the policy.[7]

– 15 Years of Free Education

The government launched the 15 years of free education program to help 12 million students in Thailand access schooling.[8] However, not every student has benefitted, especially those in remote areas. There are also some costs the policy does not cover, for example stationary, clothes, books, food, and accommodation. Thus, parents still have to spend money on these costs.

– 2,000-Baht Aid Check

The government provided a 2,000-baht aid check to all insured persons and to subscribers to the social security system who earn less than 15,000 baht per month. In 2009, There were 9.7 million people eligible to receive the 2,000-baht aid check. The implementation of this project fell under the purview of the Social Security Office, and was an attempt by the government to encourage people to buy goods and products to boost the nation's economy during the period of recession.[9]

---

6 Tangpianpant, "A Study of Thaksin's Pro-Poor Populist Policies in Thailand."

7 Democrat Party Thailand, "Progress Report," 2017, https://www.facebook.com/DemocratPartyTH/posts/10154304023861791/ (accessed June 20, 2020).

8 Democrat Party Thailand, "Progress Report," 2017.

9 "National Help Check vs Give Money to the Poor, Is it Different?," *Thairath Online*, December 2016, https://www.thairath.co.th/content/800916 (accessed June 10, 2020).

2.1.3 Populism in the Yingluck Shinawatra Period

Yingluck Shinawatra, Thaksin Shinawatra's younger sister, became Thailand's first female prime minister after the 2011 election and served as prime minister until May 7, 2014, when she was removed from office by a Constitutional Court decision. During election campaigns, her party, the Pheu Thai Party, proposed many populist policies that were then implemented accordingly. Some policies were formulated to attract support from specific groups, such as the middle class, laborers, parents of schoolchildren, and new graduates.

– First-time Car Buyer Policy

A first-time car buyer policy was implemented between September 16, 2011, and December 31, 2012, under Yingluck Shinawatra's administration. The aim of the policy was to give low-income citizens an opportunity to buy a new car at a low tax rate. However, the beneficiaries of the first-time car buyer subsidy were not the poor. Instead, the upper income groups, or the Thai middle class, benefitted most from the policy. This policy also provided an enormous benefit to automobile companies, which saw increased profits from selling their vehicles.[10]

– Rice Pledging Scheme[11]

The rice pledging scheme is one of the most well-known populist policies of the Yingluck administration. Before the general election, the Pheu Thai Party promised to buy rice from farmers at 15,000 baht per ton (20,000 baht for jasmine rice), which was double the price on the global rice market. The government believed that Thailand could manipulate global prices simply by stockpiling the rice the government bought from farmers, and eventually, when supplies on the world market fell, the global price would rise, and the government could sell the rice at a higher price. However, things went wrong when the scheme provided opportunities for massive corruption. It affected millions of Thai farmers and had an unprecedented negative impact on Thailand's agricultural industry and economy.[12]

---

10   "Overview of Thailand Reform: Populist policies effected to public debt," The Secretariat of the House of Representatives, 2015, http://library2.parliament.go.th/giventake/content_nrcinf/nrc2557-issue13-abst01.pdf (accessed June 10, 2020).

11   Vikram Nehru, "Thailand's Rice Policy Gets Sticky," *East Asia Forum*, June 13, 2012, https://www.eastasiaforum.org/2012/06/13/thailand-s-rice-policy-gets-sticky/ (accessed June 10, 2020).

12   "The Politics and Perils of Rice-Pledging Scheme and Impact of Yingluck Case," *The Nation Online*, 2017, https://www.asiaone.com/asia/politics-and-perils-rice-pledging-scheme-and-impact-yingluck-case (accessed June 10, 2020).

- One Tablet Computer per Child

  Ahead of the general election in 2011, the Yingluck government promised to give a tablet computer to all grade 1 elementary school students across Thailand. The aim of the policy was to make sure students could access digital data and use technology to improve the quality of their education via electronic devices. Approximately 2.4 million tablets were provided to Thai children during the Yingluck administration. However, after a short implementation period, it was recognized as an inefficient policy because there were problems with the buying process and the tablets that were provided were of low quality. The total spending on the scheme was 7,000 million baht, most of which benefitted the tablet companies.[13]

- 300-Baht Daily Minimum Wage

  The minimum wage of 300 baht per day was implemented for all businesses and jobs in Thailand on January 1, 2013, fulfilling a promise made to Thai workers by the government during the election campaign. The aim of the scheme was to increase the standard of living among workers. The minimum wage policy had a negative impact on many businesses in the country, especially small businesses, as the policy led to profit reductions. However, millions of Thai workers benefitted from the policy.[14]

- 15,000-Baht Minimum Wage for University Graduates

  The minimum salary for new university graduates increased from the previous level of 9,000–12,000 baht monthly up to 15,000 baht per month in 2011 during Yingluck's administration. Based on the principle of income redistribution, all graduate students received the standard minimum salary, with no conditions.[15]

2.1.4   Populism in the General Prayut Chan-o-cha Period

The government of General Prayut Chan-o-cha, the 29th Prime Minister of Thailand, began on August 30, 2014, under the National Council for Peace and Order (NCPO). His administration played an important role in stimulating the grass-roots economy via the "Civil State," or *pracharat*, project. The government

---

13   "Overview of Thailand Reform."

14   "TDRI Analyze the Benefits/Disadvantages of the Minimum Wage of 300 Baht per Day," Bangkokbiznews online, 2012, http://www.bangkokbiznews.com/news/detail/485423 (accessed June 10, 2020).

15   "TDRI Analyze the Minimum Wage of 300 Baht per Day – 15,000 for Bachelor's Degree," *Thaipublica*, 2012, https://thaipublica.org/2012/05/tdri-analysis-wage300-baht/ (accessed June 10, 2020).

also promoted the 20-year strategic plan, which is the main project under the NCPO. The details of each of these policies are as follows.

- Civil State (*pracharat*)

  Civil State is a political strategy implemented under the Prayut administration. The terms "civil" and "state" identify that the model is based on a cooperative relationship between the government and the people to create social harmony and stimulate economic, social, and political development. The Civil State project aims to improve the quality of life of poor people and reduce poverty in Thailand.[16]

- Thai Niyom Yangyuen Program

  The main objective of the Thai Niyom Yangyuen program is to improve all aspects of life for all Thais. This program is based on ten principles, including the promotion of a social contract between citizens and communities, the provision of social security to impoverished people, the creation of a self-reliant culture, the improvement of people's livelihoods and the empowerment of people in remote areas, the promotion of an anti-corruption culture, the establishment of free internet access for communities, and the advancement of an anti-drug policy. The project contributes to the national strategic plan implemented under the NCPO. The government plans to spend money in rural areas to eliminate poverty and increase equality. At the same time, this project encourages people to participate in the government development process under the principle of a sufficiency economy,[17] and also aims to increase the rate of individual savings to reduce household debt.[18]

- The National Welfare Scheme Card

  The national welfare scheme card was launched on October 1, 2017. The objective of this project is to provide 11.67 million low-income Thais with access to basic necessities such as public transportation (Bangkok-based buses, BTS, and MRT), electricity, food, and cooking gas.[19] People with an income of less than 30,000 baht (US$ 1,000) per year are eligible to receive 200

---

16 Surasak Popwandee, "What Is 'Civil State' Strategy?," *Popwandee Blog*, 2018, https://popwandee.blogspot.com/2015/12/blog-post_39.html (accessed June 10, 2020).

17 "Sufficiency economy" is a philosophy initiated by H.M. King Bhumibol Adulyadej. The aim is to encourage self-reliance and immunity, building rational economic spending.

18 "Thai Sustainable Project Focuses on Participation, Reduce Inequality, and Increase Revenue with Sustainable," *Thairath Online*, 2018, https://www.thairath.co.th/content/1293616 (accessed June 10, 2020).

19 "Welfare Card Scheme Will Help Poor Pay for Basic Needs." *The Nation*, August 30, 2017, https://www.nationthailand.com/national/30325331 (accessed June 10, 2020).

baht per month, and those whose income is higher than 30,000 baht but less than 100,000 baht (US $3,000) per year are eligible to receive 100 baht per month. All registered low-income earners can use the welfare scheme card to buy food and pay for basic necessities at eligible stores. The card could be used like a general ATM card to transfer funds at Krungthai Bank ATM s from September to December 2018.[20]

3   Results of Policy Implementation

3.1   *Success Factors*

Populism has been the mechanism and the approach to alleviating inequality and poverty in Thailand. After Thaksin implemented a populist approach, the public was satisfied with the benefits they received as a result of the policies. Under subsequent administrations, some populist policies have been created and implemented in response to public demand. Healthcare services have been extended to 48 million people, and the adoption of "citizens' rights" means that everyone in the country has equal access to social services and the same rights to welfare. Thus, many scholars agree that populism has resulted in an improvement in the quality of life for the Thai people.

Moreover, political participation, political parties, civil society, non-government organizations, and the democratic movement after the 1997 Constitution were all crucially linked to and associated with the implementation of populist policies.

Populism during Thaksin's government impacted on many aspects of social services including healthcare services, education, pensions, agrarian debt relief, and a community fund for grass-roots projects. There was widespread support for the TRT and Thaksin because they promoted much-needed redistribution policies, which had a direct impact on communities across the country. The success of Thaksin's populism also had relevance in the democratic context, affecting the approach and policies of all political parties in contesting elections. Populism became a political tool to win the majority vote in elections. Finally, the aim of many populist redistributive policies was to "eliminate poverty," and as such populism has played a crucial role in addressing poverty in Thailand.

However, populism can also lead to dissatisfaction among the elites, as in any redistribution of wealth the government needs to spend a considerable

---

20   "Approve the National Welfare Scheme Card," *Khaosod Online*, 2018, https://www.khaosod.co.th/economics/news_1502651 (accessed June 10, 2020).

POPULISM IN THAILAND   131

portion of its budget to implement the required policies. Stakeholders who
suffer a loss of benefits do not appreciate a redistributive strategy. As a result,
some elites have acted against populist policies and used the term "populism"
to delegitimize their political opponents.

3.2 *Positive and Negative Aspects of Populism*
3.2.1 Positive Aspects of Populism
First, populism has transformed Thai politics from the old election culture of
buying support to one of policy competition. Political parties increasingly use
populist policies to gain public support and win elections. Second, populism
has encouraged greater checks on the actions of the government, both through
popular movements and through the Parliament. Third, people have become
more interested in public policy, resulting in higher rates of voter turnout at
elections. Many populist policies offer basic guarantees, for example the 30-
baht healthcare scheme and accessibility to healthcare for all, but most of
them function as political tools as well. Lastly, populism can alleviate inequality, because it can lead to the promotion of aspects of social welfare such as
healthcare, education, old age pensions, and allowances for poor people.[21]

3.2.2 Negative Aspects of Populism
Populist policies can have the negative effect of encouraging people to wait
for help instead of being self-reliant, and thus many critics claim that populist
policies create a weakness in the people. Populism can also lead to massive
corruption as well as conflicts of interest among political parties. In addition,
some populist policies can lead to abuse of power in the political process and
policy implementation as well as increased public debt,[22] as happened with
the rice pledging scheme, which weakened the national economy and deeply
affected Thai farmers financially.

4 Criticism and Analysis

In a group discussion held by King Prajadhipok's Institute on December 12,
2018, experts and academic participants pointed to five problems associated
with populist policies in Thailand. Mechanisms to avoid fiscal mismanagement

---

21   Puwak   Lit   Heimahachart,   "Populist   Policies,"   Political   Science   thesis,
      Mahachulalongkornrajavidyalaya University, 2015.
22   Heimahachart, "Populist Policies."

in the policy-making process and critical recommendations to establish sustainable policies were also addressed.

4.1 Problems with Populist Policies in Thailand

1. Populist policies do not strengthen people's livelihoods by introducing income distribution, job creation, innovation, or opportunity. Rather, many policies create public reliance on the government as people wait for help rather than engaging in self-reliant behavior. The launch of the 500-baht banknote and the national welfare scheme card under the Prayuth administration are examples of this dependence.

2. Political parties and political leaders attempt to exchange benefits with stakeholders instead of maintaining national benefits, neglecting to provide welfare benefits to improve the well-being of ordinary citizens. Many populist policies have been used as a tool to increase public satisfaction with the government, a kind of political marketing to win votes. As a result, many populist policies are impractical when actually put into practice. Policies such as the rice pledging scheme and the first-time car buyer rebates during the Yingluck Shinawatra administration had an enormous impact on the economy, as did the populist policies of the Thaksin, Abhisit, and Prayuth administrations. This indicates that the government is not prepared to handle any negative consequences that arise following the implementation of populist policies.

3. Thailand does not emphasize the role of local government to the extent that most developed countries, such as Japan, do. This indicates that decentralization in Thailand is still weak. In Japan, local communities are an important mechanism for implementing government policies. This allows for better delegation of responsibility for problem-solving in rural areas compared with full implementation by the central government. Thus, increased decentralization is a crucial factor for Thailand to increase the efficiency and sustainability of its policy implementation.

4. Thailand lacks flexibility in its policy-making process due to the fact that policy-makers fail to understand that different locations face different problems. One policy cannot be applied to the entire country as a solution to varying problems. Instead, policy-makers need to craft responsive policies that can be applied in different cultures and socioeconomic contexts in order to promote the national interest to the highest degree possible.

5. Many policies in Thailand are short term. There is no continuation, no evaluation, no collection of data, no analysis, and no monitoring of

output, outcomes, consequences, and impact after implementation. In other words, there is a lack of strategy when it comes to policy implementation. As a result, the government has no evidence or output that can demonstrate the pros and cons of previous populist policies. In practice, this translates to the failure of many populist policies, some of which result in severe damage to society and the economy, as they are in fact impossible to implement.

4.2 *Recommendations to Create Sustainable Policies*

4.2.1 The Role of Political Parties and Policy-Makers

Political parties should understand the likelihood of successful policy implementation, emphasize the national interest, and be held responsible for the results and consequences of populist policies. Moreover, political parties should not merely emphasize political marketing; instead, all parties should provide opportunities to the public to participate in the policy-making process.

4.2.2 Flexibility and Decentralization

In order to achieve the greatest national benefit, populist policies should be flexible according to location, because in practice each policy should be applied with consideration given to the specific culture and context of the community. Moreover, the central government should support the participation of local communities in policy decision-making by decentralizing power and encouraging local government organizations, including local people, to design their own policies. More importantly, monitoring should be encouraged after policy implementation to ensure that each policy successfully achieves its intended outcome.

4.2.3 Preventive Measures via Laws and Regulations

Before policies are implemented, the state needs to mandate preventive measures to avoid financial mismanagement and negative consequences of populist policies. Fortunately, Article 142 of the 2017 Constitution states that the introduction of an annual appropriations bill must show the sources of revenues and estimated revenues, expected outcomes or output from payments, and conform with the National Strategy and development plans in accordance with the rules prescribed in the law on financial and fiscal discipline of the state. As a result, all governments must be fiscally disciplined and formulate policies under the guidance of the Constitution to protect against the adverse impact of populist policies.

4.2.4 Classification of Good and Bad Populist Policies

Concerning Article 142 of the Constitution, it is necessary to classify what is considered a "good" or "bad" populist policy in order to ensure that people are not prohibited from fully exercising and enjoying their rights to access social and welfare services. In other words, the law must protect people's right to welfare. Therefore, welfare benefits should be considered positive populist policies, while in contrast, unsuccessful populist policies must be terminated when they are no longer effective in addressing the problems they were meant to target.

5 Conclusion

In conclusion, populism has been embedded in Thai society since 2001. Populism in Thailand is mostly related to a political ideology,[23] and to an economically redistributive governing strategy.[24] The healthcare scheme is one such strategy intended to engender public satisfaction and trust in the government, and to provide healthcare benefits to the people.

Populism, or *prachaniyom*, has both positive and negative aspects. It is an approach that can provide benefits to the public, increase public satisfaction with political parties, and establish a culture of policy competition, but absent regulation it can result in fiscal problems and have an impact on social, economic, and political dimensions.

First, populist policies include a fiscal dimension, and thus policy budgets need to incorporate checks and balances by nongovernmental organizations or monetary institutions to ensure accountability in the implementation process. There also needs to be an economic strategy to maintain policies in the long run. Sustainability is a major challenge for the government, and proper management of economic mechanisms and economic growth are essential in order to sustain good populist policies in the future.

---

23 K. Weyland, "Clarifying a Contested Concept: Populism in the study of Latin American politics," *Comparative Politics* 34, no. 1 (2001): 1–22; K. Weyland, "Populism: A political-strategic approach," in *The Oxford Handbook of Populism*, ed. Cristóbal Rovira Kaltwasser, Paul Taggart, Paulina Ochoa Espejo, and Pierre Ostiguy (New York: Oxford University Press, 2017), 48–72; P.D. Kenny, *Populism in Southeast Asia* (New York: Cambridge University Press, 2019).

24 R. Dornbusch and S. Edwards, eds., *The Macroeconomics of Populism in Latin America* (Chicago: University of Chicago Press, 1991); D. Acemoglu, G. Egorov, and K. Sonin, "A Political Theory of Populism," *Quarterly Journal of Economics* 128, no. 2 (2013): 771–805.

Second, populist policies in Thailand often involve a redistribution of resources, and the implementation of populist policies impacts stakeholders as a result, especially the taxpayer. Therefore, the challenge is how to persuade stakeholders to support populist measures and prevent fiscal mismanagement and corruption via checks and balances.

Lastly, a populist approach can result in unsustainable policies that are implemented without good management and a strategic economic plan. In the long run, policies such as the rice pledging scheme, tablet computers for students, first-time car buyer rebates, and the launch of the 500-baht banknote will lead to fiscal problems and increased public debt. To address such problems, the introduction of laws and regulations should be considered. Thailand has experienced the negative side of populist policies, and the 2017 Constitution includes measures to prevent massive corruption and fiscal mismanagement in the future. There are strict regulations on the source of government income to implement policies. Such measures will limit the negative consequences of populism. As a result, all governments have to practice fiscal discipline and formulate policies according to regulations and the Constitution.[25]

Finally, populism poses two challenges that must be addressed. The first is how to ensure that populism functions as a mechanism to guarantee welfare benefits to the public, and how to avoid a dependency culture. The second is how the government can balance financial management and policy implementation in order to create sustainability in both the fiscal and operational dimensions. More importantly, populism can improve citizen well-being in the long run, and therefore, in the Thai context at least, political parties should be encouraged to implement positive populist policies to alleviate inequality and future conflicts of interest.

---

25   Suwanmanee, Chongkacharn. "Constitutional Mechanism for the Prevention and Suppression of Corruption," *The Secretariat of the House of Representatives*, July 2017, http://library2.parliament.go.th/giventake/content_royrueng/2560/rr2560-jul3.pdf (accessed June 10, 2020).

CHAPTER 7

Populism as a Phenomenon: Signs of Populism in Mongolian Development

Gerelt-Od Erdenebileg, Ariunbold Tsetsenkhuu, and Ganbat Damba

1 Introduction

The foundation of democracy in Mongolia was laid in 1989 when the country took its first steps towards political change. Parliamentary democracy, a multi-party system, competitive elections, an open society, freedom of thought, freedom of assembly, civil society organizations, and pluralism are clearly observable in Mongolia. In the period since 1989, right-wing, centrist, and left-wing parties have formed in the country within the scope of the political spectrum.

However, researchers suggest that the people still have a shallow understanding of fundamental concepts of democracy,[1] such as the definition of democracy itself, democratic institutions, and the market economy. This is a common phenomenon in many post-communist states, where high degrees of communist doctrine remain even after the transition to democracy.

As Mongolia has evolved towards a free and open society, media outlets have exploded in number. This abundance of media, however, has created social mistrust. In particular, social media, which is disproportionately consumed by the younger generations, is problematic. A popular Mongolian proverb, "truth and lies are only separated by four fingers," offers us an interesting glimpse into the Mongolian mindset of comparing what one hears with what one sees. In this sense, Mongolians tend to believe readily what they see on television and social media platforms without questioning the legitimacy of the source of the information.

In terms of civic education, although a sizable demographic group has a solid understanding of core democratic values, they remain in the minority, while the majority of Mongolian citizens are still in the early stages of learning. This represents one of the biggest challenges to the development of Mongolian

---

1 Asian Barometer Reports, Academy of Political Education, 2003–2018, http://www.asianbarometer.org/ (accessed June 10, 2020).

© ERDENEBILEG, TSETSENKHUU, AND DAMBA, 2021 | DOI:10.1163/9789004444461_009

POPULISM AS A PHENOMENON

society.[2] Additionally, in this stage of social development, populism is increasing in Mongolia, posing a potentially serious challenge.

While many agree that populism is evident in Mongolian society, there is a dearth of work being done on identifying the very phenomenon of populism itself. There are only a few academic works focusing on this issue. In many cases, journalists, columnists, and bloggers have only touched upon the topic to report the observable symptoms to the public. In order to fill the gap, this chapter seeks to examine populism in Mongolia by looking at its specific manifestations and its implications for Mongolian democracy.

2 Positive and Negative Implications of Populism for Society

Populism has been an object of research across many social science disciplines, not just limited to political science. However, widespread use of the term "populism" dates back to the 19th century, when it was used in the US context, while the word "populism" originates from the Latin *populus* meaning "the people." The term was introduced to political science in the 20th century. In some Arabic countries, especially in Turkey, the word *halkçılık* is used, which means "the ones who devote themselves to the people."[3] In this sense, populism expresses both national interests and the ambitions of ordinary citizens.

In modern history, populist techniques have not only been employed in democratic countries, but have also been widely used by authoritarian leaders and dictators. Fascist leaders such as the Italian Duce Benito Mussolini and Nazi Germany's Adolph Hitler based their actions, campaign platforms, and propaganda on the notions of "bread and circus." They skillfully mobilized people by offering themselves as the sole solution to the economic crises, promising income equality to the poor by curbing the power and privilege of elites and extolling the superiority of their respective nations. In particular, Hitler employed vast propaganda machines to promote his militarist and racist theories of national socialism. He was also masterful in using religious mythology, making claims such as "The Aryan is the Prometheus of mankind."

As Daniele Albertazzi and Duncan McDonnell state, "populism is an ideology which pits a virtuous and homogeneous people against a set of elites and

---

2 Asian Barometer Reports, 2003–2018.

3 Esġn Kivrak Köroğlu, "Chain of Populism from the Democrat Party to the Justice and Development Party in Turkey," PhD thesis, The Graduate School of Social Sciences of Middle East Technical University, 2016, http://etd.lib.metu.edu.tr/upload/12620594/index.pdf (accessed June 10, 2020).

dangerous 'others' who are together depicted as depriving (or attempting to deprive) the sovereign people of their rights, values, prosperity, identity, and voice."[4]

Researchers have identified four underlying reasons for the rise of populism. The first factor is a nation's socioeconomic difficulties and crises. These are associated with the second element, widespread corruption and the erosion of state power, which can lead to an increase in populism. These various factors contribute to the third stage, the undermining of democracy and widespread inequality. Fourthly, the consequent deficiencies in the nation's democracy as well as its respective pillars and institutions all contribute to the rise of populism.

In countries where the political, legal, and cultural frameworks are not well developed and information is lacking, people often want to elect a smart leader with strong and straightforward narrative. This is further shown by the fact that the populist leaders of the 21st century are especially adept at public speaking. Exploiting public frustration and problems to advance their personal agendas, populist politicians gradually rise to power by getting people to trust them. It can even be said that the main goal of populists is to gain political power as opposed to solving the problems of the people or ushering them out of financial crises.

In modern Western politics, it is quite common for populism to be described pejoratively. This trend is visible in Mongolia as well, where researchers tend to describe populism as a dangerous phenomenon. They generally conclude that populism is used by politicians as a tool to mask their flawed policies and polish their positive images while humiliating others. Many Mongolian researchers conclude that populism has introduced a number of detrimental factors to the general political process. Populist politicians often make attractive yet unrealistic promises in order to gain power and influence as well as to heighten their public reputation and perception. Oftentimes, these attractive yet unrealistic promises are directed towards the common populace. In doing so, the populist politicians aim to create fault lines in society that they can exploit. They manipulate facts to depict themselves as representatives of the common people. In the process, however, the politicians also utilize and exploit an "us vs. them" mentality in order to depict elites, oligarchs, or others in power as public enemies and sources of corruption. Furthermore, their populist agendas often have detrimental effects on existing laws and regulations because

---

4 "Популизмын ойлголтыг гуйвуулсан популистууд," ["Populists Who Corrupt Populism"] *Sonin Online*, March 17, 2015, http://www.sonin.mn/news/easy-page/40821 (accessed June 10, 2020).

POPULISM AS A PHENOMENON

the nation often lacks the sound economic foundations and mechanisms for implementing them. Populist promises may include democratic appeals, but these are largely shallow and irrational in their implications, and tend to exploit the trust of the general public. In addition, while populist leaders offer simple and quick solutions for accommodating economic recessions, such calculated proposals redirect public dissatisfaction and frustration towards existing government institutions and governing elites, and thus challenge national security and unity. As populism increases, the reputation of the democratic government and public trust in the government are both significantly eroded. These effects negatively impact on the existing political structures as well as the conduct of political parties.

Based on the above characteristics, there are a number of examples of populist policies that have negatively affected Mongolia and the Mongolian democratic process. One of the most popular examples is the idea that Mongolians could get rich by receiving millions of dollars in transit fees from a fiber optic communication network ranging from Hong Kong, Beijing, Ulaanbaatar, and Moscow to London. These promises often sound like fairy tales, since the stories are fabricated and unrealistic.

Another populist promise made by politicians is based on a vision of Mongolia being transformed into an economic powerhouse by following in the footsteps of the four Asian "tigers." Unfortunately, Mongolia has not yet witnessed this "populist miracle," although it was first promised in the late 90s and has been extensively discussed ever since. Politicians have made many unrealistic promises, such as "we will build a better economy in seventy days" or "we will overcome economic recession in 100 days."

In 2015, the well-known Mongolian columnist Baabar argued that "judging from a series of events occurring in the last ten years, populism is higher (in Mongolia) than it is in Nigeria and Latin America."[5] Politicians do not hesitate to spend national revenue from the mining and other sectors to fulfill their "pleasant" campaign promises. It seems that politicians are trying to achieve income equality by implementing cash transfer programs. However, these promises in reality represent a form of hidden robbery of the people by the authorities, as those populist promises for short-term election purposes have greatly increased budget expenditures, triggering high inflation. Many shortsighted populist promises have been made in order to attract voters. For example, many politicians have promised voters that they will build hospitals

---

5 B. Batbayar (Baabar), "Politics and Populism: An Open Discussion," Capital City Citizen's Representative Council, March 5, 2015, http://dd.cityhall.gov.mn/2015/03/baabar.html (accessed June 10, 2020).

or cultural centers in remote areas where only a few hundred people live. Although they did manage to become Members of Parliament, those relatively large facilities are not economically beneficial, since they only occasionally provide services to at most a few dozen people. In other words, in order to buy votes, politicians needlessly spend revenue from mining and other public funds to distribute a couple of thousand *tugriks* in cash handouts to voters and build unnecessary facilities.

Furthermore, Baabar writes:

Today things that are populist in nature in Mongolia are political parties and the government that those parties created. It is too naïve to label those individuals who are leading populist tides as "populists." When they discuss grand issues such as "the national interest" they are, in fact, acting out of their own hidden self-interest and greed, which is not always in line with what is best for the public. Not all political parties in Mongolia are populists, but their leaders are. These political leaders behind the scenes are just villains who are driven by the pursuit of self-interest. I imagine that the number of populist figures will increase and their successes will be widespread in countries like Mongolia where society is governed by a social lack of consciousness, a weak mindset, irresponsibility, laziness, and the moral law of the jungle. Our government is a reflection of its people. People came first, not the state. It is particularly relevant to countries like ours where the government is elected and formed by the will of people. So, the Mongolian government, political parties, mindset, and system is a direct reflection of its people.[6]

It must be noted that Baabar's insight and thoughts are not his alone but also reflect the thoughts of the general public, as his remarks are widely supported by the people.

A national consultation by leading scholars in the field and representatives of the local civil society identified common characteristics in the public image of populist politicians.[7] It was noted that these leaders "bring issues that the general public wants to hear to the forefront" while ignoring pressing concerns of a not-so-public nature; that they are "standing up for the nation and only want to serve the people"; that they act as "public diplomats concerned with the protection of ethnic Mongolians and those in diaspora communities"; that

---

6   Batbayar, "Politics and Populism: An Open Discussion."
7   Memo from National Consultation held on June 8, 2018.

they portray themselves as self-confident and determined "sons of the people"; that they rely heavily on empty but well-executed rhetoric; that they "skillfully exploit national sentiments and often with the help of famous public figures in sports and the arts"; and that they heavily utilize media outlets and social media to push their image to the public.

However, it would be biased to reflect on populism in a solely negative light. There are times when populism has redeeming qualities and even in some respects protects the national interest.[8] The most widely seen of these effects, first, is helping to resist flawed government policies and pressuring the government to respond to public opinion. The second positive effect is that populism brings to light wrongful acts committed by politicians. Third, it helps people look critically at the authorities' management of national wealth. Finally, populism motivates people to demand government to focus on campaign platforms and the promises they have made.

In other words, there are two types of populism in Mongolia: positive populism based on the public interest and negative populism based on unreasonable and unrealistic promises. For example, if a politician argues that the external debt of Mongolia is out of control, he or she is often accused of using populist rhetoric despite this being an arguably legitimate criticism. In Mongolia, criticism against government policy from the public interest perspective tends to be attacked as populist. Obviously, this type of attack is meant to minimize the impact such healthy criticism might have on public opinion. If this is truly populism, it could be considered a positive force in that it informs the public and acts as a balancing force to check the dominance of the political power. It is because of these real concerns based on facts and analysis that one can talk about the redeeming qualities of populist politicians. These relatively indirect and unofficial forms of checks and balances are growing increasingly more important as Mongolia's external debt rose in 2018 to US\$ 21 billion, representing around 180 percent of the country's gross domestic product in that year; it certainly poses a great challenge to Mongolia's economic security.

Nevertheless, these few positive aspects do not justify the harms done by populism in Mongolia. While this silver lining may be comforting argument made by populist leaders and groups that do have relevance, one cannot ignore the detrimental effects this phenomenon has in weakening political parties and the very institutions of the Mongolian state. One must keep in mind

---

8 D. Myagmarsuren. "Populism Is a Political Technology," Politics Is a Profession (blog), December 13, 2010, http://ulstur-tech.blogspot.com/2010/12/blog-post_13.html (accessed June 10, 2020).

that populism is a political tool mainly utilized to win elections and push political agendas that are not necessarily in the public interest.

3   Populism in Mongolia and the Crisis of Political Parties

In 1992, Mongolia ended the one-party system by introducing multi-party democracy. Although different political parties have been created and are helping to shape democracy in Mongolia, unfortunately, in many cases they have failed to serve society as an important player in the processes of representative democracy due to long-awaited but slow legal reforms for promoting the formation and institutionalization of political parties.

As a result, Mongolians are losing trust in politicians and growing more skeptical of political parties. Many people have little trust in political parties. This trend is likely to continue in the years to come. According to a public opinion poll conducted by the Sant Maral Foundation in 2017, 81.3 percent of respondents said that political parties often fail to respond to public opinion, while 44.3 percent of respondents believed that political parties are unnecessary. Further, 60.6 percent of respondents said they do not trust political parties at all.[9] According to a report compiled by the Open Society Forum in 2015, 67 percent of respondents said that political financing is not transparent enough, while 94 percent of those surveyed said that the names of political party donors should be declared publicly.[10] As a result, it is quite common for ordinary people to agree with statements such as "political parties are unnecessary," "the state is weak," "no politicians are patriotic," and "all politicians are greedy and corrupt."[11] This trend is clearly seen across reports conducted by all research institutes in Mongolia.

The public perception that the economy is not developing and that high percentage of distrust of people in state institutions as reported by these surveys show that it is reasonable for a large segment of the population to perceive political parties this way and draw such conclusions. These perceptions stem from the fact that political parties, in having a close relationship with the government, lack core values, principles, and political ideologies to nourish

---

9   Sant Maral Foundation, *Political Barometer Report*, 2017, http://www.santmaral.org/en/publication/politbarometer-1650-march-2017 (accessed June 2018).

10   Sant Maral Foundation, "General Population Opinion Poll on Party Financing," Open Society Forum, November 2014, http://www.santmaral.mn/mn/node/2 (accessed June 2018).

11   Asian Political Barometer Report, 2014.

and develop. In addition, many of the parties are not well structured, lacking internal democratic mechanisms. This leads political parties to tend towards clientelism, resulting in many being under the control of business interest groups and thus resulting in an even greater space for populism to thrive.

Populism, in the sense that it is depicted as "of the people" or "for the good of the people," is a political technique to advance certain agendas or ideologies without offering concrete and viable solutions to problems. The word "populist" describes politicians who opt for populist techniques. Populist techniques include quite straightforward approaches that offer simplistic prescriptions for everything that is not working. Moreover, such politicians persuade ordinary citizens to perceive social and political processes in a simplistic way and skillfully use this perception to advance their political agenda.

Political parties are facing a crisis in Mongolia. Therefore, politicians seek to play the role of populists in order to make themselves known to the public and their own party members. As researchers suggest, the specific social, economic, and political conditions necessary to give rise to populism are already in place in Mongolia. Due to the socioeconomic crisis and the transient nature of political parties in Mongolia, charismatic politicians with superior public speaking skills are trying to win mass support.

According to researcher Amantai. Kh, populist leaders win people's trust by using the concept of "the people," making ordinary citizens feel that they are the "true" representatives of the country and are ready and willing to devote themselves to the motherland and sovereignty. They also suggest that right-wing or left-wing politics are not important, because "the interests of the people" are paramount and above ideological divides.

Moreover, it is common for populists to label elites unpatriotic and to blame them for causing problems behind the scenes, whether at home or abroad. In particular, they persuade people to see elites and the authorities as public enemies who deceive common people and make unrealistic promises, overstepping their power. Populists present themselves as new or sole representations of "the people" who will overthrow the entrenched elites and devote themselves to the people.[12]

Cas Mudde, a Dutch political scientist, once wrote that "populism is an illiberal democratic response to undemocratic liberalism."[13] In countries where populism is surging, political parties fail to bridge the gap between the

---

12   Myagmarsuren. "Populism Is a Political Technology."
13   Sholto Byrnes, "Populists Are the Product of Failed Political Parties," *The National*, April 4, 2017, https://www.thenational.ae/opinion/populists-are-the-product-of-failed-political-parties-1.90099 (accessed June 2018).

government and citizens, and fail to appeal to the people who cannot see any ideological difference between parties. In other words, populism is a product of the failure of mainstream parties. Mudde's definition of populism is quite reasonable. He further explains that populists split society into "two homogenous and antagonistic groups: the pure people on the one end and the corrupt elite on the other." In this sense, populism is an ideology that states that politics is no longer the business of a few elites, but should rather be guided by the "will of the people."[14]

In a democratic society, many different interests, social classes, and groups co-exist. Yet populism can neither recognize nor appreciate social diversity. That is why populist politicians do not want to make concessions that acknowledge various interests in society. In this sense, populism eventually creates favorable conditions for a tyranny of the majority.

Moreover, by splitting society into two groups—patriots versus mixed-race people, capitalists versus workers whose labor is exploited—populism produces a greater degree of conflict in society. In this sense, "normal folks" can delineate themselves from "others" who cheat, control, and subjugate them.

Although in 1992 Mongolia became a democratic country with a multi-party system that respects and supports human rights, one can observe how the people are losing trust in the political system, especially the political parties. This in turn undermines the very concept of political parties in a functioning democracy. This is understandable, since political parties are not able to function as a bridge linking the people with the government in times of socioeconomic crisis, when people seemingly feel they are surrounded by instability and chaos. These feelings have gradually made it possible for populism to rise. It is clear that Mongolian political parties are gradually but significantly losing their legitimacy. According to researchers and thinkers focusing on the study of political parties, people should join a political party once they are motivated by personal willingness and aspirations based on certain political philosophies. However, Mongolians tend to see political parties as instruments for ensuring personal gain, so they join the party that is potentially beneficial to the pursuit of their own interests. Furthermore, political parties have begun to function as an institution that provides some people access to government jobs. Those who wish to apply for government jobs feel the need to provide contributions and donations to the political parties in power or to gain the favor of political leaders in order to achieve their desired positions. It is important for political

---

14 "Популизм гэж юу вэ? / Populism gej yu ve?," Dashka DAVAASUREN Altankhuyag (vlog), July 2, 2014, https://www.youtube.com/watch?v=kGZQklYKvGU (accessed June 10, 2020).

parties to attempt to fill the government with their "people" or their supporters whenever they desire to do so.

Political parties also see public service as a source of funding, and many of Mongolia's political parties exhibit specific characteristics of "cartel" parties. One of the underlying reasons for such a tendency is that Mongolian parties are not driven by particular political ideologies, which makes it difficult for the public to differentiate between them. Moreover, people do not have a proper understanding of the basic differences between liberal and socialist agendas. As a result, people have begun to believe that there will not be much difference in the overall social environment if they vote for one party or the other. Due to political funding that is less transparent, political parties tend to rely heavily on big companies for contributions. They gain funding for their organizations by attracting a few rich contributors, making political parties an instrument for generating extra profit. In return, businessmen receive political protection or gain political opportunities for successfully managing their endeavors. Finally, businesses also recruit puppet members to represent their interests in political parties by getting involved in internal party competition between groups or factions. In doing so, they are able to exercise greater influence during internal party decision-making processes and funding provisions, greatly undermining internal democracy in political parties.

Political parties have created a symbiotic system wherein the politics of the state indirectly funds the political parties from which certain politicians are benefitting or seeking to benefit. This system is weakening Mongolia in many ways. There are also certain groups that are benefitting or willing to benefit from the competition between politicians. Those groups include the media, small parties, and populists. Previously, the media in Mongolia was considered the fourth branch of government, acting as an instrument that controlled governing parties and politicians. However, due to the increasing number of media outlets, the media itself has become a tool to generate funds for the operations and profits of governing parties and politicians. Many media outlets are under the control of influential politicians. Small political parties, fighting not to be forgotten, have a political interest in finding a way into the pockets of strong political parties. It can be concluded that the socioeconomic crisis facing Mongolia has been caused by unfair competition among irresponsible political parties. This in turn has led to a crisis for political parties and generated fertile soil in which populism can grow.

Most Mongolian researchers and civil society organizations concluded that populism is becoming increasingly evident, as political parties are not well structured and have lost legitimacy as their ideological differences have been blurred. However, there are still opportunities to stem the populist tide in Mongolia and push political parties to adopt policy-oriented approaches by continuing the efforts to amend the Law on Political Parties that started in 2011, adding new comprehensive provisions to the Constitution to impose some legal duties on the parties, and reforming the existing election system.

CHAPTER 8

The Changing Nature of Populism in Malaysia

Faiz Abdul Halim and Aira Azhari

1 Introduction

With the rise of populist leaders and parties across Europe, the United States, and the Philippines, many of whom have been voted into power, there has been a surge of scholarly and public interest in the topic of populism and its impacts on democracy and liberal values. This discussion has begun to spill over into Malaysia. Parallels are being drawn between the nativist rhetoric of popular right-wing European parties and the ethno-nationalist and religious rhetoric of members of the former ruling party, the United Malays National Organization (UMNO).[1] There are also concerns over the potential socioeconomic and political impact and the feasibility of allegedly "populist" promises made on the campaign trail by the Pakatan Harapan (PH) coalition.

In short, populism worries Malaysians. Yet, as is common with any popular topical political terminology used in public and academic discourse, populism is not a clearly defined term. More often than not, populism is used in charged polemics to discredit political and socioeconomic policies. Far-right parties have also begun adopting populist platforms, adding more confusion to the mix—populism is then mixed up with right-leaning or extremist ideologies such as nativism or fascism.

Hence, this chapter first seeks to identify a working definition of populism and examines the current trends of populism in Malaysia. The political discourse and issues constituting populism in Malaysia will be discussed. The chapter will then look at populism within the PH manifesto. It will conclude with some thoughts on how populism in Malaysia is likely to change in the future and suggested directions for further research.

---

1 At the time of writing, the Pakatan Harapan coalition was still in power; however, the coalition fell on February 24, 2020, when Prime Minister Tun Dr. Mahathir Mohamad resigned. This triggered a change in government when the Perikatan Nasional coalition took over, with UMNO as one of its component parties. The content of this chapter should be read from the point of view of the PH coalition being in power.

© FAIZ ABDUL HALIM AND AIRA AZHARI, 2021 | DOI:10.1163/9789004444461_010

2 The Malaysian Discourse on Populism

Although definitions of populism vary, political scientist Cas Mudde's definition has gained some acceptance within the academic community and has been implicitly used within mainstream media. Mudde defines populism as "an ideology that considers society to be ultimately separated into two homogeneous and antagonistic groups, 'the pure people' versus 'the corrupt elite,' and which argues that politics should be an expression of the *volonté générale* (general will) of the people."[2] This chapter will refer to populism according to this definition.

This "ideational" definition of populism has two opposite, competing ideologies: pluralism and elitism. Elitism, the mirror opposite of populism, advocates for politics to be an expression of a moral elite rather than the amoral, vulgar masses. At odds with both elitism and populism, pluralism instead views the political sphere as a "heterogeneous collection of groups and individuals with often fundamentally different views and wishes." Hence, pluralism instead advocates for diversity, consensus, and compromise.[3]

Central to Mudde's definition of populism is the monist and moralistic dichotomy between the masses and the elites. Populists believe that the "people" share the same "pure" values and interests. Consequently, populists believe that all "elites" share the same "corrupt" values, which are diametrically opposed to those of the people. Moral conflict is at the core of this dichotomous relationship whereby the will of the people is at odds with the will of the dominant evil and corrupt elites or traditional political institutions. This "us versus them" mindset leads populists to exhibit dismissive behavior towards any opposing views. As a result, populism tends to encourage divisive stances and polarization on common political and socioeconomic issues.[4]

The definition of populism has been fairly inconsistent within the Malaysian political discourse, despite its fairly frequent usage within the media and among some academics. For instance, in the most notable writing on populism in Malaysia, *Autocrats vs The People: Authoritarian Populism in Malaysia* by Anne Munro-Kua, the term "authoritarian populism," first coined by Stuart Hall, "depicts politics as a struggle between 'the people' and some combination of malevolent, racialized and/or unfairly advantaged 'others' at home or

---

2 Cas Mudde, "The Populist Zeitgeist," *Government and Opposition* 39, no. 4 (2004): 541–563.
3 Mudde, "The Populist Zeitgeist."
4 Mudde, "The Populist Zeitgeist."

THE CHANGING NATURE OF POPULISM IN MALAYSIA   149

abroad or both. It justifies interventions in the name of 'taking back control' in favor of 'the people.'"[5]

While there are superficial similarities with the ideational definition, Munro-Kua describes authoritarian populism as an "authoritarian form of democratic class politics." The definition of "authoritarian" here refers to an "expression of the coercive function of the capitalist state" rather than a fascist or dictatorial regime. All states have the power to exert their coercive capacity, but states also possess ideological institutions to exert more subtle forms of domination over the ruled. Populism here describes a political ideological strategy used by the state to reinforce its dominance of the population rather than an anti-establishment "thin-centered ideology." Populism, according to Poulantza, "involves the creation of an ideology which can be used to manipulate the populace and to facilitate the introduction of policies which may be against their broad class interest." This strategy is used in order to exert ideological intervention into the private sphere of life to promote an ideological stance that attempts to "legitimize" the state's use of coercive authoritarian measures as being in the best interest of the people. While this chapter does not seek to discredit the term "authoritarian populism," this term and the ideational definition of "populism" are essentially two separate concepts used to describe two different political phenomena.[6]

Prior to the 14th general elections (GE14) on May 9, 2018, several articles and columns were published expressing concerns regarding populism in Malaysia. The concerns were mostly over the potentially negative political and socioeconomic impact that "populism," particularly from the "populist" PH manifesto, could have on Malaysia.

The *New Straits Times* writer Syed Umar Ariff compared the rise of populism in the United States and Malaysia.[7] The author described populism as the "best tool to use against the establishment or competition in order to rally an army of simple-minded supporters by magnifying pettiness into national-scale issues."[8] He criticized Mukhriz Manhathir's call for a two-term limit for the Prime Minister (PM) as "populist," stating that it was a little too late since the same calls arose during his father Mahathir's 20-year tenure as PM. He also

---

5   Anne Munro-Kua, *Authoritarian Populism in Malaysia* (New York: St Martin's Press, 1996; Basingstoke: Palgrave Macmillan, 1996).

6   Munro-Kua, *Authoritarian Populism in Malaysia*.

7   Syed Umar Ariff, "Rise of Populism in US and Malaysian Politics," *NST Online,* September 20, 2016, https://www.nst.com.my/news/2016/09/177061/rise-populism-us-and-malaysian- (accessed June 20, 2020).

8   Umar Ariff, "Rise of Populism in US and Malaysian Politics."

attacked the opposition's "populist" criticisms of the electoral re-delineation move, claiming that it would only benefit Barisan Nasional (BN).

The Centre for a Better Tomorrow, a think tank linked with the BN component party the Malaysian Chinese Association, asked voters to be wary of PH's populist pledges, claiming they could devastate the country's long-term socioeconomic interests.[9]

In March 2018, the *New Straits Times* published an article in which two political analysts criticized PH's manifesto as "ridiculous" and "populist," aimed at garnering votes without properly taking into account the country's current economic status. Universiti Utara Malaysia lecturer Md Shukri Shuib suggested that PH's plan to abolish the goods-and-services tax (GST) and control the price of goods was "ridiculous," as the state of the global economy meant that every country was looking for means to increase revenue. Universiti Malaya political analyst Dr. Awang Azman Awang Pawi said that PH's "populist" manifesto lacked implementation strategies and was merely aimed at attracting voters. He added that PH's promises to control the price of goods and fuel prices did not account for the importance of supply and demand, nor did they factor in the influence of fluctuating global fuel prices. He criticized PH for recycling old issues to woo voters.[10]

Malaysian leaders and parties have rarely described themselves as populist, let alone attached positive connotations to the greatly maligned word. Yet, in an odd twist, UMNO treasurer and Communications and Multimedia then-Minister Salleh Said Keruak claimed UMNO had become the longest-ruling party in the world due to its "ultra-populist" nature. It was "sensitive to the needs of the people, understood the aspirations of the people, maintained good relations with component parties, protected the people of all races, helped the poor, and took care of the people's welfare." He also claimed that UMNO was a democratic party with the undivided support of a majority of Malays and Malaysians.[11] Ironically, when directing criticism at PH's planned budget, Salleh

---

9   "Populist Pledges Will Ruin Malaysia, Think Tank Says Ahead of GE14," *Malay Mail*, February 24, 2018, https://www.malaymail.com/news/malaysia/2018/02/24/populist-pledges-will-ruin-malaysia-think-tank-urges-ahead-of-ge14/1584353 (accessed 31 October, 2018).

10 Rohaniza Idris, Khairul Azran Hussin, and Tharanya Arumugam, "Ridiculous and Populist Pakatan Manifesto, Say Analysts," *New Straits Times*, March 8, 2018, https://www.nst.com.my/news/politics/2018/03/343137/ridiculous-and-populist-pakatan-manifesto-say-analysts (accessed October 1, 2018).

11 "Umno an Ultra-Populist Democratic Party: Salleh," *Sun Daily*, February 8, 2018, https://www.thesundaily.my/archive/umno-ultra-populist-democratic-party-salleh-updated-MUARCH524778 (accessed October 1, 2018).

said that "populist" policies such as removing taxes and offering free services would put the country in jeopardy.[12]

Absent from the "populism" described in these articles and columns is any hint of a moral "people" versus a corrupt "elite" dimension, and there is also an absence of any talk of the general will of the people. Though these articles purport to talk about "populism," they generally lean towards its oft-used pejorative socioeconomic definition as a set of short-sighted, potentially detrimental, but popular economic policies aimed at quickly garnering votes. They sometimes use populism to make a charged attack on PH and its "simple-minded supporters." Salleh described UMNO as "ultra-populist," but he seems to imply that they are more of a "pluralist" party than a populist party. He described UMNO as a party that catered to the interests and demands of all Malaysians, regardless of their ethnicity. However, he too referred back to the socioeconomic definition of populism. By describing the issues addressed as "populist" through a socioeconomic lens, the authors of these articles may have implicitly acknowledged the widespread, popular support for promises that aimed to abolish highly unpopular policies and address issues that Malaysians felt were negatively affecting their livelihoods while a few select people in power were benefitting at their expense.

3 What Socioeconomic and Political Issues Resonate with the Malaysian Public?

As populism is not a substantive ideological stance, what constitutes populism in Malaysia generally varies from other countries, though there may be similarities. In Malaysian politics, populist issues might center on controversial topics regarding ethnicity, religion, education, cost of living, immigration, political corruption, repressive laws, the Constitution, and taxation, to name a few. Moreover, it must be asked how "the people" is defined in Malaysia, and what comprises their "general will."

Malaysia's diverse ethnic makeup and pluralist society make it difficult to discern to whom exactly "the people" might refer. According to 2010 census data from the Department of Statistics Malaysia (DOSM), Bumiputera (Muslim and non-Muslim) accounted for 67.4 percent of Malaysia's total population, with Malays comprising a total of 63.1 percent of the population in Peninsular

---

12   Haikal Jalil, "Populist Policies Will Only Jeopardise Our Future: Salleh," *Sun Daily*, October 29, 2017, https://www.thesundaily.my/archive/populist-policies-will-only-jeopardise-our-future-salleh-ATARCH497729 (accessed October 1, 2018).

Malaysia. Chinese accounted for 24.6 percent of the population, followed by Indians (7.3 percent). Approximately 61 percent of Malaysians professed Islam to be their religion, followed by Buddhism (19.8 percent), Christianity (9.2 percent), and Hinduism (6.3 percent).[13] The 2018 population estimates by the DOSM indicated that the Bumiputera were projected to grow to 69.1 percent of the population, up from 68.8 percent in 2017.[14]

How does one identify the pertinent issues with which most Malaysians are concerned and also take into account these ethno-religious cleavages? Opinion surveys may help us in this respect by providing a general overview of the issues that concern most Malaysians.

A survey conducted by market research firm Ipsos titled *What Worries Malaysia in 2017?* revealed that the top three concerns among Malaysians in 2017 were immigration control (of foreign workers), governance (government and corporate conduct), and unemployment (Figure 8.1).[15] Foreign immigration was of particular concern to respondents with a household income of below RM 3000 and/or those living in rural areas. Official statistics from the Ministry of Home Affairs estimated that there were around 1.9 million registered foreign workers in the country, an estimate that does not account for undocumented foreign workers. Ipsos, which conducts similar studies globally, noted that rising unemployment concerns usually correlate with rising concerns about immigration control.

In a national survey conducted by the Merdeka Center prior to the GE14 titled *Malaysia General Election XIV Outlook*, released on April 26, 2018, inflation, corruption, and job opportunities were the top three issues that concerned the survey respondents, at 57 percent, 37 percent, and 21 percent, respectively. Inflation was of particular concern among 60 percent and 59 percent of Malay and Indian respondents, while 53 percent of Chinese respondents were concerned about corruption (see Figure 8.2).

Following the GE14, in a survey in July 2018, Ipsos said that overall concerns still remained centered on financial and political corruption (60 percent), unemployment (43 percent), inflation (16 percent), and taxes (14 percent); however, in a notable change, 66 percent of Malaysians were more confident that the country was heading in the right direction.[16] In 2018, Transparency

---

13   "Population Distribution and Basic Demographic Characteristic Report 2010," Department of Statistics Malaysia, 2010.

14   "Current Population Estimates, Malaysia, 2017–2018," Department of Statistics Malaysia, Official Portal, July 31, 2018.

15   Ipsos Malaysia, "What Worries Malaysia: Post GE 2018," *Ipsos*, August 16, 2018, https://www.ipsos.com/en-my/what-worries-malaysia-post-ge-2018 (accessed October 1, 2018).

16   Ipsos Malaysia, "What Worries Malaysia: Post GE 2018."

THE CHANGING NATURE OF POPULISM IN MALAYSIA

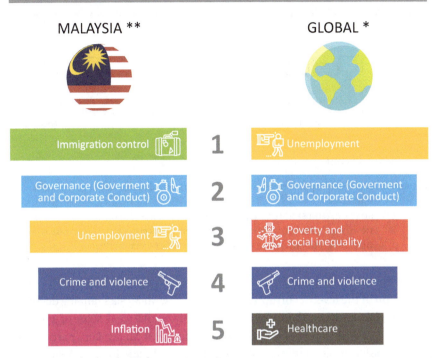

FIGURE 8.1 What worries Malaysians in 2017?
SOURCE: IPSOS MALAYSIA, "WHAT WORRIES MALAYSIA: POST GE 2018," *IPSOS*, AUGUST 16, 2018, HTTPS://WWW.IPSOS.COM/EN-MY/WHAT-WORRIES-MALAYSIA-POST-GE-2018 (ACCESSED OCTOBER 1, 2018)

Important Issues

Issues	Total	Malay	Chinese	Indian	Muslim Bumiputera	Non Muslim Bumiputera
Inflation	57%	60%	49%	59%	56%	70%
Corruption	37%	33%	53%	12%	29%	35%
Job opportunities	21%	24%	9%	40%	34%	22%

FIGURE 8.2 Malaysia general elections XIV outlook: prospects and outcome
SOURCE: MERDEKA CENTRE FOR OPINION RESEARCH, "SURVEY, KUALA LUMPUR: NATIONAL VOTER SENTIMENTS: EXCERPT OF PRINCIPAL INDICATORS," *MERDEKA CENTER*, 2019

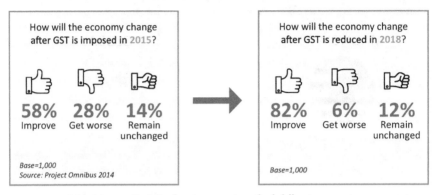

FIGURE 8.3 Malaysians optimistic about economic outlook following recent government initiatives
SOURCE: NIELSEN, JULY 12, 2018. HTTPS://WWW.NIELSEN.COM/APAC/EN/INSIGHTS/ARTICLE/2018/MALAYSIANS-OPTIMISTIC-ABOUT-ECONOMIC-OUTLOOK-FOLLOWING-RECENT-GOVERNMENT-INITIATIVES/

International's Corruption Perception Index, which surveys a country's public perception of the level of corruption in the country, Malaysia's ranking declined by seven places, from 55th in 2016 to 62nd in 2017, with a weak score of 47/100.[17]

Taxation has always been a touchy subject for most Malaysians, particularly the unpopular implementation of the GST under the BN in 2015. A survey by market research firm Nielsen saw mixed reactions among Malaysian consumers towards the impact of the implementation of the GST on the economy (see Figure 8.3). While 58 percent of respondents said it would improve Malaysia's economic situation, 28 percent of respondents said it would worsen it. Nielsen then released new survey results for 2018 post-GE14 showing that 82 percent of Malaysians believed the zeroization of the GST would improve the economy and only 6 percent thought it would worsen it. In the same survey, more than nine out of ten respondents believed the PH government would reduce or remove tolls, and 77 percent of respondents said the "fuel price fix" would be "good for consumers."

The results of these surveys may indicate that Malaysians are generally concerned about bread-and-butter economic issues. Malaysians may also link foreign immigration, the GST, and political corruption to the country's economic

---

17   Transparency International, "Corruption Perceptions Index 201," February 21, 2018, https://www.transparency.org/news/feature/corruption_perceptions_index_2017 (accessed October 1, 2018).

THE CHANGING NATURE OF POPULISM IN MALAYSIA   155

woes. Public perception may also link the 1MDB (1 Malaysia Development Berhad) scandal and the GST to inflation, a high cost of living, a weakening ringgit, and a high government debt ratio.

4 Why Were These Issues Considered Populist in Malaysia?

While public opinion surveys provide some insight into what popular issues the Malaysian public is concerned about, it is important to account for how and why the previous political elites responded to (or ignored) these issues. Populism brings controversial issues back to the forefront of the public political discourse, issues that the elites are largely uncomfortable discussing. In the case of Malaysia, which has been referred to as a competitive authoritarian regime—a hybrid regime where competitive regular elections are practiced but where the ruling party has unfair and advantageous access to state mechanisms and institutions (such as the media) that are frequently used to hinder or attack the opposition—the elites tend to apply repressive laws to censor discussion of sensitive and "uncomfortable" issues and silence those opposed to the regime.[18]

Since its independence in 1957, Malaysia has not been known as a bastion of free speech and democracy. Freedom House gave pre-GE14 Malaysia a freedom rating (a score that measures civil and political liberties in a given country) of "partly free" in its Freedom in the World 2018 report, with an aggregate score of 45/100. For comparison, New Zealand was ranked the freest country in the world, with a score of 98/100. Among the several issues plaguing Malaysia's political system, Freedom House highlighted the lack of independence within the Electoral Commission (EC), gerrymandering by the EC, rampant corruption within political institutions, repression and restrictions on civil society, and former PM Najib Tun Razak's attempt to contain the fallout of 1MDB by purging critical cabinet ministers, as well as targeting media outlets such as The Edge and the Sarawak Report covering the scandal, which were censored or suspended in the latter case for publishing incriminating investigative pieces on the scandal.[19]

International media watchdog Reporters Without Borders (RSF) placed BN-led Malaysia at 145 out of 180 countries in the 2018 World Press Freedom Index,

---

18   Steven Levitsky and Lucan A. Way, "Elections Without Democracy: The Rise of Competitive Authoritarianism," *Journal of Democracy* 13, no. 2 (2002): 51–65.

19   Freedom House, "Freedom in the World 2018: Malaysia," https://freedomhouse.org/report/freedom-world/2018/malaysia (accessed October 1, 2018).

with a score of 46.89 (the lower, the better) in 2017. By contrast, top-ranked Norway scored 7.63. RSF cites several legal hindrances to media freedom posed by repressive and draconian laws such as the Printing Presses and Publications Act, the Official Secrets Act, the Communications and Multimedia Act, and the Sedition Act. Furthermore, RSF noted how journalists and media were being harassed for being too independent and critical of the previous regime led by Najib, particularly when covering the 1MDB scandal.[20]

Calls for reforms and to tackle high-level and widespread corruption have been a staple issue in the Malaysian political discourse since the mid-2000s. Since 2006, a coalition of civil society groups and nongovernmental organizations (NGOs) called the Coalition for Free and Fair Elections (better known by its Malay name "Bersih 2.0") has organized several large-scale protests demanding substantial political, institutional, and electoral reforms. Some of Bersih's eight demands include a clean-up of the electoral roll, which is allegedly filled with "phantom voters," free and fair access to media coverage for all political parties, and the strengthening of public institutions.[21]

However, the BN regime's response to these rallies has usually resulted in crackdowns and arrests of Bersih members and rally-goers. In November 2016, Bersih organized the Bersih Five rally, which saw further calls for then-PM Najib to resign following the 1MDB scandal exposé. Authorities raided offices and detained Bersih Five leader Maria Chin Abdullah on November 18, 2016, under the Security Offences (Special Measures) Act, supposedly intended to be used for genuine security and terrorist threats. Thus, it was easy to see that political corruption and the 1MDB scandal were very sensitive subjects for the BN elites, who cracked down on any attempt to publicize the issues.

5   Current Trends in Populism in Malaysia

There are several elements of populism within PH's *Buku Harapan*, despite the fact that it contains only two mentions of the term "elite," both of which are found in a paragraph that describes UMNO and the BN's manipulation of "racial politics" to ensure that the political elite remained in power.[22] The manifesto

---

20   "Malaysia, Reporters Without Borders, 2019," https://rsf.org/en/malaysia?nl=ok (accessed February 1, 2019).

21   "Our 8 demands," Bersih 2.0., n.d., http://www.bersih.org/about/8demands/ (accessed October 1, 2018).

22   Pakatan Harapan, *Buku Harapan: Rebuilding Our Nation, Fulfilling Our Hopes* (Putrajaya: Pakatan Harapan, 2018).

THE CHANGING NATURE OF POPULISM IN MALAYSIA

also makes clear that it aims to cleanse Malaysia of "corruption, malfeasance and kleptocracy," citing the 1MDB case as the primary example.

The general language of the manifesto attempts to appeal to popular dissatisfaction towards a small elitist and racist UMNO-dominated BN government. PH promises to save Malaysia from the BN, returning it to the right path in order to bring glory to the country again. The manifesto emphasizes the socio-economic discrimination perpetuated by the BN against the "common people." PH also echoes the slogans of the 2008 Great Recession populist movement Occupy Wall Street by evoking the disparity between the "99 percent" and the "1 percent":

> Pakatan Harapan is determined to stop UMNO and Barisan Nasional's failure to guarantee the welfare of the common people, especially those who live in rural areas, the Indians, and the indigenous people, as well as the lower middle class who are often forgotten. Our promises are for the 99 percent, and not just for the 1 percent cronies of UMNO and Barisan Nasional.[23]

Public perception may have attributed the rising cost of living and price of goods to the imposition of the GST, despite BN leaders claiming that the GST would gradually help reduce prices while providing substantial increases in government revenue. These justifications may have failed to assuage public perceptions that linked implementation of the GST to the 1MDB scandal and media coverage of the lavish, luxurious lifestyles of high-level politicians that coincided with the implementation of the GST. PH made sure to capitalize on this and establish links between the two issues, stating: "Today Malaysians are being forced to pay the regressive GST, only for that money to be used to pay for the luxurious lives of politicians who fly in private jets around the world."[24]

PH describes the GST as a regressive tax imposed by UMNO and the BN as a result of their failure to properly manage the economy. In its second promise to "reduce the pressures causing burdensome price increases," PH states that the GST is the main cause of higher inflation rates of 4 percent in 2017 compared with the 1 percent inflation in 2015. The coalition also criticized then-BN leaders for being detached from the realities of life for regular Malaysians.

The second pillar of the manifesto, institutional and political reform, echoes some of the demands put forth by Bersih to address corruption within

---

23   Harapan, *Buku Harapan.*
24   Harapan, *Buku Harapan.*

the government by placing checks and balances on the PM, ministers, and other government institutions. PH blames Najib, UMNO, and the BN for most of these political failings due to their constant consolidation and abuse of power: cronyism and kleptocracy are the name of the game, and the existing checks and balances put in place by the founding fathers of the nation can no longer function. PH then promises to restore dignity to the defiled institutions.

While the manifesto does use populist language to direct much of the blame towards the BN elite, it is important to note that much of the content of the promised solutions is pluralistic in nature. For instance, the section titled "Special Commitments" accounts for the interest groups that tend to feel marginalized, such as women and youth, as well as minority groups such as Indians, Felda settlers, and senior citizens.

Moreover, the political, electoral, and institutional reforms PH proposes are very much anti-populist in nature as they seek to reform the public institutions and abolish repressive laws to ensure that there are more check-and-balance mechanisms at work on the government. This would open communication channels with the government for opposition parties, reform committees, the media, NGOs, interest groups, and citizens to allow them to voice their opinions, concerns, and grievances on relevant issues more freely. Furthermore, the manifesto places an anti-populist emphasis on decentralization. For instance, the fourth pillar of the manifesto sets out to return Sabah and Sarawak to the status accorded by the Malaysia Agreement 1963. The manifesto also promises to revive the true spirit of federalism to encourage decentralization and strengthen the role and power of local authorities.

Many parts of the PH manifesto seek to introduce pluralistic and liberal reforms to improve the governance structure and allow dissenting and competing views to have input into the government. This is antithetical to populism, which emphasizes the so-called "people's" will—a one-size-fits-all solution for how the government ought to function that ignores minorities and in some cases may repress dissent. Thus, while the manifesto borrows populist concepts and language to direct the blame toward the BN regime for recent grievances, the content of the manifesto encourages a move towards a more plural system.

6   One Year On—Has PH Stayed True to Its Promises?

At the time of writing, the PH government had been in power for almost a year. There is a need to assess how successful they have been in implementing their promises. The most notable success has been the zero-rating of the GST and the reintroduction of the Sales and Services Tax (SST) in its place. The government clearly made this move a priority for its administration, knowing full well that any indication otherwise would trigger a backlash from the public and risk losing its hard-won support. As a result of this policy, there was an initial sharp drop in prices, and the lower prices were enjoyed during the tax holiday before going up again on September 1, 2018, when the SST came into place. Malaysians have begun to realize that lowering the cost of living does not simply entail removing an unpopular consumption tax but requires deeper structural reforms to tackle problems such as stagnant wages and changing consumer habits. The GST is a good example of how populist economic promises do little to serve citizens' (the *rakyat*'s) interest in the long term.

A 2019 survey conducted by the Merdeka Center revealed that the top three concerns among Malaysians were inflation, corruption, and the preservation of Malay rights/fair treatment of all races.[25] Interestingly, all three concerns can be linked to populist narratives. The tide of dissatisfaction with the PH government was largely due to their failure to reduce the price of goods or to curb practices of money politics and patronage, as well as the perception that they were not adequately protecting Malay rights. Following the general elections on May 9, 2018, there were eight by-elections between August 2018 and January 2020,[26] three of which were won by BN. Signs of dissatisfaction were becoming more apparent, and the same Merdeka Center survey showed that the PM's approval rating plummeted from 83 percent in May 2018 to just 46 percent in March 2019. Many commentators attributed this loss of support to the PH's failure to bring down the price of goods and the perception that Malay-Muslim rights were being threatened.

It is important to note that this dissatisfaction, while natural in a maturing democracy such as Malaysia, is also a sign that despite the watershed election results of 2018, the political discourse in the country has not changed much. Populist narratives that feed into larger problems of inequality, rising costs of living, and widening social divides continue to distract the people from having concrete conversations about the policy direction necessary to alleviate these concerns.

---

25   "Survey, Kuala Lumpur: National Voter Sentiments: Excerpt of Principal Indicators," Merdeka Center, 2019.

26   In Malaysia, if a parliamentary/state legislative seat falls vacant, a by-election is held to elect a new representative for that seat.

7 Conclusion: Changing Currents of Populism in Post-GE14 Malaysia?

Following Pakatan Harapan's surprise victory in the GE14, their first 100 days in government saw the "zeroization" of the GST and its eventual replacement with the SST. In 2018–2019, the government focused on dealing with the 1MDB scandal and prosecuting figures associated with the scandal, renegotiating project contracts, and attempting to slowly reform institutions. However, they had also rolled back or delayed some popular promises, such as the promise to abolish tolls, though it was still too early to see where PH's numerous promises would head in the coming years. After PH came to power, its populist language changed somewhat, whereby government ministers began to talk about how the challenges faced by the government are linked to and said to be caused by the failings of the BN.

Between May 2018 and September 2019, the opposition Islamic Party of Malaysia (PAS) and UMNO tried to find their feet in the new political climate. By taking note of populist electoral victories and successful platforms from right-wing, typically nativist parties in Europe and the United States, there may be a possibility that the opposition will also adopt a more populist stance, which may be combined with political Islam and Malay nativist sentiments, particularly since the PH government is attempting to encourage a greater degree of pluralism in the political system. Furthermore, UMNO and PAS leaders have always had the not-so-subtle tendency to frame Malaysia's political narrative as a Malay versus non-Malay and/or a Muslim versus non-Muslim political struggle despite their attempts to exhibit superficial ethnic tolerance. The potency of a populist Malay nativist and/or a populist Islamist platform should not be underestimated, especially when one considers that in GE14 only 25–30 percent of Malays voted for PH while the remaining 70 percent were divided between the PAS and the BN.[27] However, there are voices within UMNO and BN component parties that are seeking to reform their parties in a new direction, though it is uncertain where the reform will lead the party or how it will alter its core ideology.

Further research should also raise questions as to how the Malaysian "people" are educated and informed on policy and social issues. Populism plays on the popular sentiments of the people, but how do the "people" come to adopt these views and is there is any factual basis for such views? This is particularly

---

27 "Report: 95% Chinese but Less Than 30% Malays Voted for PH," *FMT Reporters*, June 14, 2018, https://www.freemalaysiatoday.com/category/nation/2018/06/14/report-95-chinese-but-less-than-30-malays-voted-for-ph/ (accessed October 1, 2018).

pertinent due to the rise of post-truth narratives that are challenging basic assumptions about information, data, and facts. Furthermore, we now live in a world where social media plays a huge role in the dissemination of alternative narratives and conspiracies, which in turn allows political echo chambers to thrive.

PART 4

Ethnic and Religious Populism

∵

CHAPTER 9

Populism in Indonesia: Learning from the 212 Movement in Response to the Blasphemy Case against Ahok in Jakarta

Sri Nuryanti

1 Introduction: Popular Rallies around the Ahok Blasphemy Case

Indonesia is a multicultural and very diverse country largely inhabited by Muslims. Although the citizens of Indonesia live for the most part in harmony, there were mass rallies of Muslims in Jakarta and many other cities in Indonesia as a response to the so-called blasphemy case of Basuki Tjahaja Purnama (Ahok). This event began when a Facebook user named Buni Yani uploaded a portion of a video featuring Ahok in the Thousand Islands (Pramuka Island) with the title "Blasphemy Against Religion?" The video immediately went viral, becoming a trending topic in the mass media. The responses to the content of the video were varied. Many Muslims were not happy with what Ahok had said and considered his statement that the Qur'anic Verse 51, Al-Ma'idah was a "tool to deceive the public" to be blasphemous. This verse states that Muslims should not accept non-Muslims as leaders with different religion.

In the speech Ahok touched on the issue of religious opposition, speculating that some groups might use this verse to undermine support for him in the governor's election on February 15, 2017. Ahok said that people who would not vote for him because he is a Christian had been "fooled" by Verse 51, Al-Ma'idah, explaining that the verse was used particularly against his candidacy, for political gain. However, most people concluded that Ahok intended his words as an insult to Muslims. Following Ahok's statement, people became angry as they felt that Ahok actually was insulting the Qur'an, and the issue quickly spiraled beyond the contestation for the Jakarta gubernatorial elections. Islamic groups throughout the country mobilized to host rallies and demand that Ahok be detained.

While some have interpreted Verse 51, Al-Ma'idah literally to mean that Muslims should not choose Christians or Jews as leaders, there are actually many interpretations of this verse, including those that take into account the historical context in which the verse was spoken.

© SRI NURYANTI, 2021 | DOI:10.1163/9789004444461_011

Several rallies were held by Muslims to protest against Ahok's speech. The first rally was held in the main street of Jakarta on November 4, 2016. The rally was initiated by the National Fatwa Guards Movement (*Gerakan Nasional Pengawal Fatwa*/GNPF) to guard *fatwa* (the *ulama* order) issued by the Indonesian Ulama Council as a continuation of the previous demonstration on October 14, 2016, which was initiated by the Islamic Defenders Front (*Front Pembela Islam*/FPI). The FPI designated November 4, 2016 as the second Islamic Defense Action. After the blasphemy accusations were first leveled against Ahok, he made an apology on October 10, 2016, explaining that he did not intend to insult Muslims or the Qur'an. He stated that he had simply mentioned that someone might use this verse to prevent people from voting for him in the 2017 gubernatorial elections in Jakarta. He also explained that he has Muslim relatives and that during his tenure as Governor of Jakarta, he supported Jakarta's Muslim community by opening Islamic schools. In his apology, Ahok tried to show that it was not his intention to insult Muslims, stating: "I do not intend to harass the holy verses of the Qur'an, but I do not like to politicize the holy verses, whether the Qur'an, the Bible, or other books." Ahok's apology had little effect. On October 11, 2016, the MUI issued a fatwa stating that Ahok had insulted Islam, including the *ulama* (Islamic clerics), and also stating that: (1) Verse 51, Al-Ma'idah explicitly contains a prohibition against making Jews and Christians leaders, and thus this verse is one basis for prohibiting non-Muslims from being leaders; (2) the *ulama* must admit the content of Verse 51, Al-Ma'idah to Muslims, stating that choosing Muslim leaders is mandatory; and (3) every Muslim must believe in the truth of the content of Verse 51, Al-Ma'idah as a guide in choosing a leader.

After the MUI issued the fatwa in the blasphemy case against Ahok, a movement arose advocating for the strongest possible justice against him. MUI's National Fatwa Guards Movement (GNPF), commanded by Ustad Bachtiar Nasir, was formed to secure the implementation of the MUI fatwa, condemning the blasphemy against Ahok. A series of mass rallies took place on October 14, November 4, and December 2, 2016 in many cities as a response to the lack of legal action against Ahok. The people protested that, despite an official police announcement that Ahok was considered a "suspect" in violation of the law, he was still roaming free and not in detention. This angered people who claimed to be defenders of Islam.

The second rally was soon followed by the biggest rally held on December 2, 2016. Taking inspiration from that date, the groups in attendance called themselves the 212 movement. The rally was attended by thousands of people across Indonesia, following *jum'ah* (Friday prayer). Although the rally was held peacefully, many scholars see this event as marking the emergence of an Islamic political identity among the people in opposition to the non-Islamic identity represented by Ahok.

Some may see this event as the continuation of political battles that utilize the sharp dichotomy of non-religious identities versus Islamic ideology. Islamic identity in this context is seen as strong symptom of the emergence or revival of Islamic populism in Indonesia, regardless of the political interests underlying it. It is assumed by many that since the Islamic population in Indonesia is quite dominant, it has become an important source of support that can be used by anyone for political gain. In this context, the opposition tried to use the 212 movement as its main source of supporters in various elections, particularly the 2017 Jakarta gubernatorial elections and the 2019 concurrent legislative and presidential elections.

In response to the December mass rallies, the government attempted to mitigate the tension by having a so-called dialogue and meetings with the protestors at the rally sites. Indeed, government officials even joined in Friday prayer on the day to show that the government understood the case and supported potential legal action. "Legal action" at this stage meant subjecting the case to an investigation to determine whether or not Ahok had violated any laws. If Ahok were to be charged with any violations, the government promised to enforce the law to the fullest extent. Although on this occasion the police and government officials urged people not to rush to the conclusion that Ahok had intentionally insulted Islam, the media still regarded the rallies as a movement to defend Islam against the insult made by Ahok. The media interpretation was justified by the demands of the crowd that Ahok had to be arrested and jailed for violating the Blasphemy Law No.1/PNPS/1965 Article 156a.[1]

In the context of populism, the rallies claiming to be in defense of Islam led to the rise of Islamic populism. Many people believe that if the police had acted quickly and immediately, enforcing the law against Ahok in response to his alleged blasphemy, the rally that clearly engendered the Islamic populist movement likely would not have happened. Although the 212 mass rallies were bigger than the November 4 (known as the 411) rallies, the participants promised to maintain peace. The mass rallies of the 212 took place peacefully and received praise from various groups as a result.

Learning from the past, the 212 rally participants also worked hard to convince others that Islam is a peaceful and tolerant religion with a love for cleanliness. During these rallies, participating Muslims held Friday prayer together

---

1 "Populisme Islam (2)," *Republika.co.id*, January 4, 2018; Benjamin Arditi, *Politics on the Edges of Liberalism: Difference, Populism, Revolution, Agitation* (Edinburgh, UK: Edinburgh University Press, 2007).

at the rally sites in an orderly manner, and demonstrators voluntarily brought along garbage bags and collected any visible waste. The sense of an Islamic bond was also seen in the distribution of food to the rally participants. Many participants helped the street cleaners cleaning up the sidewalks and streets by collecting bottles and plastic waste.

2 Understanding Populism: The Indonesian Context

In trying to understand the emergence of populism in Indonesia through the case discussed above, the political situation in Indonesia at the time must be factored in. In the sociopolitical context of Indonesia, as the country with the largest Muslim population in the world, has experienced political ups and downs. Islamic politics in parliament, especially during Suharto's New Order period, was represented by the United Development Party (*Partai Persatuan Pembangunan*/PPP). Although there were many institutions representing associations of Islamic groups, such as the *Nahdlatul Ulama* (NU) and Muhammadiyah, the Indonesian Muslim Intellectual Association (*Ikatan Cendekiawan Muslim Indonesia*/ICMI), and other Islamic student organizations, the ability of Islamic politics to accommodate their various interests was limited.[2] After the reforms that took place at the beginning of 1998, Islamic politics had more room to develop, as many political parties were allowed to compete in elections in Indonesia. In this connection it can be seen that Islamic politics are represented by many political parties that do not necessarily have an Islamic name or symbol such as *Partai Kebangkitan Muslim Indonesia* (Indonesian Muslim Awakening Party), *Partai Umat Islam* (Islamic Ummah Party), *Partai Masyumi Baru* (New Masyumi Party), and many others. The crowds claimed that the populist activities reflected in the mass rallies in support of the blasphemy case against Ahok represented the *ummah* (community of believers). According to Margaret Canovan, populism in modern democratic societies is best seen as an appeal to "the people" against the established structure of power. Populism is "of the people but not of the system." The rallies represented a revolt against an individual who represented the established structure of power in the name of the people (in this case, the *ummah*). According to Canovan's categories, the rallies employed a populist ideology to claim legitimacy in speaking for the people and were influenced by the leadership of Habib

---

2 Donald J. Porter, *Managing Politics and Islam in Indonesia* (London and New York: Routledge Curzon, 2002).

POPULISM IN INDONESIA 169

Rizieq Syihab, chairman of the FPI. Habib Rizieq Syihab made a strong public speech stating that they were hosting rally because they were defending Islam. This is in line with the theoretical framework that populist leader often claim that they speak for the silent majority. In this context, Muslim is the majority. People cannot remain silent when they are insulted and Habib Rizieq Syihab was there to provoke them.[3]

Further, Canovan argues that populism may be seen as a politics of pragmatism, which uses populist activities to pursue pragmatic goals, or as a politics of skepticism, which believes that government is not capable in fulfilling the needs of the people. From this perspective, the rallies represent a politics of pragmatism rather than skepticism, as they occurred in the context of local political contestation. If the populist activity had been successful it could have overthrown Ahok, the Chinese Christian Governor of Jakarta, from the contestation of Jakarta local election. The blasphemy case against Ahok evolved during local election contests in Jakarta province. Ahok was the incumbent Governor of Jakarta who was contested to rerun as Jakarta Governor for the second time. He was finally overthrown from the candidacy. This is in line with the views of Allan Knight, who argues that populism is a particular political style that demonstrates close relations with the people.[4]

As mentioned earlier, the rally was influenced by Habib Riziq Syihab, the head of the FPI, who strongly advocated for Ahok to be jailed for insulting the Islamic community. The role of strong leadership is emphasized in a number of theories of populism. For example, Kenneth M. Roberts states that populism is a top-down mass political mobilization carried out by leaders with strong personalities to oppose an elite group in the name of the people's suffering. As a political movement, populism can be observed when a particular leader mobilizes people to challenge elite groups.[5] However, populism can also have a different meaning. Kurt Weyland argues that populism is a political strategy used by populist leaders to achieve power by making direct contact with the masses who are not organized by a certain organization or institution.[6]

---

3 Habib Rizieq Syihab's speech during rally of 212 was broadcast by many television companies. According to Canovan this is in line with the theory of populist leaders. See Margaret Canovan, "Trust the People! Populism and the Two Faces of Democracy," *Political Studies* 47 (1999): 2–16.

4 Alan Knight, "Populism and Neo-populism in Latin America, Especially Mexico," *Journal of Latin American Studies* 30, no. 2 (1998): 223–248.

5 Kenneth M. Roberts, "Latin America's Populist Revival," *SAIS Review of International Affairs* 27, no. 1 (2007): 3–15.

6 Kurt Weyland, "Clarifying a Contested Concept: Populism in the Study of Latin American politics," *Comparative Politics* 34, no. 1 (2001): 1–22.

According to Benjamin Moffit, populism is a political style that is translated into the political mainstream. In this case, the rally, which was claimed by them to be a populist activity due to support gained during rally by so many people in many cities in Indonesia and to the claim that they were defending Islam, was then used for the political purpose of fighting against Ahok's candidacy in the local election. The speech during the rally was intended to denigrate Ahok for committing blasphemy. The populism demonstrated in the rally represented a so-called destabilizing element within democratic politics.[7] Based on this definition, it seems clear that populism in Indonesia is populism in the sense of ideology, as it is influenced by Islamic ideology and is seen by leaders as a strategy to achieve power by showing their closeness to the people.

The above explanation is in line with the argument made by many scholars that populism generally involves a political ideology that mobilizes the masses to fight the elites (i.e., the people versus the elites). It also involves the role of so-called religious-based groups (organized or unorganized groups) to some extent, which in this case comprised the FPI and the many unidentified groups that make up the *ummah*. The political scientist Cas Mudde calls populism a "political position that places the 'common people' and 'corrupt elites' in an antagonistic position, and sees politics as an expression of the passions of the common people."[8] Other analysts see populism as a political expression that has several elements. First, it is anti-establishment, in the sense of representing groups that feel marginalized; second, the leader has authority, whether through charisma or otherwise, and delivers strong messages that differ from those of the opposition. Populism produces an in-group or out-group feeling, as it usually refers to the notion of "us versus them," our group versus their group, liberal versus republican, left wing versus right wing, progressive versus conservative, minority versus majority, the rich versus the poor, the mass versus the elite, and so on. The diversity of these aspects demonstrates the wide range of events that can trigger the rise of populism. However, it is also possible to witness a blurred dichotomy between the two opposing sides, due to various dynamics that impact on populist theories. Therefore, it is true that populism is a thin ideology that may consist of several aspects mixed together. The populism of the 212 movement can be seen from various angles and does not constitute a pure form. The populism in Indonesia as expressed in the 212 rallies can be seen as a reaction against blasphemy, and it can also be seen as a political tool used to defeat the opposition by exploiting religious sentiment.

---

7 Benjamin Moffit and Simon Tormey, "Rethinking Populism: Politics, Mediatisation and Political Style," *Political Studies* 62, no. 2 (2013): 381–397.

8 Cas Mudde, "The Populist Zeitgeist," *Government and Opposition* 39, no. 4 (2004): 541–563.

Ernesto Laclau understands populism as a multi-class and supra-class political movement that is present in the fragile political moment of dominant hegemonic political power that gives birth to new structures for political movements led by charismatic leaders to articulate radical anti-establishment discourses.[9] According to Laclau, populism itself must be understood in two contexts: (1) as structurally related to the conditions of economic crisis and political economy that encourage the emergence of the politics of populism; and (2) as a discourse that connects every element of social and political movements. From this point of view, the 212 rallies would be portrayed as involving multiple social classes led by a "charismatic leader" (in the eyes of rally participants). However, they were held during a stable political period. The 212 movement was assumed to be a tool to achieve a political purpose in both the short and long term—political gain in the gubernatorial elections in 2017 as well as in the concurrent legislative and presidential elections in 2019. Therefore, an analysis of the 212 movement from Laclau's perspective will lack the inclusion of a fragile political moment, as the 212 rallies were held in preparation for a scheduled political contestation in a stable political situation. It can be said that the 212 movement is a populist phenomenon, judging from the number of people who participated and the presence of a so-called "vocal leader" seen by followers as charismatic. However, it cannot be said that the rallies were held during a political crisis.

3 Roots of Islamic Religious Populism

In his book *Islamic Populism in Indonesia and the Middle East* (2016), Vedi Hadiz compares Islamic populism in Indonesia with religious phenomena in Turkey and Egypt. He states that what distinguishes the pattern of populism in Indonesia is the fact that the bourgeois elite is the representative of Islam. The loss of an elite leader as the most important component in the formation of Islamic populism has meant that the influence of Islamic populism in Indonesia is not as strong as that of the Muslim Brotherhood in Egypt or the Justice and Development Party (AKP) in Turkey. Even though historically there was a major rebellion based on an Islamic political movement (the 212 movement), this was the result of a conflict between certain Islamic identities and the established bourgeois or oligarchic elites in Indonesia. To some extent, though this form

---

9 Benjamin Arditi, "Review Essay: Populism is Hegemony is Politics? On Ernesto Laclau's on Populist Reason," *Constellations* 17, no. 3 (2010): 488–497.

of populism is rooted in an Islamic group, because it is a diverse group that is in fact also influenced by the involvement of non-organized groups, Islamic group movements will not have a permanent effect in altering the politics as they do in Turkey and Egypt.[10]

Hadiz also argues that the Islamic political movement in Indonesia will not be able to become as powerful as the Muslim Brotherhood in Egypt, which is able to control civil society and the extraordinary opposition movement. The power of the richest members of society or the political oligarchs in Indonesia, who are also the representatives of Islamic groups, means the Islamic movement is only of a momentary nature. As a result, Islamic populism will not be able to take control of political and social life permanently.

The 212 rallies invoked the defense of religion as a justification to bring people onto the streets. As a result, many people arrived from various areas and gathered in the central places in town and at the big mosques in the city. Most of those who participated in the rallies felt they were there to defend their beliefs. Although the question of whether people truly mobilized in defense of Islam is still open to debate, the leaders of the movement successfully mobilized people based on their sensitivity towards their Islamic identity rather than based on political contestation per se. Islamic populism mobilizes a kind of political identity in order to forge alliances to contest power. It does not necessarily defend discrimination against or marginalization of those outside the *ummah*, but the organizers of the rally employed religion to justify their presence.[11] Once again, apart from infighting in Indonesia's oligarchic political elite, illustrated in the elections every five years, the FPI is an important force showing that there is a power behind Islamic populism's battle against the established elite. As of 2020, the bond of Islamic populism formed during the 212 rallies continued to thrive. Those who participated in the rallies refer to themselves as the 212 movement.

The 212 rallies to protest Ahok's case were assumed to be the continuation of protests against his actions towards the *ulama*. Hence, Ahok was not only accused of insulting the Holy Qur'an, but also of insulting the *ulama* by saying that the head of the MUI, K.H. Ma'ruf Amin, was involved in a conspiracy to undermine his candidacy as the incumbent Governor of Jakarta. Ahok's attitude towards the *ulama* meant he was considered an unacceptable candidate by Muslims. Although after his trial Ahok requested an apology from Islamic

---

10   Vedi R. Hadiz, *Islamic Populism in Indonesia and the Middle East* (Cambridge, UK: Cambridge University Press, 2016).

11   Hadiz, *Islamic Populism in Indonesia and the Middle East*, p. 14.

society, the discourse in the public space justified the ruling that he had committed blasphemy by insulting the Holy Qur'an and the *ulama*.

During the mass rallies of 212, some people joined not to support the purpose of the rallies or to become part of the 212 movement, but just to show their sympathy, for example by taking Friday prayer with the protestors. Although K.H. Aqil Siraj, the Central Board of *Nahdlatul Ulama* (*Pengurus Besar Nahdlatul Ulama*/PBNU) chair, banned the *Nahdlatul Ulama* (NU) followers from taking part in the 212 movement, many NU's members joined anyway and also took part in the post-trial session that brought in K.H. Ma'ruf Amin. K.H Ma'ruf Amin was present at the 212 movement as a sort of mediator to calm down the situation. He called on the 212 movement to conduct a peaceful protest around the National Monument by sitting and chanting.[12] The teacher-student relationship between Ma'ruf Amin and Habib Rizieq Syihab may have been seen as evidence of Ma'ruf Amin's support for the FPI, which was more radical than NU.[13] At the beginning, Ma'ruf Amin was regarded as part of the 212 movement. But then PBNU asked the 212 movement not to associate Ma'ruf Amin with the movement and their other rallies.[14] This indicates that the fragmentation in the NU was the result of the understanding that one of their clerics had been insulted. Although the chair of the NU formally refused the idea that Ahok had insulted one of their *ulama*, the mass movement could not be stopped. Ma'ruf is a respected NU cleric and so when he was suppressed and treated improperly, fragmentation in the NU suddenly became an inevitable phenomenon.

If we look at Laclau's categories, the Islamic Defense Action Movements, the 411 and the 212 movements, were the products of the tension between the elite and the people, which gave birth to a sharp dichotomy. Yet, according to Laclau, this type of movement where populist politicians take advantage of a movement for their own political gain, may arise out of populist criticisms of the government made to accommodate the call of populist political interest.[15] Furthermore, Laclau states that the massive involvement of the people

---

12 See detik.com Interview with KH. Ma'ruf Amin, "Blak-blakan Ma'ruf Amin, Aksi 212 dan Gerilya untuk Jokowi," https://www.youtube.com/watch?v=RQVVrUxoAJM (accessed June 15, 2020).

13 See rmco.id, "Soal Habib Rizieq Syihab. KH. Ma'ruf Amin: Dia Murid, Saya Guru," https://rmco.id/baca-berita/parpol/302/soal-habib-rizieq-shihab-kh-maruf-amin-dia-murid-saya-guru (accessed June 15, 2020).

14 Antara News.com, "PBNU minta Aksi '212' tak catut Nama NU, Ma'ruf Amin tak hadir," February 20, 2017 at https://jateng.antaranews.com/berita/161332/pbnu-minta-aksi-212-tak-catut-nama-nu (accessed June 15, 2020).

15 Ernesto Laclau, *On Populist Reason* (London and New York: Verso, 2005).

in populist movements makes them ideologically thin, because people are assumed to have different interests.[16]

In Hadiz's view, "Islamic populism" can be seen as a variant of the broad form of populism. Populist Islam is a form of populism based on certain Islamic symbols that are able to unite all classes in one spirit of religion to respond to a particular political need. Previously, Hadiz also explained that the creation of a populist order not only involves the bourgeoisie, but also requires other layers of society to be present, such as an educated middle class. If these components are present, the people may be empowered to create a populism that can facilitate a joining of all classes. Hadiz defines populism as an "asymmetric multi-class alliance."[17]

There is some concern that the strength of Islamic political propaganda is potentially weakening state nationalism, which is based on diversity. Therefore, this propaganda has received much attention from state officials. A PERPU, or interim government regulation in lieu of a law, was enacted to prevent the enlargement of radical groups. This was part of the response to the fear that Islamic political propaganda may weaken nationalism and strengthen a hidden religious identity assumed to strengthen the radical mind. Therefore, the discourse of nationalism has been upheld vis-à-vis non-nationalist identity.

4 Conclusion

From this point of view, the mass rallies of the 212 were regarded as a moment in which the *ummah* became a narrative that united society with the momentum of "condemning" Ahok for his misleading words. Then, the reactions to the event were politicized by the use of shared Islamic identity that triggered Muslims' religious sentiment. This identity was used to mobilize certain groups of people to protest against the incumbent government. Although the initial protests took place locally in Jakarta, the movement later expanded to other regions. It should be said that the narratives that led to people's involvement in the 212 movement were varied and did not take a singular form. The movement also demonstrates how the discourse of defending Islam was able to unite Muslims at all levels of society at the time, despite the fact that the social and economic backgrounds of those present at the 212 rallies were

---

16   Ben Stanley, "The Thin Ideology Of Populism," *Journal of Political Ideologies* 13, no. 1 (2008): 95–110.

17   Hadiz, *Islamic Populism in Indonesia and the Middle East.*

varied. It also suggests that the political backdrop for the emergence of populist activities does not necessarily need to be a crisis.

From the above insights, it can be concluded that the trend of Islamic populism in Indonesia will be temporary given the fact that the emergence of the 212 rallies involving mass participation in 2016 was triggered by political contestation for the gubernatorial election in Jakarta. The continuation of the so-called the 212 movement is uncertain, and presumably it will vanish after a short period due to the resolution of the issue that created such a strong reaction in the first place. It is also suggested that the strong bond among members of the 212 movement was not sustained in the context of the concurrent legislative and presidential elections in 2019 due to the fact that the original issue that gave rise to the rallies was resolved, and the vice-presidential candidate of the incumbent president was K.H. Ma'ruf Amin, the cleric who was undermined by Ahok in the blasphemy case.

CHAPTER 10

Hegemonic Populism: Sinhalese Buddhist Nationalist Populism in Contemporary Sri Lanka

Pasan Jayasinghe

Populism has become a subject of much scholarly interest, driven by its numerous and intensifying expressions in politics across the Western world. In many polities beyond the West, however, and particularly in Asia, populism is not a novel phenomenon but one that has been a longstanding feature of politics. This has certainly been the case in Sri Lanka, whose entire history as an independent country is marked by frequent populist impulses feeding deep ethnic division. The most severe consequence of this, a three-decade-long armed civil conflict, ended in 2009, and the subsequent period warrants study to evaluate populism's contemporary dynamics in the country.

This chapter undertakes such an assessment. It first looks at theorizing populism in the Sri Lankan context, and then identifies Sinhalese Buddhist nationalism (SBN) as the dominant force animating populism in the country since its inception. The chapter next moves to an examination of populism inflected with SBN over the past decade. This examination moves through three phases: the rule of Mahinda Rajapaksa from the end of the country's armed ethnic conflict in 2009 until 2015; the "moment" of his surprise electoral defeat; and the operation of the succeeding *yahapālanaya* (or "good governance") government.

This examination uncovers the intensification of populism along SBN lines over the course of the Rajapaksa regime; examines the emergence of a liberal democratic politics in opposition to this and its relative strength; and surveys the continued function of SBN populism despite the lack of an SBN populist leader in power or in control of the state. This leads to the concluding argument that SBN populism is a hegemonic force in Sri Lanka and one that importantly is not simply an instrumental, elite-driven project but rather one that operates at multiple sociopolitical strata with a dynamic and constitutive character.

© PASAN JAYASINGHE, 2021 | DOI:10.1163/9789004444461_012

HEGEMONIC POPULISM   177

1   Theorizing Populism in Sri Lanka

Contemporary literature commonly identifies populism as a phenomenon that places "the people" against "the elite" and imagines politics as an expression of the Rousseauian "general will" of the people.[1] Populism accounts for "the people" in various ways: as the sovereign from which true political power is derived; as a silent majority excluded from political power due to their socio-cultural and economic status; and as a collective centered on a civic national identity or ethnicity.[2] To create such common identities, populism tends to encourage divisive stances and polarization on political and socioeconomic issues. This consequently creates conflict with pluralism, as minority interests and viewpoints can be placed in opposition to those of the majority.[3] Accordingly, while populism advocates for a deeper form of democracy than merely representative democracy (to allow for the greater expression of the "general will"), certain forms of it also tend to legitimize recourse against minorities in illiberal and anti-democratic ways.[4]

Mainstream accounts of populism in Sri Lanka tend to characterize it as a force external to, and used instrumentally by, elite actors.[5] The dynamics these actors exhibit are classed as processes of "ethnic outbidding" or "intra-group" competition in which these elites attempt to outdo each other in the pursuit of populist goals.[6] Such accounts also understand the state and its institutions as channels for the production and dissemination of populist discourse and policy. The end result of this is the categorization of the state and governance of Sri Lanka as in crisis which hinges on elite politicians manipulating the electorate

---

1   Cas Mudde, "The Populist Zeitgeist," *Government and Opposition* 39, no. 4 (2004): 541–563.
2   Cas Mudde and Cristóbal Rovira Kaltwasser, *Populism: A very short introduction* (New York: Oxford University Press, 2017).
3   Bhaskar Dutta, "What is Populism?—Voters Have Not Booted Out Re-distributive Schemes in India," *Telegraph India*, January 14, 2014.
4   Mudde and Kaltwasser, *Populism*.
5   Pradeep Jeganathan and Qadri Ismail, "Introduction: Unmaking the Nation," in *Unmaking the Nation: the politics of identity and history in modern Sri Lanka*, ed. Pradeep Jeganathan and Qadri Ismail (Colombo: Social Scientists' Association, 1995), 2–9. Kristian Stokke, "Sinhalese and Tamil Nationalism as Post-colonial Political Projects from 'Above', 1948–1983," *Political Geography* 17, no. 1 (1998): 83–113; Kenneth Bush, *The Intra-group Dimensions of Ethnic Conflict in Sri Lanka: Learning to read between the lines* (Basingstoke: Palgrave Macmillan, 2003); Neil DeVotta and Jason Stone, "Jathika Hela Urumaya and Ethno-religious Politics in Sri Lanka," *Pacific Affairs* 81, no. 1 (2008): 31–51.
6   Bush, *The Intra-group Dimensions of Ethnic Conflict in Sri Lanka*; DeVotta and Stone, "Jathika Hela Urumaya and Ethno-religious Politics in Sri Lanka."

using populism in order to win the rewards of power.[7] Such a focus on elites and institutions consequently leads to a glossing over of the actions and agency of non-elite actors, and of how they can inform both elite and institutional activity.

Mainstream accounts of Sri Lankan populism also accord with the broader literature on populism in focusing on dualities centered on divisions such as elite–masses, local–foreign, urban–rural, and so on.[8] The dichotomous nature of such conceptualizations generally leads to a deep focus on the practical dynamics underlying populism rather than their discursive manifestations. According to David Rampton,[9] however, such discourse is key to understanding how practices of populism can "construct" the world in which they are located.

Accounting for the actions and agency of both elite and non-elite actors, as well as considering both physical and discursive manifestations of populism, then, enables a broader perspective on populism. From such a viewpoint, populism can be understood not simply as an ideology limited to the elite as its progenitors and the state as its vehicle, but as a phenomenon that incorporates a diverse range of social strata in its production and uses a variety of instruments as sites of this production. As this chapter will demonstrate, using such an expansive lens on populism is especially helpful in understanding the particular dynamics of populism in Sri Lanka.

2 Sinhalese Buddhist Nationalism as a Driver of Populism

Examining the development of Sinhalese Buddhist nationalism throughout Sri Lanka's modern history exposes it as the predominant driver of populism in the country. While it is beyond this chapter to provide a detailed account of its development, a brief overview helps situate the examination of the 2009–19 period that this chapter will undertake.

---

7   See, for example, Jonathan Goodhand, Bart Klem, Dilrukshi Fonseka, S. I. Keethaponcalan, and Shonali Sardesai, *Aid, Conflict, and Peacebuilding in Sri Lanka, 2000–2005*, Vol. 1 (Colombo: Asia Foundation, 2005).

8   B. Kapferer, *Legends of People, Myths of State* (Washington and London: Smithsonian Institution Press, 1989); B. Kapferer, "Nationalist Ideology and a Comparative Anthropology," *Ethnos* 54, nos. 3–4 (1988): 161–199; Manu Goswami, "Rethinking the Modular Nation Form: Toward a Sociohistorical Conception of Nationalism," *Comparative Studies in Society and History* 44, no. 4 (2002): 770–799.

9   David Rampton, " 'Deeper Hegemony': The Politics of Sinhalese Nationalist Authenticity and the Failures of Power-sharing in Sri Lanka," *Commonwealth & Comparative Politics* 49, no. 2 (2011): 245–273.

Sri Lanka's demographic composition is central to discussions about populism in the country. Of its population of around 21 million people, 74.9 percent are Sinhalese, 15.3 percent are Tamils (of which 11.2 percent are Sri Lankan Tamil and 4.1 percent are Upcountry Tamil), and 9.3 percent are Moors.[10] Over 70 percent of the population is Buddhist while Hindus, Muslims, and Christians constitute 12.6 percent, 9.7 percent, and 7.4 percent of the population, respectively. The overall demographic dynamic wherein the vast majority of the population are Sinhalese Buddhists thus facilitates the production of a sociopolitical hierarchy that places Sinhalese Buddhists at the apex.[11]

Anthony Smith explains how SBN sought to assert itself and its character during periods when the community came into contact with different ethnic and religious forces and experienced crises of identity.[12] This was especially true during the British colonization of Sri Lanka in the 19th century (which followed Portuguese and Dutch colonization in the two centuries prior). British colonial rule sparked the self-organization of members of the *sangha*, or Buddhist monks, in order to combat British imperialism and Christian proselytization. The *sangha* found support from laypeople, foremost among them Anagārika Dharmapāla (1864–1933), who rallied Sinhalese Buddhists to oppose British rule and to see themselves as civilizationally and morally superior to both the British and the island's ethnic minorities. Resentment towards minorities was driven especially by the divide-and-rule tactics of Sri Lanka's European colonizers, which resulted in the overrepresentation of particularly the Tamil population in the civil service, universities, and professional bodies.[13]

Central to the mobilization of Sinhalese Buddhists was the creation of an "axiomatic identity"[14] that coupled Sinhalese ethnic identity with the Buddhist religion. This identity was derived especially from the *Mahāvamsa* (Great Chronicle), which was written around the 6th century CE. The *Mahāvamsa* is essentially a part-mythological narrative "written to legitimize, cement and propagate the Buddhist association with Sri Lanka."[15] Despite its clear discrepancies with modern historical accounts, it is treated as an indisputable

---

10   *Census of Population and Housing of Sri Lanka* (Department of Census and Statistics, 2012).

11   Kapferer, *Legends of People, Myths of State*; Kapferer, "Nationalist Ideology and a Comparative Anthropology."

12   Anthony D. Smith, *The Ethnic Origins of Nations* (Oxford, UK: Basil Blackwell, 1986), 249–264.

13   DeVotta and Stone, "Jathika Hela Urumaya and Ethno-religious Politics in Sri Lanka."

14   David Rampton, "Deeper Hegemony: The Populist Politics of Sinhalese Nationalist Discontent and the Janatha Vimukthi Peramuna in Sri Lanka," PhD diss., SOAS, University of London, 2010.

15   DeVotta and Stone, "Jathika Hela Urumaya and Ethno-religious Politics in Sri Lanka," 1.

historical record by most Sinhalese Buddhists, enabling the construction of the Sinhalese as "sons of the soil" of Sri Lanka and custodians of the Buddhist religion. The veneration of the *Mahāvamsa* also inversely defines all other ethnicities on the island as having lesser or no claims to the country and existing at the behest of the Sinhalese. In essence, it provides a conceptual basis for Sinhalese Buddhist dominance.

SBN by itself is simply an expression of identity politics—it is when it is used to mobilize and give form to mass politics that it can be termed a manifestation of populism. In practice, this has meant the deployment of SBN in and through electoral politics.

While SBN was not explicitly adopted by the leaders of the independence movement, matters quickly changed after independence was achieved in 1948. Electoral politics in the island state quickly became a fierce contest of appeals to ethnicity, with the country's two major parties, the Sri Lanka Freedom Party (SLFP) and the United National Party (UNP), both taking up its mantle. While the parties have different economic orientations—with the SLFP being committed to more statist economics and the UNP being more market-oriented—the leaders of both have always been Sinhalese. The demographic advantage of the Sinhalese allowed the two parties to take control of the state using the democratic process and then to express Sinhalese Buddhist nationalism through the state in a number of distinct, trenchant ways.

First, the Sri Lankan state and its practices were recast along Sinhalese Buddhist nationalist lines. This included through maneuvers such as the passage of the Official Language Act of 1956, which declared Sinhalese as the sole official language of the country, and education reforms through the 1960s and 1970s that further entrenched the linguistic dominance of the Sinhalese language over the Tamil language.[16] These overtures extended to the very definition of citizenship—the Ceylon Citizenship Act of 1948 disenfranchised practically the entire Malaiyaha (or Upcountry) Tamil population, who were brought over by the British to work on tea plantations and who represented some 11 percent of the national population at the time.[17]

---

16   Heinz Bechert, "Buddhism in Ceylon and Studies on Religious Syncretism in Buddhist Countries," in *Buddhism in Ceylon and Studies on Religious Syncretism in Buddhist Countries: Report on a symposium in Göttingen* (Göttingen: Vandenhoeck & Ruprecht, 1978).

17   Michael Roberts, *Exploring Confrontation: Sri Lanka—politics, culture and history*, Vol. 14 (Abingdon: Taylor & Francis, 1994); P. P. Devaraj, *Constitutional Electoral Reform Proposals and Indian Origin Tamils* (Colombo: Foundation for Community Transformation, 2008), p. 11.

Constitutionally, the 1972 Republican Constitution removed the already weak safeguards for minorities contained in the 1948 Constitution that the British left the country with,[18] and gave the state an explicit role in protecting and promoting Buddhism. The subsequent 1978 Constitution (which remains in force as of 2020) retained this status and further introduced a system of semi-presidentialism in place of a pure parliamentary system.[19] The powerful office of executive president as the head of state featured minimal checks and balances, a weakened parliament, and very weak local governing structures. These moves heightened the centralization of a state that, due to demographics, would always be Sinhalese-dominated, in the process further weakening minority access to political power.

Second, regular junctures at which Sinhalese political elites were willing to make moderate reform concessions to decentralize the state were frequently met with strong SBN populist backlash mobilized as protest, riots, or insurgency. These reforms include the Bandaranaike–Chelvanayakam Pact of 1957, the Senanayake–Chelvanayakam Pact of 1965, the 13th Amendment to the Constitution in 1987, the draft Constitution of 2000, and the Norwegian-brokered Ceasefire Agreement of 2002, all of which promised various degrees of autonomy, federalism, or self-rule to the Tamil minority.[20] The reforms were quickly diluted, withdrawn altogether, or not fully implemented due to pressure from SBN populists who saw any derogation from the state's centralized powers as symbolizing the disintegration and corruption of the Sinhalese Buddhist nation.

Finally, and as a culmination of all these factors, SBN populism provoked a reactive Tamil nationalism that grew increasingly forceful in both its demands—from federal autonomy to a separate state—and its tactics—from political engagement to insurgency. The response of SBN populism itself to this

---

18 Asanga Welikala, "5. An Anatomy of Failure: The 2014–18 Sri Lankan Constitutional Reform Exercise in Context," in *Annual Review of Constitution-Building Processes: 2017* (Stockholm: International IDEA, 2018), 80.

19 David L. Rampton and Asanga Welikala, *The Politics of the South* (Colombo: Asia Foundation, 2005); *Report of the Commission of Inquiry into Local Government Reform* (Colombo: Government of Sri Lanka Publishing, 1999); Sirivardana, Sirivardana, "Innovative Practice amidst Positive Potential for Paradigm Shift: The Case of Sri Lanka," in *Pro-Poor Growth and Governance in South Asia*, ed. S. Sirivardana and P. Wignaraja (New Delhi: Sage 2003).

20 Neil DeVotta, "Sri Lanka's Political Decay: Analysing the October 2000 and December 2001 Parliamentary Elections," *Commonwealth & Comparative Politics* 41, no. 2 (2003): 115–142; Rampton and Welikala, *The Politics of the South*; *Report of the Commission of Inquiry into Local Government Reform*.

reaction—expressed by both elite state actors and the non-elite citizen elements compelling them—was to completely rebuke any idea of separatism. Thus, the Sinhalese-dominated state would politically and legally delegitimize separatism while militarily sustaining a three-decade-long armed conflict with the Liberation Tigers of Tamil Eelam (LTTE), who took up the mantle of demanding a separate state for Tamils in the country's North and East in the early 1980s. Outside the state, non-elite SBN populist actors mobilized to support a military response to Tamil separatism, and to oppose and derail any political engagement or compromise with the LTTE or Tamil political leaders to resolve the conflict.

An instructive example of this non-elite SBN populism is the second armed insurrection led by the Marxist Janatha Vimukthi Peramuna (JVP) party against the state. Unlike its first insurrection in 1971, the one the JVP instigated in 1987 took on a distinct Sinhalese nationalist ideology that opposed any political compromise with the Tamil insurgency.[21] The insurrection was ostensibly provoked by the signing of the Indo-Sri Lanka Accord in 1987 in which the government agreed to constitutionally devolve power to the provinces in exchange for the LTTE surrendering its arms to the Indian Army. The second JVP insurrection is seen to have derailed the full implementation of devolution, caused the Indo-Sri Lanka Accord to implode, and ushered in a stage of intensified warfare between the Sri Lankan state and the LTTE.[22] In this manner, SBN populism regularly asserted itself both as a deterrent against any peace process and as an incitement to a military end to the conflict. The latter is indeed what transpired when the Sri Lankan government militarily defeated the LTTE in 2009.

3   2009–14: The Rajapaksa Regime

3.1   *Dynasty as Destiny*
SBN populism witnessed an "extraordinary resurgence" in the immediate aftermath of the war's conclusion, which was interpreted by many Sinhalese Buddhists as a "victory" for Sinhalese Buddhist nationalism itself. In both image and action, the Rajapaksa regime, which oversaw the end to the war, represented a near perfect confluence with SBN ideals. Mahinda Rajapaksa himself

---

21   Rajesh Venugopal, "Sectarian Socialism: The Politics of Sri Lanka's Janatha Vimukthi Peramuna (JVP)," *Modern Asian Studies* 44, no. 3 (2010): 567–602.

22   Rampton, "Deeper Hegemony."

can be seen as a populist leader who merged SBN with both his image and the state, representing a distinctive variant of an elite populist actor.

First, on a symbolic level, Mahinda Rajapaksa conformed to SBN foundational myths as laid out in the *Mahāvamsa*. Rajapaksa's military defeat of the LTTE and its leader Vellupillai Prabhākaran was functionally equivalent to the Sinhalese King Dutugamunu defeating the Tamil King Elāra and reuniting the territory of the country.[23] The conclusion of the war was thus a (re-)fulfillment of historical lore and was accompanied discursively by Rajapaksa being anointed as "the nation's father" and as a "living Dutugamunu."[24] While all Sinhalese politicians since independence had used SBN ideals to bolster their legitimacy, none had gone as far as Rajapaksa in merging those ideals with his image and the state. Rajapaksa's "ending" of the ethnic conflict (in the eyes of the Sinhalese people) along the lines of SBN foundational mythology thus provided a powerful basis to complete this transformation. It allowed him to cast himself as *the* representative of "the people," where "the people" are implicitly defined as the hitherto imperiled but now liberated Sinhalese Buddhists.

The narrative elevation of Rajapaksa to divine monarch status provided aesthetic justification for the nearly complete takeover of the Sri Lankan state by the Rajapaksa family. Rajapaksa's immediate family held multiple key positions in the state—his brothers Gotābhaya, Basil, and Chamal respectively as Secretary to the Ministry of Defense, Minister of Economic Development, and Speaker of Parliament, and his son Namal as a Member of Parliament. Members of the extended Rajapaksa family occupied numerous positions within the state apparatus, and at one point, the Rajapaksas were said to control over 70 percent of the Sri Lankan budget.[25] This form of dynastic rule, though antithetical to liberal democratic norms, made sense in the context of SBN populist ideals, which anointed him a "living king." Rajapaksa's overwhelming electoral victories in the presidential election of 2010, and in parliamentary elections later that year, confirmed this stature.

Such potent symbolism was also used to justify the authoritarian excesses of the regime, which began to escalate following the war. The post-war period saw a near total collapse of liberal and democratic notions of the rule of law. The nadir of this came with the impeachment of the Supreme Court Chief Justice in 2013, who was seen as being targeted for making a crucial judicial

---

23 Nira Wickramasinghe, "After the War: A New Patriotism in Sri Lanka?" *Journal of Asian Studies* 68, no. 4 (2009): 1045–1054.

24 Wickramasinghe, "After the War."

25 Neil DeVotta, "Sri Lanka: From Turmoil to Dynasty," *Journal of Democracy* 2 (2011): 130–144.

ruling against one of the regime's flagship development projects.[26] Rajapaksa also managed to use his party's supermajority in Parliament to force through the 18th Amendment to the Constitution, which, among other measures, removed presidential term limits (allowing him to run for president for a third time) and crippled the autonomy of the country's independent commissions, including its Human Rights Commission.[27] All of these moves were largely justifiable from an SBN populist perspective—as a monarch-like figure instead of a democratically elected leader, any actions to consolidate power on the part of Rajapaksa were both expected and necessary, so long as his commitment to SBN values remained intact. Broadly, this demonstrates how SBN populism in policy practice has tended to run counter to democratic values.

SBN populism also provided the discursive means to defend these actions. Opposition to the Rajapaksa agenda, be it from the judiciary, media, nongovernmental organizations and civil society, or human rights activists, was essentially treated as traitorous, and the use of dichotomous categories such as "patriot" (*dēshapremi*) and "traitor" (*dēshadrōhi*) became prevalent. Such a dichotomy was not new within SBN discourse historically among non-state actors such as Buddhist monks; however, they acquired state sanction under Rajapaksa, ostensibly indicating whether one wanted the armed forces to triumph over the LTTE or not, and were especially used to single out those critical of the government's numerous abuses both during and after the war.[28] The ubiquitous adoption of these discursive categories by citizens—indeed, with even government critics constantly defending their patriotism—shows how effectively SBN operates as a motivator of populism.

A foundational premise of this discourse was the charge that these actors were secretly funded by, and working for, foreign governments who were leveling war crimes charges against the government and the military and demanding investigations at international fora. The notion of a "Western conspiracy" against Sri Lanka accorded with the SBN populist resolve to protect the sovereignty of the country and act against those who seemingly sought to compromise it.[29] These discursive dynamics were also abetted by Rajapaksa's complete control of state media and domination of non-state-owned media

---

26   Nira Wickramasinghe, *Sri Lanka in the Modern Age: A history* (Oxford, UK: Oxford University Press, 2014).

27   Piyadasa Edirisuriya, "The Rise and Grand Fall of Sri Lanka's Mahinda Rajapaksa: The End of an Era?" *Asian Survey* 57, no. 2 (2017): 211–228.

28   Neil Devotta, "Religious Intolerance in Post-Civil War Sri Lanka," *Asian Affairs* 49, no. 2 (2018): 278–300.

29   Wickramasinghe, *Sri Lanka in the Modern Age*.

HEGEMONIC POPULISM

through intimidation and violence: the post-war period saw a continuation of the regime's attacks on journalists and private media organizations. The resulting atmosphere of state obeisance and self-censorship by media actors ensured that SBN populism remained the dominant sociopolitical ideology in the media. In these ways, SBN populism in this period bounded a particular narrative of ethno-nationalism through the state both rhetorically and institutionally, engaging non-elite actors in its orbit.

3.2   *Anti-Minority Violence*

SBN populism's operation, however, was not limited to elite agency. It also operated outside of Rajapaksa and the state apparatus, most distinctly through the frequent episodes of violence directed at ethnic minorities. While attacks against Christians (particularly evangelicals) and their places of worship had been commonplace since the late 1980s and continued apace in the post-war period,[30] non-state SBN populist actors found a new target in the country's Muslim population from around 2010 onwards.[31] The sentiment underlying the SBN populist gaze shifting to Muslims was that with the end of the war, the "Muslim problem" could at long last be tended to.[32]

SBN populist mobilization against Muslims is motivated by several factors. Muslims are seen to have higher fertility rates than Sinhalese, and thus as able to "take over" the country. This is compounded by the corresponding belief that Muslims wish to suppress the fertility of the Sinhalese people through covert sterilization efforts executed through food and apparel.[33] Muslims are also seen to represent a territorial threat, mirroring the fears of separatism that drove SBN populism against Tamils. Unlike Tamil nationalists, who eventually took up arms to achieve their cause, however, Muslims are seen to use wealth—both their own and that from overseas Muslim countries[34]—to acquire land and set up exclusive Muslim enclaves.[35] The perceived wealth of Muslims compared with the Sinhalese, who were evidently not enjoying many

---

30   Verité Research, "Religious Violence in Sri Lanka: A New Perspective on an Old Problem," *Insights* 5, no. 1 (2017); National Christian Evangelical Alliance of Sri Lanka, *Summary Report on Religious Freedom* (Colombo: NCEASL, 2017).

31   "Attacks on Places of Religious Worship in Post-War Sri Lanka," Centre for Policy Alternatives (CPA), March 8, 2013.

32   Devotta, "Religious Intolerance in Post-Civil War Sri Lanka."

33   Devotta, "Religious Intolerance in Post-Civil War Sri Lanka."

34   Athambawa Sarjoon, Mohammad Yusoff, and Nordin Hussin, "Anti-Muslim Sentiments and Violence: A Major Threat to Ethnic Reconciliation and Ethnic Harmony in Post-War Sri Lanka," *Religions* 7, no. 10 (2016): 125.

35   Ruwan Laknath Jayakody, "BBS Calls for a Religious State," *Ceylon Today*, October 6, 2014.

post-war economic dividends, is a strong current throughout these contentions (historically, Muslims have engaged in trade and commerce, and thus have more apparent visible markers of wealth such as retail stores).

The chief progenitor of anti-Muslim sentiment in the post-war period was the Bodu Bala Sēna (BBS, Buddhist Power Army), which was formed in 2012 by monks formerly involved with the Jāthika Hela Urumaya (JHU, National Heritage Party), itself an SBN party formed in 2004 to contest parliamentary elections, where it fielded monks as candidates.[36] Unlike the numerous SBN populist organizations formed in the country since independence, BBS is unique for being almost exclusively an anti-Muslim front.[37] It has been accused of inciting and committing numerous acts of violence against Muslims and their places of residence, business, and worship. A series of anti-Muslim attacks countrywide since 2011 culminated in the Aluthgama anti-Muslim riots of June 2014 in which Sinhalese Buddhist mobs destroyed numerous mosques, Muslim-owned shops, and places of residence, resulting in four deaths and the displacement of thousands.[38]

While the Rajapaksa regime has never been directly linked to these episodes of anti-minority violence, its wholehearted embrace of SBN populism provided the atmosphere for such episodes to continue. The Rajapaksas repeatedly made Islamophobic statements and suggested that SBN populist perpetrators of anti-minority violence, particularly Buddhist monks, would receive state protection.[39] The BBS is also widely believed to have received patronage from the Rajapaksa regime; for instance, Gotābhaya Rajapaksa ceremonially opened a BBS leadership academy in Galle. None of these incidents of violence ever saw prosecutions being advanced, and in the case of Aluthgama, the government was later found to have pressured local media not to report on the violence. The widespread assumption that minorities favored the opposition UNP also meant the Rajapaksas had little fear of electoral repercussions for their direct and implicit incitements against minorities.

The lack of censure of such violence underlies a level of impunity that greatly empowers violent expressions of SBN populism. Such impunity has always

---

36 Farzana Haniffa, Harini Amarasuriya, Vishakha Wijenayake, and Gehan Gunatillake, *Where Have All the Neighbours Gone? Aluthgama riots and its aftermath: A fact finding mission to Aluthgama, Dharga Town, Valipanna, and Beruwela* (Law & Society Trust, 2014).

37 Devotta, "Religious Intolerance in Post-Civil War Sri Lanka."

38 Haniffa, Amarasuriya, Wijenayake, and Gunatillake, *Where Have All the Neighbours Gone?*

39 Hilmy Ahamed, "Yahapalanaya Lapses—Is Mahinda the Option for Muslims?" *Daily FT*, January 17, 2017, http://www.ft.lk/article/592912/Yahapalanaya-lapses-%E2%80%93-Is-Mahinda-the-option-for-Muslims (accessed June 20, 2020).

existed for Sinhalese violence against minorities—Sri Lanka has witnessed a series of pogroms against minorities, from the 1958 and 1983 anti-Tamil riots to the 1999 anti-Muslim outbreaks—and the continuation of such violence in the post-war period reaffirms its often blatant validation by the state.[40]

Underlying anti-minority violence is a particularly existential fear shared by SBN populists—Sinhalese Buddhists, while a "relative majority" on the island, are believed to constitute a "global minority."[41] SBN populists perceive themselves as having only Sri Lanka as a "motherland," whereas Tamils and to a greater extent Muslims have numerous other "motherlands."[42] This is used as a justification to resist minority demands to make the country secular and to respect pluralism, arguing that those minorities will take advantage of Sinhalese "generosity" and attempt to take over the country.[43] It also provides a reason to constitute Sri Lanka as an ethno-religiously homogeneous state—titled Sinhalé—where the Sinhalese people are not just a majority but a constituent whole within the country.[44] It is in these SBN populist efforts to close the gap between majority and totality that the most potent expressions of violence can be found.[45] In this context, the anti-democratic bent of SBN populism—in being resistant to providing democratic space for minority political expression, self-determination, and even existence—is clear.

4   2014–15: The Fall of Rajapaksa

4.1   *Rajapaksa's Electoral Defeat*
After changing the Constitution, Rajapaksa called for presidential elections in early 2015. With a greatly weakened opposition and nearly complete control of the state apparatus,[46] he was widely expected to win an unprecedented third term and to consolidate the Rajapaksa dynasty's rule well into the

---

40   Gehan Gunatilleke, "The Constitutional Practice of Ethno-Religious Violence in Sri Lanka," *Asian Journal of Comparative Law* 13, no. 2 (2018): 359–387.

41   Chamila Liyanage, *Encountering the Demise of a Race: An enquiry into the population trends in Sri Lanka*, trans, Kaligna Tudor Silva (Colombo: Bodu Bala Sena Scholars and Professionals Front, 2014).

42   Robin Noel Badone Jones, "Sinhalese Buddhist Nationalism and Islamophobia," Honors Thesis, Bates College, 2015.

43   Jones, "Sinhalese Buddhist Nationalism and Islamophobia in Contemporary Sri Lanka."

44   Arjun Appadurai, *Modernity at Large: Cultural dimensions of globalization*, Vol. 1. (University of Minnesota Press, 1996).

45   Jones, "Sinhalese Buddhist Nationalism and Islamophobia."

46   Edirisuriya, "The Rise and Grand Fall of Sri Lanka's Mahinda Rajapaksa."

future. Just three months before the election, however, Maithripala Sirisena, who served as Defense Minister under Rajapaksa, announced he would be defecting and running against him for president. Sirisena would run as the "common candidate" of a broad coalition, including the opposition UNP led by Rajapaksa's long-time rival Ranil Wickremesinghe. Sirisena positioned himself as the candidate of *yahapālanaya*, or "good governance," which consisted of a platform of reinstituting constitutional checks and balances and abolishing the executive presidency in particular; fighting corruption and nepotism; and reorienting Sri Lanka's foreign policy away from China towards engagement with the West.[47]

Sirisena's unexpected candidacy proved surprisingly popular and, despite Rajapaksa's deployment of considerable resources against him, Sirisena managed a narrow victory.[48] Once in office, Sirisena immediately appointed Wickremesinghe as prime minister and initiated a "100 day program," the centerpiece of which was the 19th Amendment to the Constitution, which reduced presidential powers, restored presidential term limits, and reinstated independent commissions. Parliamentary elections were called for August 2015, and the UNP campaigned on introducing a new constitution and the maximum possible devolution of power within a unitary state.[49] In the elections, the UNP-led alliance won the most seats and, despite falling short of a majority, created a coalition with Sirisena's supporters in the SLFP to form a National Unity Government.

4.2 *Liberal Democratic Opposition*

Sirisena's victory and its reaffirmation at the parliamentary elections, and the broad civil coalition that coalesced in support, appeared to constitute a popular politics centered on liberal democratic values that could offer an effective counter to SBN populism. Aside from the support it received from political outfits across the political spectrum, a broad range of civil society organizations and actors mobilized in support of Sirisena. *Yahapālanaya*, or "good governance," provided both a policy-based and a discursive foundation for a liberal democratic politics. The issues of curtailing executive power and combatting corruption proved to be especially salient across large parts of the electorate. Sirisena's candidacy was a feasible outlet to challenge the authoritarian

---

47   Jonathan Goodhand and Oliver Walton, "The Tangled Politics of Postwar Justice in Sri Lanka," *Current History* 116, no. 789 (2017): 130–135.

48   Goodhand and Walton, "The Tangled Politics of Postwar Justice in Sri Lanka."

49   Goodhand and Walton, "The Tangled Politics of Postwar Justice in Sri Lanka."

excesses of the Rajapaksa regime and its pervasive corruption—which was widely known of but seldom challenged by the media or civil society for fear of repercussions.[50] Moreover, Sirisena had a quiet, unspectacular profile while serving under Rajapaksa, suggesting that his victory was predicated on his electoral platform rather than his personal popularity. The combination of these issues could render Sirisena as an analogue to an "outsider" battling the entrenched and powerful from the perspective of populist theory, thus blunting part of Rajapaksa's appeal as being the same.

The more salient question here is where the liberal democratic politics that arose in late 2014 lies in relation to SBN populism. Several factors suggest that this liberal democratic politics did not arise in response to SBN populism, but is instead a separate phenomenon. First, its substance does not directly address or correspond to the core tenets of SBN populism. The elements of anti-authoritarianism and anti-corruption, and a program of restoring democratic checks and balances, are not direct responses to the ethnic supremacy inherent in SBN populism. They can instead be viewed as aimed more squarely at Rajapaksa as a political figure, and in particular at elements of the Rajapaksa persona that lie outside direct SBN populism, such as corruption, graft, and the mismanagement of public funds.

If such a politics was reactive to SBN populism, then the Sirisena program, or even its advocacy by civil society actors, would have demanded, for instance, the secularization of the state by removing preferential treatment for Buddhism from the Constitution and state institutions; stronger redress of Tamil concerns following the war; and a deeper reflection on the country's ethnic conflict that sought alternative historical perspectives. Such advocacy likely would not have enabled the defeat of Rajapaksa in 2015, but it is nevertheless the case that, in their absence, liberal democratic politics as seen in 2015 left SBN populism largely untouched.

Second, advocates of liberal democratic values validated key tenets of SBN populism in expressing support for Sirisena during the 2015 presidential election campaign. Most were quick to preface their criticisms of Rajapaksa by expressing gratitude to him for "ending the war" and "reuniting the country." Those criticisms themselves rarely extended to reprimanding him for his encouragement of ethno-religious supremacy. The eulogizing of Rajapaksa after his electoral defeat reiterated the rhetoric of gratitude perhaps even more strongly, validating the SBN populist image of Rajapaksa as a national savior. Rajapaksa himself capitalized on this, playing the role of a disappointed father

---

50   Edirisuriya, "The Rise and Grand Fall of Sri Lanka's Mahinda Rajapaksa."

slighted by his children's ingratitude in reaction to his electoral defeat. While the repression and violence directed at minorities were crucial factors in turning them against Rajapaksa, this was not acknowledged explicitly on a political level as a repudiation of SBN populism, either by Rajapaksa or by Sirisena's coalition.

Finally, SBN populist agents were themselves divided at the elections. While Rajapaksa counted on the support of ultranationalist parties such as the National Freedom Front (a breakaway from the JVP), the key SBN populist party Jāthika Hela Urumaya left his administration to back Sirisena.[51] Sirisena made sure to present himself as an exemplary Buddhist who was motivated to turn on Rajapaksa not by a desire for power but by love of country, and that Sinhalese Buddhists should trust him on that account. In any case, the Sinhalese vote itself fell heavily to Rajapaksa, with some 58 percent estimated to have voted for him.[52] The overwhelming support Sirisena received from ethnic minorities—some 85 percent of the total minority vote—led to him being immediately branded as a president installed by minorities and not a "president for Sinhalese" by SBN populists.[53] Certainly, Rajapaksa's losses in both elections indicate an erosion in the support he had previously enjoyed from Sinhalese Buddhists, on whom he had an iron grip;[54] however, it is unlikely that this was a wholesale exodus.

These factors suggest that the significant "constitutional moment" of 2015 took place on a plane somewhat removed from that of SBN populism,[55] and did not react to or counter it in any meaningful way. Subsequent events, which this chapter now turns to, confirm this fact.

---

51   "Buddhist Party Quits Sri Lanka Government," *Al-Jazeera,* November 19, 2014, https://www.aljazeera.com/news/asia/2014/11/buddhist-party-quits-sri-lanka-government-201411894525420326.html (accessed June 20, 2020).

52   Ranjiva Munasinghe and Ruwanthi de Silva, "Deconstructing the 2015 Sri Lanka Presidential Election through Data," *Daily FT,* February 13, 2015, www.argylex.com/wp-content/uploads/2014/10/2015-Sri-Lanka-Presidential-Election-Daily-FT-Write-Up-Web-Version-2.pdf (accessed June 20, 2020).

53   Neha Sinha, "Sri Lanka: Hope for minorities?" *The Diplomat,* February 3, 2015, https://the-diplomat.com/2015/02/sri-lanka-hope-for-minorities (accessed June 20, 2020).

54   Suranjith Gunasekera, "Sri Lanka's Historical Failure to Accommodate Ethnic Diversity," in *Dealing with Diversity: Sri Lankan discourse on peace and conflict* (The Hague: The Netherlands Institute of International Relation, 2005).

55   Asanga Welikala, "Sri Lanka's Long Constitutional Moment," *The Round Table* 104, no. 5 (2015): 551–562.

HEGEMONIC POPULISM

5 2015 Onwards: The Yahapālanaya Government

5.1 *A Test of Liberal Democracy*

The period from 2015 onwards shows the liberal democratic politics that emerged in 2015 in practice. In the early days of Sirisena's administration, the promise of a more restrained, consensual style of conducting politics seemed to have materialized; the 19th Amendment to the Constitution was ratified unanimously in Parliament and signaled the close cooperation of Sri Lanka's two major parties, who had always been bitter rivals. In addition to initiating a process to draft a new constitution, the new government also co-sponsored a United Nations Human Rights Council resolution in October 2015 promising to institute an ambitious transitional justice program in Sri Lanka,[56] which included setting up offices on missing persons and reparations, a truth commission, and an independent special court for war crimes with the participation of foreign judges.

The promise of a clean break with the past and the passage of an expansive reform agenda by a government comprised of many different and conflicting political actors and ideologies always presented the risk of exposing a large gap between perception and reality.[57] The *yahapālanaya* government, however, affirmed this risk rapidly and spectacularly. Sirisena and Wickremesinghe quickly emerged as two distinct and opposing centers of power in the government; Wickremesinghe and the UNP's neoliberal economic policies and wider reform agenda proved to be anathema to Sirisena's more statist economics (which were more in line with Rajapaksa's in the first place) and his rural and suburban Sinhalese voter base.[58] Investigations and prosecutions of the Rajapaksa regime's corruption and rights abuses were also evidently stymied by alternating influence from Sirisena and Wickremesinghe, respectively intent on consolidating or fracturing the SLFP.[59] The new government seemed to slide quickly into the old politics of patronage, horse trading, and deal-making.[60] This provided ample space for both the Rajapaksa base and SBN populism to mobilize in multiple ways.

---

56 Goodhand and Walton, "The Tangled Politics of Postwar Justice in Sri Lanka."
57 Goodhand and Walton, "The Tangled Politics of Postwar Justice in Sri Lanka."
58 *Sri Lanka's Transition to Nowhere* (International Crisis Group, 2017).
59 *Sri Lanka's Transition to Nowhere.*
60 Goodhand and Walton, "The Tangled Politics of Postwar Justice in Sri Lanka."

5.2 Sinhalese Buddhist Nationalist Populism against State Reform

It is in the arenas of transitional justice and constitutional reform where SBN populism is most apparently re-galvanizing itself. Transitional justice measures such as the establishment of the Office on Missing Persons (OMP) sparked SBN populist accusations of foreign interference in domestic affairs and the specter of prosecuting members of the armed forces, who are widely revered by Sinhalese as "war heroes."[61] Such populism is responsible for immobilizing the transitional justice program—it took nearly two years for the OMP to become operationalized, and the remaining mechanisms did not materialize.[62] The truth commission and special court for war crimes, in particular, have been victims of the government's fears of upsetting SBN populists; Rajapaksa had resolutely resisted any foreign involvement in questions of justice and accountability.

Similarly, while the constitutional reform process began with much fanfare and cross-party consensus in 2016, progress became extremely protracted over the course of the next two years, with apparent contention among the involved parties over the central powers of the state, the form of the presidency, and the place of Buddhism.[63] The gridlock in the process allowed Rajapaksa and his supporters to propagate a narrative that the new constitution would break down the unitary nature of the Sri Lankan state (thereby allowing the provinces, the North and East in particular, to secede) and remove the special constitutional position given to Buddhism.[64] The government has been non-responsive to these charges, taking little ownership in the process and leaving its defense and advocacy mainly to the minority Tamil National Alliance (thereby further strengthening the narrative of the new constitution as a minority-driven project). Accordingly, prospects for a new constitution being promulgated seem remote.[65] The fates of the transitional justice and constitutional reform processes thus demonstrate the enduring power of SBN populism to weaken and halt even modest measures to decentralize the state and to provide redress to minorities, as seen throughout Sri Lanka's history.

5.3 Sinhalese Buddhist Nationalist Populism by Non–State Actors

SBN populism's resurgence was also confirmed in an alarming manner with the return of attacks on minorities by non-state actors. In Gintota in the South in November 2017 and Ampāra in the East in February 2018, Sinhalese mobs

---

61   *Sri Lanka's Transition to Nowhere.*
62   *Sri Lanka's Transition to Nowhere.*
63   Welikala, "5. An Anatomy of Failure."
64   Welikala, "5. An Anatomy of Failure."
65   Welikala, "5. An Anatomy of Failure."

attacked a number of Muslim businesses and mosques.[66] These were followed by a series of prolonged riots in the central Kandy district in March 2018, resulting in hundreds of Muslim businesses, mosques, and residences being burned down and at least one person being killed. It took the government declaring a state of emergency and banning social media platforms, and more than four days, for the riots to be halted.[67] While over one hundred alleged perpetrators were apprehended, they are yet to be formally charged as of September 2019.

The incidence of anti-minority attacks of this type and at this juncture is significant. They demonstrate that the capacity for anti-minority violence in Sri Lanka remains strong even in the absence of an overtly sympathetic and validating government. More deeply, it shows that SBN populism as a force is able to mobilize easily both through and independent of the state, in ways both peaceable and not.

5.4   *Constitutional Crisis*

The local government elections in February 2018, the first nationwide elections since 2015, saw the Podujana Peramuna (PP), a new political vehicle formed by Rajapaksa and his loyalists, receive 40 percent of the vote and the control of an overwhelming number of local authorities. The UNP and Sirisena-aligned parts of the SLFP, contesting separately, managed 32 percent and 11 percent of the vote respectively.[68] The elections confirmed the persistent salience of SBN populism, which recrystallized support behind Rajapaksa through the deep dissatisfaction with the government's incompetence and its reform agendas. The country's faltering economy and the rising cost of living were clinching factors in Rajapaksa's triumph.

In the aftermath of the elections, political instability only intensified, with Sirisena openly undermining Wickremesinghe.[69] This culminated in late October 2018 when Sirisena unilaterally dismissed Wickremesinghe as prime minister and, to the shock of many, appointed Rajapaksa in his place, sparking

---

66   Devotta, "Religious Intolerance in Post-Civil War Sri Lanka."

67   Amalini De Sayrah, "Kandy: The Damage and the Distrust," *Groundviews*, June 12, 2018, https://groundviews.org/2018/06/12/kandy-the-damage-and-the-distrust/ (accessed June 20, 2020).

68   Tisaranee Gunasekara, "From an Electoral Drubbing to a Manufactured Crisis," *Groundviews*, February 18, 2018, http://groundviews.org/2018/02/18/from-an-electoral-drubbing-to-a-manufactured-crisis (accessed June 20, 2020).

69   Eshan Jayawardena and Punsara Amarasinghe, "The Winds of Change in Sri Lanka? Rajapaksa's Charisma and Foreign Factors in Sri Lankan politics," *South Asia @ LSE*, blog entry, http://eprints.lse.ac.uk/89135/1/southasia-2018-03-13-the-winds-of-change-in-sri-lanka-rajapaksas.pdf (accessed June 20, 2020).

an unprecedented constitutional crisis with two persons making claims to the position of prime minister.[70] Sirisena proceeded to prorogue Parliament in order to buy time to gain enough parliamentary support for Rajapaksa, and when this failed, he attempted to dissolve Parliament and call for a general election. The crisis, which paralyzed governance and took a heavy toll on the economy, continued for nearly two months until a series of court decisions declared Sirisena's actions unconstitutional, forcing him to reappoint Wickremesinghe.[71]

The crisis can be seen as representative of multiple dynamics of populism in contemporary Sri Lanka. Rajapaksa's declared motives in accepting the Premiership in this manner instead of simply waiting for parliamentary elections in 2020 (which he was expected to win easily) was that he wished to prevent the introduction of a new constitution that would divide the country, and to stymie "the forces that seek to destroy" Sri Lanka.[72] During the crisis period, Rajapaksa quickly assumed control of the state machinery, including state media, with little internal protest, revealing the state's easy acquiescence to explicit SBN populism (and, indeed, its default setting as a vehicle of such). Citizen protests during the crisis also displayed emerging inflections of populism with democracy. Those supportive of Rajapaksa's purported government were demanding democracy by insisting on elections to reflect the will of the people, whereas protests opposing Rajapaksa or supportive of Wickremesinghe and the UNP made arguments for democracy on institutional grounds, calling for adherence to constitutional procedure.[73] While these protest dynamics are reflective of the ongoing contestation between SBN populism and liberal democratic values since late 2014, the "resolution" to the crisis cannot be said to have quelled the former in any way.

6   Conclusion: Sinhalese Buddhist Nationalist Populism as Hegemonic

The examination of the 2009–19 period undertaken by this chapter indeed demonstrates how SBN populism has manifested itself multilaterally and

---

70   Tisaranee Gunasekara, "What the Coup Taught Us," *Groundviews*, January 6, 2019, https://groundviews.org/2019/01/06/what-the-coup-taught-us/.

71   Gunasekara, "What the Coup Taught Us."

72   Mahinda Rajapaksa, "Our Pledge to the People," *Colombo Telegraph*, December 15, 2018, at https://www.colombotelegraph.com/index.php/our-pledge-to-the-people (accessed June 20, 2020).

73   Gunasekara, "What the Coup Taught Us."

multi-modally. As posited by theorists on populism, these manifestations have been borne out through the state and political elites; however, the case of Rajapaksa represents a distinct merging of populism with an elite leader and the two with the state. SBN populism has also operated at a non-elite level through numerous non-state actors who have engaged in politics, protest, and anti-minority violence, frequently influencing the state's actions, both when overtly SBN populist leaders and parties are in power and when they are not.

With this near omnipresence, SBN populism has come to gradually and incrementally hegemonize the social field so that the idea of the Sri Lankan space as a Sinhalese Buddhist one is no longer solely in the imagination of elites or driven exclusively by the state vehicle.[74] It is actively propagated, often in violent ways, by actors entirely outside the state. This hegemony is proven particularly when compared with oppositional politics based on liberal democratic values. Just as this chapter's discussion on the 2015 "moment" suggested that the liberal democratic politics that arose then was not necessarily reactive to SBN populism, the experience of 2015–18—featuring a steady stream of liberal democratic reforms being quashed or obstructed and ending in a crisis of governance—suggests that it cannot challenge SBN populism in any meaningful sense.

Importantly, this chapter's examination showed the highly fluid and adaptive nature of SBN populism. Its ability to be expressed through elite and non-elite actors and to be channeled through various institutions of the state, whether it receives explicit state validation or not, underscores both the highly entrenched nature of SBN populism and its dynamism. Indeed, the decade of Sri Lanka's post-war experience conforms to the country's entire seven-decade-long independent history as one that continually reaffirms SBN both in a discursive sense—in nullifying any symbolic challenges to it and in constructing various minorities as intolerable quantities—and in an institutional sense—in fostering institutions that consolidate, entrench, and support SBN. Its aversion to pluralism in particular demonstrates the threat it represents to liberal democratic norms, in both supporting and encouraging autocratic governance and disavowing the presence and participation of minorities in the Sri Lankan polity.

These dynamics are likely to play a central role in the presidential and parliamentary elections slated for 2019 and 2020, as Sirisena and Rajapaksa, now in alignment, and Wickremesinghe all vie to retain or regain power. This political nexus is in effect one of Sinhalese political elites expressing and

---

74   Rampton, " 'Deeper Hegemony'."

accommodating SBN populism to varying degrees and relying on it to access political power. Ultimately, this can only provide further space for an unchallenged and hegemonic SBN populism to flourish, both within and outside the Sri Lankan state, and spells a worrying future for the country's turbulent democracy.

CHAPTER 11

Populism in Myanmar

Myat Thu

1   Introduction

Shortly after the liberalization process, starting from 2011 when U. Thein Sein became President, in 2012, Myanmar witnessed a series of religious conflicts and communal violence between the Buddhist majority of the population and the Muslim minority. That time period coincided with the birth of Ma Ba Tha, the ultranationalist Buddhists who claimed religious nationalism as the basis for their organization. Before 2012, media and research coverage on Myanmar limited its focus to student movements, the then opposition leader and democratic icon Aung San Suu Kyi and her party, the National League for Democracy (NLD), authoritarian resilience, and democratization and ethnic conflict. Although there were several periodic and recurring religious communal conflicts during the rule of the authoritarian regime, especially from 1988 to date, it was only after 2010, in particular in 2012, that these issues came to light and received unprecedented attention from international media and scholarly discourse. Most interestingly, this was also the year when the NLD, led by Aung San Suu Kyi, decided to take part in the by-elections. Within this context, populism around religious nationalism arose with unprecedented force and overwhelmingly dominated the political arena.

It is generally accepted that there are three main traditions in the study of populism around the world, namely populism as ideology, populism as a discursive style, and populism as political mobilization or political strategy.[1] According to political scientist Cas Mudde, populism is "a thin-centered ideology that considers society to be ultimately separated into two homogenous and antagonistic groups, 'the pure people' versus 'the corrupt elite,' and which argues that politics should be an expression of the *volonté générale* (general will) of the people."[2] Populism as a discursive style considers populism a largely fixed attribute of political actors, an attribute of the message and not the speaker. As

---

1   Bart Bonikowski and Noam Gidron, "Multiple Traditions in Populism Research: Toward a Theoretical Synthesis," *APSA Comparative Politics Newsletter* 26, no. 12 (2016): 7–14.

2   Cas Mudde, "The Populist Zeitgeist," *Government and Opposition* 39, no. 4 (2004): 541–563, quoted in Bonikowski and Gidron, "Multiple Traditions in Populism Research."

© MYAT THU, 2021 | DOI:10.1163/9789004444461_013

Kurt Weyland put it, "populism is best defined as a political strategy through which a personalistic leader seeks or exercises government power based on direct, unmediated, uninstitutionalized support from large numbers of mostly unorganized followers."[3]

Although populism in Myanmar maintains a binary nature, with the presence of discourses such as "the pure people" versus "the corrupt elite" as in left-wing populism and "insiders" versus "outsiders" as in right-wing populism, it is not primarily intended as well to pave the way for the "expression of the *volonté générale* (general will) of the people" to gain popular support in elections. Although there are some political figures, mostly from the democratic activist side, who try to gain "direct, unmediated and uninstitutionalized support from a large number of mostly unorganized followers," it is not the case with the most dominant populist movement in the country. Populism in Myanmar is mostly right-wing, with an emphasis on Buddhist religions and members of the Bamar (Myanmar) nationality representing the "core values" of society.

2   Historical Development of Religious Nationalism

After almost five decades of authoritarian rule, in 2010, Myanmar inaugurated its Constitution (2008) and held elections (albeit very controversial ones) for its bicameral Parliament, made up of the Amyotha Hluttaw (House of Nationalities) and the Pyi Thu Hluttaw (House of Representatives).[4] Thein Sein became the first president of the new regime. By-elections were held on April 1, 2012, and the largest opposition party, the NLD, won in a landslide victory, taking 43 out of 45 available seats.[5] The NLD enjoyed a second sweeping victory in the 2015 elections as well, and Aung San Suu Kyi assumed the office of State's Counsellor.

Pre-colonial Myanmar was by no means a secular state. Not only was Buddhism regarded as the religion of the kingdom, but its religious institutions were also crucial for the life of the ancient Burmese. The head of the *Sangha* (a Pali word for monks), the Sasanabai, also assumed the official status of

---

3 Kurt Weyland, "Clarifying a Contested Concept: Populism in the Study of Latin American Politics," *Comparative Politics* 34, no. 1 (2001): 1–22, quoted in Bonikowski and Gidron, "Multiple Traditions in Populism Research."

4 Constitution of the Republic of the Union of Myanmar.

5 They contested only 44 seats. Olarn Kocha, "Myanmar Confirms Sweeping Election Victory for Suu Kyi's Party," *CNN*, April 4, 2012.

Minsaya, the immediate mentor of the king, who was required to comply with the ten Buddhist criteria of "good kingship" to be a just ruler. The same applied to the ordinary citizen. The nationwide education system was in the monastic form. As such, we can find Buddhism at the heart of ancient Burma's moral values. However, education had only an indirect influence. In fact, the King regularly had to accept moral directives from the Minsaya for his day-to-day management. The country's sub-national administration found itself in a similar situation. Local *sayadaws*, or monastic heads, had a certain influence over the Village Headman in administration and judgments. Simply put, these regular consultations and influence represented the checks and balances of the church and state of pre-colonial Myanmar. Buddhism in Myanmar became "a provider of the images and precepts for society, for the foundations of state and for the regulation of social life."[6]

With the introduction of colonial capitalism, rural Burma underwent rapid economic change. Between 1860 and the end of the 1920s, the acreage under cultivation in Lower Burma increased by 600 percent. In addition, there was a 23-fold increase in the volume of rice cultivated over the same period.[7] To accommodate the urgent need for labor for the large, newly emerging rice-exporting economy, a massive number of Indian farmers and their families arrived from various provinces of British India following the Second Anglo-Burmese war (1852–1853). The result was that, in the 1930s, Indian descendants made up over 1 million of Myanmar's total population of 14.5 million. Half of Rangoon's population of 400,000 were of Indian descent (only 127,000 were Burmese).[8] In addition to the Indian farmers, new waves of Europeans, Chinese, and other Asians searching for prosperity changed the demographic proportion of Rangoon in a very short time. Rangoon became the world's leading port in receiving immigrants, with even more temporary or permanent settlers than New York Harbor at that time.[9] The economic dominance of Europeans and other Asian newcomers exacerbated the anger of the excluded Burmese. Burmese who tried to make a living in Rangoon found themselves getting nowhere while more experienced immigrant laborers from different parts of

---

6   Emilie Biver, "Religious Nationalism: Myanmar and the Role of Buddhism in Anti-Muslim Narratives" (2014), https://www.researchgate.net/publication/268153592_Religious_nationalism_Myanmar_and_the_role_of_Buddhism_in_anti-Muslim_narratives (accessed October 5, 2018).

7   Ian Brown, *A Colonial Economy in Crisis: Burma's rice cultivators and the world depression of the 1930s* (New York: Routledge Curzon, 2005), 9–11.

8   Bo Bo, "The Black Spot in Myanmar's History," BBC Burmese, July 27, 2018.

9   John L. Christian, "Burma Divorces India," *Current History and Forum* 46, no. 1 (1937): 82.

India and China monopolized all the jobs.[10] They also faced social discrimination. The best railway carriages were only for Europeans.[11] The inferior prefixes Nga and Mi were added to Burmese names in tax revenue receipts and summonses. Furthermore, in rural Burma, resentment grew as agricultural lands were alienated to moneylenders from the Chettyars, South India's trading caste. From that time, a negative image of Chettyar moneylenders was formed in the Burmese discourse and everyday speech that remains in circulation in the 21st century.

In this context, the first Indo-Burman conflicts took place in 1930, after Myanmar workers were hired to replace Indian port workers who were boycotting their jobs. The conflict started when the latter went back to work, finally leading to a four-day community riot. The situation was resolved with a decision by the British government to employ an equal number of Burmese and Indian workers. In January 1931, there was another riot in Rangoon, this time between Chinese and Burmese, which caused 12 deaths.[12] Another much larger Indo-Burman conflict took place in 1938. A mass riot commenced in Rangoon after the publication of a book titled *Mawlawi and Yogi*, by U. Shwe Phi, a Burmese Muslim. The crisis broke out as Buddhist monks gathered in Shwedagon and riots erupted in most of the Indian wards, lasting for a month.[13]

New generations of Burmese Buddhist nationalist leaders arose against the background of the resentments generated by all these incidents. The Young Men's Buddhist Association (YMBA) was founded in 1906 and became formalized in 1908. A broad coalition of Buddhist associations, the General Council of Buddhist Associations (GCBA), was founded in 1911. Although the GCBA grew more politically prominent in later years, initially it was of little political significance and merely supported the decisions made by the British government, just as the Indian National Congress did in its early days.[14] However, the most important nationalist organization was Dobama Asi-ayone (the We Burman Association), which became the birthplace of many independence heroes and leaders of independent Burma.

---

10 Alister McCrae, *Scots in Burma: Golden times in a golden land* (N.p.: Kiscadale Publications, 1990), 70, 71.

11 Michael W. Charney, *A History of Modern Burma* (Cambridge, UK: Cambridge University Press, 2009), 28.

12 U. Ba Maw, *Breakthrough in Burma: Memoirs of a revolution, 1939–1946* (New Haven, CT: Yale University Press, 1968), 13.

13 Bo Bo, "The Black Spot in Myanmar's History," BBC Burmese, July 27, 2018, https://www.bbc.com/burmese/in-depth-44966771 (accessed October 5, 2018).

14 H.B. Zöellner, ed., "Material on Ba Khaing, Political History of Myanma," Myanmar literature project, Working Paper no. 10:5, 30–40.

Nationalism in independent Burma did not take the form of populism. Nevertheless, this part of history can, as in previous eras, explain much about the populist movements of the 21st century. Laws enacted and activities carried out by General Ne Win's regime provided the justification for modern-day populism. The roots of many of the contemporary religious or ethnic conflicts in Myanmar can be found in this period. After the coup in 1962, a constitution was ratified in 1974, which divided the country into seven ethnic states and seven Burmese regions, a division that has persisted. Another move towards division was the passage of the 1982 citizenship law. This law identified and recognized 135 ethnic groups of the union of Myanmar. It also prohibited certain marginal groups, such as the Rohingya from Northern Rakhine State, from ever becoming citizens. Without the status of citizenship, Rohingyas were deprived of the right to own property, the right to travel, and the right to marry or have children without government permission.[15] Moreover, during the military regime, various deliberate crimes were committed against these marginal groups by means of military operations and government-led campaigns. Most prominent among these were Naga Min (Dragon King) and Pyi Thar Yar (Clean and Beautiful Nation), which led to the forced flight of 200,000 Rohingya in each case and other serious crimes such as murders, raids, arrests, and rapes.[16]

3 The Rise of Populism Based on Religious Nationalism

Although the message of religious populism is primarily endorsed and propagated by a certain sect of religious institutions in the country, namely Ma Ba Tha and the 969 movement, this message has been co-opted by political elites as a strategy for political gain. It was only following this co-optation that populism in Myanmar assumed its current form (as of 2019) and began to have a comprehensive and significant impact. One of the greatest challenges facing those who study populism in Myanmar is differentiating populism as a discourse, such as that of Ma Ba Tha and the 969 groups, from populism as a political strategy, such as that of the military, the Union Solidarity and Development Party (USDP), and other minority parties, especially those who were threatened or sidelined when the NLD came to prominence after Aung San Suu Kyi's release from house arrest in 2010.

---

15 Mary Kate Long, "Dynamics of State, Sangha and Society in Myanmar: A Closer Look at the Rohingya Issue," *Asian Journal of Public Affairs* 6, no. 1 (2013): 79–94.

16 Biver, "Religious Nationalism."

202   THU

Ma Ba Tha is an organization meant to protect race and religion—that is, the Bamar race and Buddhism—from being threatened by other religions or races, particularly Muslims and other groups that are well established in the country. Although they were used in the past for political purposes by successive authoritarian governments, these discourses were always checked in one way or another. Mikael Gravers, an anthropologist and an expert on nationalism, ethnic conflict, and peace and reconciliation, noted:

> After General Ne Win and the army took power in a coup in 1962 the *sangha* gradually came under stricter political control and was "purified" in 1980. Ne Win did not want the monasteries to be political centers and potential bases of resistance to his mixture of military rule and the one-party Burmese way to socialism. Ne Win regulated monastic education and banned the use of photos of the Buddha and pagodas on calendars, books, cassette tapes and other commercial objects. He prohibited monks' political activities, and removed women and other persons who were not allowed to live in monasteries.[17]

Ashrin Wirathu, the well-known leading figure of the Ma Ba Tha movement, or "the face of Buddhist terror" as *Time Magazine* put it, was detained in 2003 and released only in 2012 for the same anti-Muslim rhetoric and subsequent movement that he promoted. This may be explained by a combination of several factors. One possible explanation could be that the military generals did not want any unnecessary instability in the community and were ready to repress any potential rival powers that developed influence on any basis, including religion, so harshly that any religious conflict was barely able to rise to the national level, despite the fact that the military always tried to portray itself as the primary guardian of nationality and religion.

The other official Buddhist religious institution, Mahana, is controlled by the government and has been used whenever necessary, particularly for issues relating to religious affairs. However, it was Ma Ba Tha that gained influence over the majority of the populace and whose message became widespread among the public. When the forces of Ma Ba Tha, the military, and the military-backed USDP combined, populism in Myanmar became both prominent and active. Here, it is worth noting that it is not only the military, but also other political parties who try to exploit Ma Ba Tha's influence as a political strategy.

---

17   Mikael Gravers, "Anti-Muslim Buddhist Nationalism in Burma and Sri Lanka: Religious Violence and Globalized Imaginaries of Endangered Identities," *Contemporary Buddhism* 16, no. 1 (2015): 1–27.

POPULISM IN MYANMAR

The shift in government policy from attempts to control the monks to their successful exploitation can be found during the military government as officials began to impose their power in religious circles. The trend can be traced through the integration of Buddhism into the military's slogans for Myanmar nationalism, such as "one race, one language, and one religion,"[18] as well as the rumors that were spread about the involvement of fake monks placed and controlled by the military in demonstrations and riots against Muslims in Mandalay in 1993 and 1997, as well as in Kyaukse in 2003.[19]

There was also so-called government interference in fostering religious sentiment among the people. As in 1997, when the booklet titled "969" was published in Moulmein to create unrest, a similar publication written by a monk under a pseudonym and titled "If You Marry a Man of an Evil Race and Religion" appeared in 2010, highlighting 11 hearsay stories of forced conversion and sexual abuse of Buddhist women by Muslim men.[20] As the former case occurred under the military government, which controlled all access to information, and in the latter case the Religious Affairs Ministry permitted publication,[21] it was alleged that the government was exploiting the religious sentiment of the people. It is still questionable whether there is a direct link between the publication in 2010 and the communal violence that followed over the next two years, but the activities provoked or instigated in the 1997 publication to put 969 stickers and emblems on the walls and windows of homes, businesses, and vehicles was also pervasive in the 2012 violence.[22]

However, the intention of the religious nationalism adopted by Ma Ba Tha and the 969 movement was not to gain political power, but rather to safeguard race and religion in Myanmar. This does not necessarily mean, however, that Ma Ba Tha and the 969 movement would not cooperate with those in power; and, interestingly, they have even tried to use state power to realize their goals. Emilie Biver observed:

> It is important to note that the religious nationalism taking place in Burma does not seek control over material resources or the state machinery, but it is rather directed towards the promotion of the Buddhist cosmology and code of values, the maintenance of its purity and the preservation

---

18 Gravers, "Anti-Muslim Buddhist Nationalism in Burma and Sri Lanka."

19 Gravers, "Anti-Muslim Buddhist Nationalism in Burma and Sri Lanka."

20 Gravers, "Anti-Muslim Buddhist Nationalism in Burma and Sri Lanka."

21 Kyaw Zwa Moe, "Burma's Time Bomb," *The Irrawaddy*, July 18, 2014, https://www.irrawaddy.com/opinion/burmas-time-bomb.html (accessed June 20, 2020).

22 Kyaw Zwa Moe, "Burma's Time Bomb."

of the Buddhist Burmese state . The Burmese monks ... they make use of a certain politicized religion that utilizes faith as the basis for the national identity, as well as the source for ultimate values and authority. Like abovementioned, the criterion of judgement is racial and religious purity, beyond the compelling interest of the state.[23]

The question, then, is why did the military and the USDP co-opt Ma Ba Tha after years of repression? Throughout history, Myanmar's military dictatorship was very unpopular, a sentiment that people expressed in many political protests, particularly the Saffron Revolution in 2007. Since the USDP comprises ex-military officials, they do not have a popular base. With the introduction of elections in 2010, it became crucially important for all political parties and institutions to have popular support to win elections. It therefore became suddenly quite advantageous to co-opt an organization such as Ma Ba Tha, which already had a large popular base and widespread influence in the allegedly Buddhist-majority country, and this was much easier than trying to build a base from scratch after a long history of oppression and repeated human rights violations. Monks hold the highest social status in the country, and it remains a common tradition and custom that even if one disagrees with a monk one cannot openly challenge him. Doing so would be disrespectful to the robe the monk wears, which is regarded by many as sacred.

Ma Ba Tha and individual monks have created an atmosphere in which people see Muslims as undesirable in Myanmar society. One of the most prominent monks, Sitagu Sayadaw, once referred to Muslims as "visitors" and Buddhists as "hosts," implying that Muslims do not belong to the land. This atmosphere has never been challenged openly by any authority or even any political figure out of fear of losing popular support. Leading monks also foment hatred against Muslims. Wirathu once told *The Guardian* that "the local Muslims are crude and savage because the extremists are pulling the strings, providing them with financial, military and technical power."[24] This attitude was clearly visible when the military staged a cleansing operation in response to an ARSA (Arakan Rohingya Salvation Army) attack in Rakhine State and people unprecedentedly supported the military, rejecting international intervention by asserting that this was an internal affair and any intervention would infringe on national sovereignty. The military and Ma Ba Tha also use international affairs

---

23   Biver, "Religious Nationalism."

24   Kate Hodal, "Buddhist Monk Uses Racism and Rumours to Spread Hatred in Burma," *The Guardian*, April 18, 2013, https://www.theguardian.com/world/2013/apr/18/buddhist-monk-spreads-hatred-burma (accessed June 20, 2020).

to stoke hatred against Muslims and to justify their atrocities. Neil Thompson wrote in *The Diplomat* that the destruction of the Buddha statues (the Taliban government demolished two ancient statues of the Buddha in Afghanistan's Bamiyan province in 2001) and the 9/11 attacks in New York and Washington that same year fueled resentful local perceptions of Muslims as violent and untrustworthy neighbors, and local actors quickly exploited this to launch another round of persecution against non-Buddhist minorities.[25]

The rapid and widespread dissemination of the comments made by U. Wirathu targeting other religious groups illustrates the important role that media and telecommunications have played in the spread of such rhetoric. The media has not only facilitated the spread of anti-Muslim speech, but also allowed images and stories of violence perpetrated by Muslims to reach far beyond the scope of the small groups from which they originate. Contrary to depictions of Ma Ba Tha by international media and scholars as an extremist group, Ma Ba Tha has a strong base and a wide audience. Matthew Walton has called for the introduction of a new approach that would "recognize nuance and variation among Buddhist and nationalist groups, and acknowledge that the sentiments that have at times motivated unacceptable anti-Muslim violence and discrimination are also connected to more acceptable religious and community-building activities," pointing out that "the organization (Ma Ba Tha) has built up its base of support through aligning with Buddhist Sunday Schools, volunteer groups, legal clinics, relief campaigns, donation drives, and other community-oriented activities."[26]

State institutions are also vulnerable to exploitation by these populist groups. To create a secular or religiously neutral institution, the 2008 Myanmar Constitution stipulates that "every citizen is equally entitled to freedom of conscience and the right to freely profess and practice religion subject to public order, morality or health and to the other provisions of this Constitution." Even so, due to the open-ended language of this right concerning the concept of freedom of conscience or religious practice, and the role of the state in the infringements on religious freedom among non-state actors, state secularity is being questioned despite its assurance in the Constitution.

---

25 Neil Thompson, "Terrorism in Asia: The Global Village Effect," *The Diplomat*, August 1, 2018, https://thediplomat.com/2018/08/terrorism-in-asia-the-global-village-effect/ (accessed June 20, 2020).

26 Matthew J. Walton, "Misunderstanding Myanmar's Ma Ba Tha," *Asia Times*, June 9, 2017, https://www.asiatimes.com/2017/06/article/misunderstanding-myanmars-ma-ba-tha/ (accessed June 20, 2020).

Last but not least, education also plays a vital role in lifting the spirit of religious sentiment because it is essential for the creation and maintenance of identities, and changes to the educational system and curricular materials will be a key part of a revised nation-building project in Myanmar. The dominant Burman Buddhist identity has been reinforced through government textbooks that privilege a particular historical narrative of the founding of the Burmese polity and depict non-Burmans either as minor players or as attempting to split the national community. Even the textbooks rewritten since the early 1990s generally reflect Burman Buddhist history and cultural norms and practices. In addition, non-Burman figures are often de-ethnicized and appropriated as "Myanmar" heroes when they are included as prominent or consequential actors.[27] All these factors demonstrate that it is hard to deny that state institutions, such as constitutions and the education system, have been conducive to the spread of nationalist sentiments and thus have provided fertile ground for populism.

4 Religious Nationalism under NLD Rule

As fundamentalist Buddhism transformed into nationalist Buddhism, monks began to attack the NLD as *Mus Daung*, meaning "Muslim peacock,"[28] implying that the NLD favored and would protect Muslims. The NLD, fearful of losing popular support over being linked to Muslims, rejected every Muslim on their candidate list in the 2015 elections. As a result, Myanmar's Parliament became the first Muslim-free Parliament. In contrast, three Muslim MPs from Rakhine State were elected in 2010 under the USDP. This clearly shows that the military and the USDP exploited this fear of losing popular support and narrative to attack the NLD for political gain during the 2015 elections. The military, the USDP, and other small parties engaged in this strategy to win the elections with the knowledge that anti-Muslim sentiment was widespread throughout the whole country, not least in the Bamar Buddhist majority areas. Sayadaw Wirathu once said in a speech that he would commit suicide if Daw Khin Wine Kyi, a supporter of the Ma Ba Tha movement from the NDF party, was not elected in 2015. He also "instructed his followers to vote for the USDP after his movement managed to extract some concessions from them in recent years, such

---

27   Adam Simpson, Nicholas Farrelly, and Ian Holliday, eds., *Routledge Handbook of Contemporary Myanmar* (Abingdon: Routledge, 2017).

28   In Myanmar, the fighting peacock symbolizes the unflinching revolutionary who fights injustices and dictatorship to the death.

as the halting of construction projects near pagodas and the passing of laws governing interfaith marriage, religious conversion, and monogamy."[29]

The fact that the NLD won the elections in 2015 does not undermine the claim that Ma Ba Tha and other nationalist groups have a great deal of influence over the majority populace, after they sharply attacked Aung San Suu Kyi and the NLD before the elections. Aung San Suu Kyi's victory can be attributed to her status as the daughter of General Aung San, who is considered one of the very few political leaders who was uncorrupted, pure, and dedicated to national independence, and thus is cherished and revered by most of the country. When any confrontations arose between Ma Ba Tha and the NLD the majority sided with Aung San Suu Kyi and the NLD. This became obvious when the declaration by Phyo Min Thein, Chief Minister of Rangoon Division, that Ma Ba Tha should be banned was met with minimal outcry. However, there remains the worrying possibility that these combined forces of the military, USDP and Ma Ba Tha could win after the Aung San Suu Kyi era has passed.

The cooperation between the military, the USDP, and Ma Ba Tha culminated when they proposed the four "Race and Religion Protection Laws." As reported in the *Global Monitor*, "four laws known collectively as the Race and Religion Protection Laws, which were submitted to the Parliament of Burma (Myanmar) in December 2014, were adopted this spring by the Parliament and recently signed by Thein Sein, Burma's President."[30] According to Al Jazeera, "hundreds of supporters from the ultra-nationalist Ma Ba Tha group formed a convoy of trucks and buses that sneaked through the main city of Rangoon on September 14 to welcome the introduction of four Race and Religion Protection Laws, which the group drafted itself."[31] Prominent monks of Ma Ba Tha said in this rally that people should vote only for the USDP since it is the only party that can protect the race and religion of the country.[32] Interestingly, the partnership between the political elites and a better part of the group of Ma Ba Tha has created tension within the Ma Ba Tha itself. Dissenters were

---

29   Zoltan Barany, "Democracy in Myanmar: A Long Way to Go," *Foreign Affairs*, December 1, 2015, https://www.foreignaffairs.com/articles/asia/2015-12-01/democracy-myanmar (accessed June 20, 2020).

30   Shameema Rahman and Wendy Zeldin, "Burma: Four 'Race and Religion Protection Laws' adopted," *Global Monitor*, September 14, 2015, http://loc.gov/law/foreign-news/article/burma-four-race-and-religion-protection-laws-adopted/(accessed June 20, 2020).

31   Joshua Carroll, "Buddhist Monks in Myanmar Celebrate Repressive Laws," *Al-Jazeera*, September 23, 2015, https://www.aljazeera.com/indepth/features/2015/09/buddhist-monks-myanmar-celebrate-repressive-laws-150922111750765.html (accessed June 20, 2020).

32   Radio Free Asia, June 23, 2015.

vindicated when one of the leading monks quit the organization in frustration over the Ma Ba Tha being exploited politically by political elites.[33]

However, it should be noted that this cooperation is a recent phenomenon that was not present during past violence. Further, while it can be argued that their cooperation served a populist purpose, it does not necessarily mean that the two groups have moved beyond the violence of the past. Rather, they are exploiting the existing atmosphere that is widespread in the Buddhist community, which emanates from cultural differences, economic resentments, and a historical legacy, for their populist project. The groups that have tried to shape the religious and nationalist populist discourse may go even further and exacerbate the hatred against Muslims by using stories about events that happened in other places. In the article "The Contentious Politics of Anti-Muslim Scapegoating in Myanmar," Gerry van Klinken and Su Mon Thazin Aung wrote:

> The first step towards a new anti-Muslim project was taken in 2001. Young monks led several rowdy events at which they spoke indignantly about the Taliban's destruction of the Bamiyan Buddhas in Afghanistan and of the Al-Qaeda attacks on the West. By adopting this internationalized discourse these monks proclaimed a new identity-based framing of the anti-Muslim riot that was not related to specific economic or political grievances. One of those young monks was U. Wirathu, born in 1968.[34]

In other words, although they did not create the anti-Muslim atmosphere, they have continued to fuel and exploit it to shape the discourse.

Despite some claims that there is no systemic exploitation led by the government or military, some research literature has alleged that there were "hidden hands" behind some of the violence, stating that the conflicts and violence were not spontaneous but rather planned by outsiders. A policy report by Justice Trust states that "the conclusion that the Mandalay riots were planned and instigated is supported by facts on the ground as confirmed by multiple eyewitnesses, extensive on-site investigation, and informal discussions and meetings conducted over six months with a wide range of stakeholders by Justice Trust's team of local and international lawyers."[35] These events, at least the more recent ones, point to elite mobilizations for the populist agenda, and

---

33　Radio Free Asia, June 8, 2016.

34　Gerry van Klinken and Su Mon Thazin Aung, "The Contentious Politics of Anti-Muslim Scapegoating in Myanmar," *Journal of Contemporary Asia* 47, no. 3 (2017): 353–375.

35　Justice Trust, "Hidden Hands Behind Communal Violence in Myanmar: Case Study of the Mandalay Riots," Justice Trusty Policy Report, 2015.

POPULISM IN MYANMAR

undermine claims that violence has emanated spontaneously from cultural or religious differences, economic resentment, or the historical legacy. However, it must be admitted that there is widespread dislike, if not hatred, of Muslim minorities.

5   The Threat of Populism to Democracy

No action was taken by the police, nor by the Ministry of Home Affairs, which was under the direct control of the Commander-in-Chief, in response to any of the legal violations committed by Ma Ba Tha U. Wirathu is still at large and has suffered no consequences from his numerous instigations and hate-filled speeches. On the other hand, a journalist was charged when he criticized U. Wirathu.

Populist political strategy alongside widespread support for an organization such as Ma Ba Tha overshadows Myanmar's nascent democratic transitions and human rights situation. Many violations against minorities, predominantly religious, have occurred including the closing of Islamic religious premises, infringements on Christian religious property, and many others. In 2015, local authorities and Thein Sein's office denied Muslims, who were born and raised in Union of Myanmar, permission to hold a nationwide conference in Rangoon, citing its "potential for instability." In the same year, "on June 2, a court in upper Myanmar sentenced a writer and former National League for Democracy official to two years in jail with hard labor for 'insulting religion' over a 2014 speech defending the purity of Buddhism from Ma Ba Tha's political distortion."[36] This is clear evidence that freedom of speech has been curtailed in Myanmar, and there are many similar instances happening in the country.

It will be extremely difficult for one party or one organization alone to handle or contain this overwhelmingly dominant atmosphere. Even the NLD government has to be very cautious in this delicate situation. Political figures are also reluctant to make any comments lest they lose support. There have been no open challenges from civil society organizations (CSOs). Only when there is a concerted effort by the government, CSOs, religious leaders, and political figures together with reform of the education system will there be any chance of countering this serious threat to democracy. The urgent need to change the

---

36   David Scott Mathieson, "Religious Extremism Looms Over Myanmar," *Human Rights Watch*, June 16, 2015, https://www.hrw.org/news/2015/06/16/religious-extremism-looms-over-myanmar (accessed June 20, 2020).

norms and values of society should be recognized by the government and political elites, especially those on the democratic side.

6   Conclusion

Populism in Myanmar is like a "time bomb," and to ignite it would result in tragedy and severe violations of human rights. As populism appears strongly correlated with the election cycles in the country, it is likely to remain a chronic problem in Myanmar. Instead of building their own base, many populist political parties try to use the already existing influence of dominant religious movements, which has thus far shown the potential to be a threat to democracy. The religious nationalist discourse set out by religious groups such as Ma Ba Tha targeting religious minorities, especially Muslims, has been co-opted by the populist main opposition party, the USDP, and the military. As long as this phenomenon continues, the outlook for Myanmar's transition to democracy will remain bleak.

Conclusion: Sources and Features of Asian Democracies

Chin-en Wu, Sook Jong Lee, and Kaustuv Kanti Bandyopadhyay

Asia is a heterogeneous region in terms of levels of economic development, political development, cultural diversity, and ethnic composition. The main social cleavages are different across countries. Therefore, emerging populism in this region exhibits several distinct types, which include redistributive populism, ethno-religious populism, progressive populism, and authoritarian populism. Based on a study of 11 country cases, we find that each type of populist movement has different targets, rhetoric, and strategies. In addition, populism's impacts on the function of democracy are also different. Throughout this book, country chapters elaborate on different types of populism. In this concluding chapter, we briefly review these types and pay special attention to the reasons behind their rise. To address the populism problem, one needs to understand not only the symptoms but also the causes. Some of the reasons pertain to specific countries, while others are relevant to the majority of countries. Next, we extend our discussion to countries that do not have strong populist movements. Why are they immune from the populist appeals? We then compare the similarity and differences between populisms of the same type in Asia and in other regions. Finally, we discuss policy recommendations.

1 Sources of Populism in Asia

1.1 *Redistributive Populism*
Redistributive populism stems from high levels of income inequality and rural poverty; namely, the division between the urban political and business elite, and the rural and urban poor. With modernization, income in urban areas tends to increase while a large portion of people in rural areas remains poor. Over time, the rural–urban wealth gap becomes entrenched, creating a strong sense among rural farmers that the urban political elite are neglecting their demands. In this way, redistributive populism is launched by the elite which mobilizes the poor masses. Populist politicians deliver targeted economic benefits while paying insufficient attention to long-term fiscal stability. This allows

them to capitalize on the perception of economic inequality. They launch policies that dole out resources under the garb of social protection and redistribute public resources to garner support.

Redistributive populism has emerged in Thailand and India, and to a lesser extent in Malaysia, Mongolia, and the Philippines. Different types of populism and their primary sources are summarized in Table C.1. Thai governments since the administration of Thaksin Shinawatra in 2001 have introduced policies including 15 years of free education, an elderly allowance, the rice-pledging scheme, and the 300-baht minimum wage. In India, contemporary redistributive populism dates back to the Mahatma Gandhi National Rural Employment Guarantee Act (MNREGA) in 2005 that provides short-term public work for adult members of rural households. At the state level, several states have launched various populist schemes ranging from free laptops for students to free meals. Following the redistributive populist tradition, since 2018 the Modi government in India also gave cash allowances to poor farmers annually to gain their support. The same government launched a populist demonetization policy that invalidated 500- and 1,000-rupee notes and reissued new notes to crack down on black money, terrorism, and corruption. In Mongolia, political leaders make many unrealistic promises such as the claim that the country can become wealthy in just three months. In addition, governments use revenues from mining to build wasteful public buildings and facilities.[1]

Malaysia also represents a case of redistributive populism, but to a limited degree. For example, during the 2018 Malaysia elections, the opposition party used populist rhetoric against the ruling elite, emphasizing the less fortunate 99 percent of the population against the 1 percent cronies of the ruling alliance. The party attempted to appeal to the public who were disenchanted with the performance of the government and the scandals of top government officials. In addition to criticizing the elite, the opposition party proposed various policy reforms that were pluralistic in nature and encouraged greater civil society participation. Some of these included populist economic policies such as fuel price controls and the provision of free public services. However, after assuming office, the new government delayed a number of these populist policies, revealing its partial adherence to redistributive populism.

The roots of redistributive populism lie in a country's developmental trajectory, which decides the extent to which the urban manufacturing sector is able to absorb surplus labor from the rural agricultural sector. At first an abundance

---

1 Note that redistribution is an integral part of economic populism but it does not cover all aspects of economic populism. Some economic policies such as price control also cater to the interests of the business sector.

of cheap labor from the countryside enables the growth of the manufacturing sector or service sector. As these sectors expand, average wages increase and more labor from rural area moves to the cities. But when wages increase to a certain level, the country is not able to compete with more advanced economies to produce high value-added goods. This situation forces countries into a middle-income trap in which income per capita is stagnant and the labor transition between the two sectors stalls. Foreign capital and cheap labor boosted Malaysia and Thailand's economies in the 1960s and 1970s, but soon after China and Vietnam entered the global market, both countries faced serious challenges and failed to upgrade their industries. Richard Doner, Reda Cherif, and Fuad Hasanov point out that the foreign-dominated manufacturing model adopted by many Southeast Asian countries makes it difficult to implement import substitution, develop alliance companies, and upgrade domestic industries.[2] In countries such as India which rely heavily on the service sector, the ability to absorb rural labor is also very limited. Given a stagnant economy, redistributive policies become the only way to improve the life of the rural people. To break the income trap, a country needs to implement structural reforms. Inclusive and structural economic reforms require a much broader consensus, making structural reforms difficult to push through. A detailed discussion of the sources of development paths is of course beyond the scope of this book.

As a result, these countries still have a sizable population in rural poverty. For example, the rural population in Thailand still accounts for around 50–60 percent of the total population. In contrast, some countries such as South Korea and Taiwan had successfully upgraded their economies and were able to absorb the rural poor into urban areas during the 1960s and 1970s. Shortly before South Korea's democratic transition in 1987, only around 30 percent of the population was living in rural areas, while the corresponding figure for Taiwan was around 17 percent. Given the sheer number of rural farmers in Thailand, income redistribution measures such as cash handouts and rice pledging schemes are not financially sustainable. It is natural for business and the conservative elite to oppose such populist measures. This provides a fertile ground for politicians in these countries to employ populist rhetoric to emphasize the

---

2   Richard F. Doner, *The Politics of Uneven Development: Thailand's economic growth in comparative perspective* (Cambridge, UK: Cambridge University Press, 2009); Reda Cherif and Fuad Hasanov, *The Leap of the Tiger: How Malaysia can escape the middle-income trap.* Nos. 15–131 (Washington, DC: The International Monetary Fund, 2015), https://www.imf.org/en/Publications/WP/Issues/2016/12/31/The-Leap-of-the-Tiger-How-Malaysia-Can-Escape-the-Middle-Income-Trap-43021 (accessed June 17, 2020).

TABLE C.1   Types of populism and their primary sources in Asia

	Redistributive Populism	Ethnic and Religious Populism	Progressive Populism	Authoritarian Populism
Case countries	India, Thailand, Mongolia, Malaysia	Indonesia, Sri Lanka, Myanmar	South Korea, Taiwan	The Philippines, Pakistan
Targets	Urban elites	Ethnic and religious minority groups	Former authoritarian parties and large businesses Pro-China politicians	Drug dealers and criminals Ineffective representative institutions
Popular Policies	Providing social welfare and targeted public goods without paying enough attention to their costs	Refusing to grant minorities equal political rights Violence	Tackling corruption and strengthening checks and balances *Chaebol* reforms Promoting direct democracy	Extrajudicial killings and openly lashing out at elected officials Popularizing courts
Sources	High income inequality and rural poverty Income traps	Ethnic and religion divisions Legacy of imperialism	Liberal values Legacy of former authoritarian parties China factor	Incompetence of representative institutions Prevalence of corruption and crime
Impacts on democracy	Long-term government deficits Divisive politics More equitable income distribution	Infringement of minority rights Harming pluralism and rule of law	Enhancing participatory democracy Infringing on the autonomy of representative institutions	Damage to the rule of law and repression of CSOs Delegitimizing representative institutions

CONCLUSION: SOURCES AND FEATURES OF ASIAN DEMOCRACIES 215

division between the urban elite and the rural poor and initiate redistributive and pork barrel policies to mobilize support from the poor.[3] We see similar populist platforms in Thailand, India, Mongolia, and the Philippines.

The long-term impact of such policies on democracy and the economy is mixed. Redistributive programs are inclusive policies that improve the lives of rural farmers. Such programs make income distribution more equitable, which in turn helps to foster social harmony and democratic stability. Redistribution, however, also has its downsides. In the long run, governments face fiscal imbalances and an abundance of wasteful public works projects. In extreme cases, political and economic threats posed by populist parties induce the conservative elite to seek extra constitutional ways to end such threats. In the case of Thailand, the urban elite and the military remain concerned about the cost of populist economic policies and the electoral popularity of populist leaders. The coalition between the urban elite and the military has eventually led to the fall of the democratic government.[4] On the surface, economic populism seems as though it is not correlated with the weakening of the rule of law and the diminishing of civil society, but it actually imposes serious negative effects on democracy. When redistributive policies are pushed too far and damage the core interests of the conservative elite, they may induce the elite to work with the military to oust populist leaders and halt populist policies.

1.2   *Ethnic and Religious Populism*

The second model of populism is ethnic and religious populism, which applies to the cases of Sri Lanka, Myanmar, and to a lesser degree, Indonesia. This type of populism is mainly concerned with claiming the mainstream ethno-religious identity as the sole legitimate one over other minority identities. Populist political leaders hence often remain silent about violence against minorities and anti-minority statements. They also use language associated with the division of the population into "us vs. them" and "patriots versus traitors." The sources of ethnic and religious populist movements involve ethnic and religious heterogeneity and overlapping ethnic and religious hegemonies. However, countries that exhibit such populism, while they may largely disregard minority identities, hold back from recognizing the majority religion as the official belief system of the state due to the modern principle of separation

---

3   By contrast, in Taiwan for years there were also cash handouts for elderly rural farmers. The number of people who received such benefits was much smaller and thereby does not arouse much debate.

4   A similar case happened in Chile in the 1970s. The left-leaning populist president Allende was overthrown by the army and police, which were backed by the conservative business elite.

between the secular state and religion. Yet the dominant religious group is still able to rally around its religion to attack minority ethnic groups and assert its religious hegemony within the official realm. For example, the dominant group can list majority group membership as a condition for candidate eligibility in elections and fundamental citizenship entitlement for security and sustenance. Overall, ethnic and religious populism is not restricted to the elite, but rather spans a diverse range of social strata, making it a deviation from the pure top-down populist model.

The people of Sri Lanka and Myanmar often identify British imperialism as the root of their ethnic and religious conflicts because British rules brought in minority populations from surrounding nations due to labor needs. They justify minority discrimination by arguing that minorities do not share the same legitimate rights or equal political status with the majority group, which is native to the country. In Sri Lanka, those belonging to the majority ethnic group—the Sinhala Buddhists—contend that they have a right to govern the country and that minorities have no such claim. Furthermore, non-elite Sinhalese Bala Mandalaya populist actors oppose any political compromise with the minority Tamil forces and reject ethnic policies that seek to protect minority ethnic groups. Myanmar's religious nationalism is another example. Mabatha and the 969 movement are both civil society organizations that claim they do not intend to gain political power, but are, rather, promoting and defending Buddhist beliefs and values. In Myanmar, the ruling National League for Democracy party also does not prioritize the protection of minorities, even distancing itself from Muslims. Furthermore, while Myanmar might be relatively accepting of Muslims from other countries, the country does not welcome the Rohingya population that was introduced there during British imperialism. These populist movements lead the population away from compromise and do not encourage the government to make effective concessions for minimizing conflicts.

Indonesia has also witnessed the rise of Islamist populism after 2015. The movement was led by various opposition and religious leaders against the former Jakarta governor, Ahok, an ethnic Chinese Christian who ran for re-election. The religious populist leaders used social media and mass rallies to mobilize the people, giving rise to increased and more frequent conflicts and violence within the country. Overall, this example indicates that ethnic and religious populist movements damage the rule of law and judicial independence, infringing upon minority rights.

Asia also displays country cases where, due to a strongly grounded political system and cooperative policies, ethnic or religious division does not necessarily lead to populist movements. Malaysia is an example of such a case,

CONCLUSION: SOURCES AND FEATURES OF ASIAN DEMOCRACIES   217

where despite its heterogeneous ethnic composition, there have not yet been clear instances of ethnic populism. Malaysia's majority Bumiputeras, which accounts for almost 70 percent of the population, has been able to maintain Islam as its official religion in a peaceful manner although around a quarter of the population is comprised of non-Muslim Chinese. An important factor that contributes to its peaceful coexistence between different ethnic groups is its political institution. Malaysia has a parliamentary system where people elect representatives instead of a single political leader. Under this political system, it is difficult for an ethnically Chinese candidate to be elected as prime minister to pose a threat against the native Malays. The latent threat that the Malays feel towards the ethnic Chinese, however, is clear since they backlashed against Mahathir for selecting an ethnic Chinese as finance minister in 2018. In addition to the political system, Malaysia's institutional arrangement and sharing of power between the economic and political branches also help quell potential conflicts. While Chinese citizens control a significant portion of the business sector, the Malaysian government maintains affirmative-action based economic policies that benefit ethnic Malays primarily.

However, one must also pay attention to the fact that Malaysia is a competitive authoritarian regime and not a democracy, at least as of the 2018 general election. Unlike the past, when the long-time ruling Barisan Nasional Party did not need to secure Islamic votes to win the elections, over the past few elections and as the party gradually lost support from urban ethnic Malays, Chinese, and Indians, conservative Islam votes have become important. Since the Barisan Nasional Party lost power in 2018, it is very likely that the party and the Islamic party of Malaysia may pursue a populist platform combining political Islam and Malay nativists in the future.

1.3   *Progressive Populism*

Progressive populism is the third model that has emerged in South Korea and Taiwan, both of which enjoy higher incomes and vibrant democracy compared to the rest of the region. Both countries have experienced the so-called two turnover test of democratic consolidation. The objectors of the populist movements include former authoritarian parties and large businesses, *chaebols* in Korea and companies with large Chinese operations in Taiwan. In South Korea, the movement aims to prosecute corrupt politicians, tackling the conventionally close relationship between *chaebol* and the government. In Taiwan, people question whether the Kuomintang (KMT) and the representative institutions deliver social justice and make secret deals with China. In response, many people support direct democracy. These countries represent a bottom-up model in that the movements are launched by civil society organizations and rely on frequent large-scale street protests. These movements subsequently partly transform into political parties and in the case of Taiwan are partly absorbed by the Democratic Progressive Party, while those in South Korea remain adrift, by neither being absorbed into established parties nor creating an alternative party.

Underlying the two movements is concern for the quality of democratic governance. Among South Koreans corruption and misuse of power are particular concerns; among the Taiwanese, local factions, vote buying, and party assets are the main focus. This factor is associated with the legacy of former authoritarian governments, party business, and political allies (conservative parties and *chaebol* in Korea, and the KMT and local factions in Taiwan). These problems date back to the authoritarian periods of each country. In addition, Korea and Taiwan also demonstrate cases of confrontation between modern and post-modern values. This involves popular attitudes toward the legacy of former authoritarian parties, social issues, and economic development models. For Taiwan, the rise of populism also relates to the looming threat of China. Liberal-minded people are more likely to worry about the threat of China against Taiwan. Trade deals between Taiwan and China incite fears about China's power. In addition, in both countries, the working class and youth face difficult economic challenges and are concerned about rising income inequality. They believe that the ruling party and large businesses rig the economy. Thus, economic factors are important contributors to the rise of bottom-up populist movements in South Korea and Taiwan.

In terms of progressive populism's impact on democracy and the economy, liberal sources of populism strengthen democracy by tackling corruption and contributing to a level playing field. This is consistent with literature that argues that populism arising from opposition movements tends to do less harm and may even contribute to some good. Both South Korea and Taiwan are fully committed to democratic values and the progressive movements within these countries do not pose threat to pluralistic democracy.

However, progressive populism also has some potential negative effects on the functioning of democracy. First, once the opposition has taken office with the help of progressive populism, the new government and the ruling party may attempt to reverse major policies and decisions of the previous government. However, delegitimizing the former government on the basis of popular demand for change imposes disruption on the political system. This is pertinent to South Korea, where those making administrative and judicial decisions are pressured to follow prevailing public opinions that are further divided along the lines of political cleavages. In addition, the populist movement in Taiwan has blocked contentious trade deals with China, but it also

CONCLUSION: SOURCES AND FEATURES OF ASIAN DEMOCRACIES 219

has also interrupted the legislative review process and harmed the ability of the government to govern. While liberal values and ideals serve the push for reforms in both countries, progressive populism also impairs their democratic governability.

1.4 Authoritarian Populism

The last populist model discussed here is the authoritarian model, which includes the cases of the Philippines and Pakistan. The background of authoritarian populism is government incompetence and weak governance. People become frustrated with representative democracy and long for a strongman, in the case of the Philippines, or an alternative power, in the case of Pakistan, to deal with critical national issues. In return, politicians seek to strengthen their power by making populist appeals.

In the Philippines, there is widespread discontent among the middle class in respect of government performance, corruption, and the short supply of government goods and services. As a result, people support a strongman who seems to have the ability to address these issues. Among issues of top concern, Filipino voters rank the crime issue only sixth, after economic and governance issues such as controlling inflation, increasing wages, reducing poverty, creating jobs, and fighting corruption. President Duterte, as an autocratic-leaning populist, was able to frame crime fighting as the most important issue that the Philippines faces. He launched a campaign to reduce crime, especially drug dealers, by committing extrajudicial killings and prosecuting corrupted officials.

Pakistan is an interesting case where the populists are not elected politicians but rather the Supreme Court judges. The reason for the rise of judicial populism in Pakistan is the perceived incompetence of the executive branch, which has enabled the judiciary to intervene in many policy issues. In order to gain popularity, the Supreme Court has sought to label itself "the People's Supreme Court" by frequently issuing *suo motu*, visiting schools and hospitals, and initiating and monitoring public works projects. In this way, the alleged corruption of top government officials creates the social expectation that the courts need to be more active in checking elected officials. In the name of the people, the Court frequently criticizes and humiliates publicly elected politicians, parties, and civil servants and is extensively involved in the adjudication of political disputes. For example, in 2017, the Supreme Court dismissed Prime Minister Sharif for not declaring his salary from a foreign company.

However, the Court's overarching power and connection with the military also raise concerns. The 2017 decision by the Supreme Court to dismiss Prime Minister Sharif, for instance, was widely perceived as being orchestrated by the military, signaling military interference with representative democracy. In fact, After its independence, Pakistan has experienced several military coups which abrogated the constitution and imposed martial law. After each coup, the Supreme Court approved martial law by calling it a necessary action. The active role of the Court and the fact that the Court is a tool of the army suggest that the military–court coalition uses populist actions to illustrate and criticize the incompetence and corruption of the representative branches. In doing so, the coalition gains the legitimacy needed for restricting the power of elected governments. Therefore, a more fundamental issue of Pakistan's populism is the unrestricted power of the military that buttresses the Supreme Court's authority and damages representative institutions.

The negative impact of authoritarian populism on democracy is significant as the government relies on violence, pays little attention to the rule of law, and represses critical civil society organizations and journalists. This situation is particularly clear in the Philippines. Judicial populism in Pakistan interferes with the functioning of elected governments and delegitimizes representative institutions. Thus, populism in Pakistan also harms checks and balances and the rule of law.

2   General Background of the Emergence of Populism

In addition to the specific factors that contribute to each type of populism, there are some general background issues that influence almost all countries in this region. First, democracy opens the door for parties to use ethnic divisions and income inequality in mobilizing the masses. In many countries, the roots of populism persisted throughout the authoritarian or military regimes of the past, but the rulers had no use for populism since sheer repressive control was enough to rule the country. However, with democratic transition, the same underlying causes are facilitating populism because elected leaders are now in need of expanding their popular support. Democratization also allows for the revival of religious and ethnic organizations that had been previously oppressed under authoritarian regimes. In several cases, populism has emerged immediately following democratic transition. Economic populism emerged in Thailand after its democratic transition. Ethnic populism in Indonesia also arose after the fall of the Suharto regime. In Myanmar, the military coopted religious organizations with large followers to secure votes and win elections to accommodate their radical agenda.

Another factor affecting populism in East Asian countries is the influence of external factors. In countries that have significant ethnic divisions, external factors that are associated with one side of the ethnic division play an important role. The first example is Muslims in Indonesia, who have gradually become more conservative after 2010. This is the result of the rise of social media that has allowed young Indonesians to connect directly with the conservative ideology of extreme Islamic forces in the Middle East. It is also related to Saudi Arabia's promotion of conservative Islamism in the Muslim world. For example, the Gulf countries provide scholarships to Indonesian youth and fund conservative mosques and religious schools. These factors contribute to the rise of conservative Islam and the ethnic populism in Indonesia. A similar external factor has also played a significant role in Sri Lanka, escalating tensions between Buddhists and Muslims. Taiwan is another interesting case. Although the two main ethnic groups are all Chinese immigrants, the main ethnic group, native Taiwanese, came to Taiwan 130 to 200 years ago, while the other ethnic group, the Mainlanders, came just 60 years ago. The latter group prefers a more moderate relationship with China. Since President Xi took office in 2013, the Chinese government tightened its domestic control and became more assertive in its foreign relations. Economic agreements initiated by the Mainlander elite have incited concerns about national security and democratic stability among the native Taiwanese and liberal-minded members of the public. This external factor is one of the most important backgrounds of the populist movement in Taiwan.

Developments in communications technology—the internet and social media in particular—play an important role in directly connecting populist leaders to their followers. The relative deprivation, anti-elite sentiment, and a strong sense of "us vs. them" are also inflamed by social media. Surrounding each populist leader is a media army in different social media outlets that supports the leaders and attacks critics. This environment essentially creates an echo chamber and provides less room for compromise and deliberation. In the Philippines, Duterte uses social media to reach out to ordinary people, bypassing traditional political parties, established media, and representatives. Even in Pakistan, Supreme Court judges use social media to connect with the general public. Social media also allows social groups to coordinate with each other and disseminate information among members. For example, in South Korea and Taiwan, social media and internet forums play an important role in allowing civil society organizations to orchestrate protest movements. Lastly, as suggested above, in some countries social media facilitates direct communication between young people and foreign extremist Islamic organizations. This situation could also play a role in affecting the emergence of religious populism.

The ethnic, economic, and authoritarian forms of populism are mainly top-down models wherein the masses are mobilized by political leaders. But even so, the general public's attitude plays an important role in shaping and sustaining the emergence of populism. First of all, populist platforms and measures must be acceptable to the general public to begin with—otherwise, the populist movement will not flourish. For example, in the Philippines, around half the population inclines toward some form of autocracy. This tendency builds the foundation for the rise of an autocratic-leaning populist movement. Moreover, following the initiation of the violent campaigns against drug trafficking, the number of robbery and theft crimes has decreased significantly. Such partial evidence of the success of the War on Drugs is important in sustaining Duterte's populist movement. In another example, as demonstrated through a public poll, a great majority of Malaysian people believe that popular economic policies such as removing value-added tax and fuel price controls benefit the economy and consumers. This provides the foundation for economic populist platforms. These observations suggest that the outcomes of the populist movements are also critical in deciding whether people are likely to continue supporting them

3   Mixed Models

Of course, the actual picture of populist movements in Asia is more complicated than the four types discussed above. First, economic populism emerges not only in Thailand, India, Mongolia, and Malaysia. To a different degree, it also appears in the Philippines, Indonesia, South Korea, and Taiwan. For example, in the Philippines, which has a high level of income inequality, former President Estrada adopted a inflammatory rhetoric claiming that he was a friend of the poor. Following his suit, President Duterte has also implemented several economic welfare populist measures such as the waiving of college fees for students and irrigation fees for farmers. These economic populist policies, however, appear to be smaller in scale than those adopted by other countries that exhibit economic populism.[5]

---

5   In addition, many Asian countries already have intense patron–client relations. Politicians attract votes by delivering for special interests. Economic populism is largely an upgraded version of this clientelist relationship. Many of the policies in economic populism are about providing direct economic benefits, such as guaranteeing rice purchase prices, fuel subsidies, and subsidies for farmers to win voters. However, the policies of economic populism differ from the traditional clientelist relationship in two aspects. One is that these economic policies are basically legal. There are fewer illegal behaviors involved such as vote-buying or grafting and bribery. Next, some of the populist policies belong to the traditional left-and-right policies, such as raising the minimum wage. The benefits apply to everyone who meets the requirements. In contrast, in the clientelist relationship, people are able to receive benefits only when they live in a particular geographical district or belong to a specific social network.

CONCLUSION: SOURCES AND FEATURES OF ASIAN DEMOCRACIES

Similarly, ethnic and religious populism also emerges in other countries such as India, which we categorize under the model of redistributive populism. Since the Bhartiya Janata Party came into power in India under the leadership of Narendra Modi in 2014 with an overwhelming majority, the values and principles of secularism enshrined in the Indian Constitution and written by stalwarts such as Mahatma Gandhi, Jawaharlal Nehru, and Sardar Ballavbhai Patel have been undermined by the government. Since 2014, the Indian government has downplayed pluralism and endorsed religious nationalism with the belief that India belongs to the Hindu majority. As a result, many Muslims, who constitute around 14 percent of the Indian population, have been subjected to attacks by fanatical Hindu groups, while the government has generally kept silent.

4   Some Special Features of Asian Populism

We discuss four types of populism in Asia, but similar types of populism also emerge in other parts of the world. There are, however, some significant differences between populism in Asia and that in other regions.

First, like Asian countries, Latin American countries also display economic populism. For example, various socialist policies have been implemented since 2000 in Venezuela, including large-scale social welfare policies and nationalization. This is one of several left-leaning populist governments that have arisen in Latin America since the turn of the 21st century.[6] However, there is a significant difference between Asian and Latin American leftist populism. Asian countries are highly dependent on trade and are more focused on market mechanism. Therefore, economic populism in Asia is less likely to promote either large-scale nationalization or anti-globalism, unlike Latin America. The populist platforms in Asia focus primarily on redistributive policies such as purchasing rice at guaranteed prices, providing subsidies to the poor, and pork barrel spending. In some cases, governments implement price controls that affect production decisions, but, in general, economic populism in Asian countries is centered more on redistribution than production. Moreover, given the size of most Asian democracies, it is also quite unlikely that the populist leaders will use trade barriers to achieve economic and political ends.

---

6   Kurt Weyland, "The Rise of Latin America's Two Lefts: Insights from Rentier State Theory," *Comparative Politics*, January 41, no. 2 (2009): 145–164.

The different degrees of economic populism in Asia and Latin America are also rooted in their respective developmental models and industrial structures, as mentioned above. Asian democracies do not implement import-substitution industrialization that fosters large-scale state-owned enterprises and adopts highly protected trade policies. Following the export-led growth model, the extent of market regulation has been reduced and is much less debated in the politics of Asian countries. In contrast, Latin American governments continue to choose between deregulating and re-regulating the market.[7] Thus, economic populism in Asia is more focused on redistribution and less on market regulation than that of Latin America.

Like the situation in many other developed countries, the hollowing out of industries remains a critical problem for South Korea and Taiwan. With rising labor and land costs, many factories have moved out of the countries, leaving low-skilled workers unemployed or uncertain about their economic prospects. As a result, many people support the anti-establishment movement from the perspective of pro-distribution over growth-first policy and pro-decentralization. Many people are also concerned about unequal income distribution stemming from economic liberalization and rising globalization. However, given the size of the two economies and their dependence on trade, few people challenge free trade and globalization. In Taiwan, many people are concerned about the trade deal with China because of the national security concern. At the same time, however, they do not question free trade agreements with other countries such as New Zealand or Singapore to the same degree.

As mentioned in the introductory chapter, immigrants are not a salient issue within the region. Although there are many migrant workers in Asia, they are generally not immigrants seeking permanent residence. Asia is relatively immune from the refugee problem that countries in Europe and North America have faced in after 2010. Ethnic and religious populism in Asia only emerges in countries with entrenched ethnic and religious divisions. Even so, the content of Asia's ethnic populism is also different. In contemporary Europe and North America, populists mainly care about how to prevent the entry of new refugees and restrict the extent to which refugees may share in economic resources. In Asian countries with ethnic populism, migration flows have taken

---

7   The difference in industrial structure explains why Asian countries do not have clear left-wing or right-wing parties. Hellmann argued that Asia does not have clear populist movements because there is no clear left–right division: Olli Hellmann, *Populism in East Asia* (New York: Oxford University Press, 2017). The left–right division is indeed less clear in Asian countries, while redistributive-based populism is present.

place over the past two hundred years. Emigrants have already settled down in new countries for generations. The issue at stake is mainly about preventing the minority from weakening the majority's dominant position and sharing economic resources.

5 Conclusion

Each chapter in this book relating to a specific country elaborates the different types of populism in Asia. There is no single definition of populism in Asian democracies. Populisms' symptoms, sources, solutions, and impact on the functioning of democracy differ across countries. With different ethnic and religious compositions, economic development paths, and urban–rural divides, several types of populism have developed in different countries. Similar types of populism also exist in other regions of the world, but the details and driving forces are in many cases different. One significant difference is that Asian populisms of various types do not resist globalization or employ anti-globalization populist rhetoric, especially regarding trade. This suggests that economic populism in Asian countries focuses more on the redistribution side and less on the production and investment side.

As for the influence of populism on the functioning of democracy, various chapters find that ethnic- and autocratic-leaning populism adversely affect checks and balances, civil space, and the protection of minority rights. Economic populism makes income distribution more equitable, favoring social harmony and democratic stability. However, in the long run it is not fiscally sustainable and may even cause democratic recession. The bottom-up model of progressive populism is in stark contrast to the top-down model of autocratic-leaning populism. In both types of countries, there was widespread discontent about the performance of representative democratic institutions. Populist leaders in the former choose to weaken checks and balances and the public tends to support the rise of a strongman. In contrast, populist movements in the latter type seek to check representative institutions by confining the power of elected leaders and enhancing direct democracy.

Index

Page references in **bold type** *indicate a more in-depth treatment of the subject.*

1Malaysia Development Berhad (1MDB) scandal 12, 155, **156–157**, 160
9/11 attacks (New York/Washington) 205
30-Baht healthcare scheme (Thailand) 11, 121, 123, 124*t*, **125**
212 movement/rallies (Indonesia) 14, **166–167**, 169n3, 170, 171, 174–175
969 movement (ultra-nationalistic group, Myanmar) 15, 201, **203**, 216

Abhisit Vejjajiva 121, 123, 124*t*, 126, 132
ABS-CBN (commercial television network, Philippines) 72
ABS (Fourth Wave Asian Barometer survey) 39, 42–43, 43*f*, 44, 45*f*
ABS Party (Philippines) 76
"accumulated evils" reform (South Korea) **34–36**, 37
Acemoglu, Daron 3
Adivasis (tribes of Indian subcontinent) 105, 114
AfD (Alternative for Germany) 5n9
Afghanistan 205, 208
agricultural development *see* rural and agricultural development
agricultural sector, shift of labor to urban manufacturing and service sectors 212–213
Ahok (Basuki Tjahaja Purnama), blasphemy case/rallies against 13, 14, 17, **165–170**, 169n3, 172–173, 174–175, 216
AKP (Justice and Development Party, Turkey) 171
Alam, Mohammad 114
Alam, Shabir M. 114
Albertazzi, Daniele 137–138
Al Jazeera 207
Al-Ma'idah, verse 5:51 165–166
Al-Qaeda 208
Alternative for Germany (AfD) 5n9
Aluthgama anti-Muslim riots (Sri Lanka, 2014) 186
Alvarez, Pantaleon 73, 76

Amantai, Kh. 143
Amin, K.H. Ma'ruf 173
Amma Unavagam ("mother's canteen", subsidized prepared food program, Tamil Nadu) 11, **106–108**, 115, 116–117
Ampāra (Sri Lanka) 192–193
Amyotha Hluttaw (House of Nationalities, Myanmar) 198
Ancient Rome 97
Andaya Jr., Rolando 76
Andhra Pradesh (India) 107
anti-elite/anti-establishment ideologies/ populism 1, 3, 4, 7, 9, 18, 36, 97–98, 119, 137–138, 143, 149, 151, 170, 177, 214*t*
see also India; Indonesia; Malaysia; Philippines; South Korea; Taiwan
anti-EU sentiments/nationalism 5n9
anti-globalization/anti-globalist populism 1–2, 7, 64, 223, 225
anti-immigration 5n9, 64
anti-pluralist populism 3, 7, 98
see also India; Philippines
Aqil Siraj 173
Aquino III, Benigno Simeon 62, 65, 74
Arakan Rohingya Salvation Army (ARSA) 204
Argentina 68, 97
Ariff, Syed Umar 149–150
Armitage, Richard 30
ARSA (Arakan Rohingya Salvation Army) 204
ASEAN Conference (Laos, 2016) 66
Asia
authoritarian past 6
democratization 2, 6, **16–18**
globalization 2, 7, 69, 224, 225
Asian populism *see* populism
Association of Southeast Asian Nations (ASEAN) 66
astroturfing 68
Aung San 207
Aung San Suu Kyi 15–16, 197, 198, 201, 207
Australian Coalition Party 68

228 INDEX

authoritarian populism   8, 9–11, 14, 103n25,
    137, 221
  definition/term   148–149
  impact on democracy   214t, 220
  roots/sources of   10, 214t, 219
  targets of   214t
  see also Pakistan; Philippines
authoritarian regimes   16–17, 22, 43–44,
    76, 155
  see also Malaysia; Myanmar
autocratic-leaning populism   219, 222, 225
Awang Azman Awang Pawi   150
Azerbaijan   68

Baabar (R. Batbayar, Mongolian
    columnist)   139–140
Bala Mandalaya populists (Sri Lanka)   216
Balochistan (Pakistan)   81, 91
Bamar (ethnic group, Myanmar)   14, 198,
    202, 206
Bamiyan (province, Afghanistan)   205, 208
Bandaranaike-Chelvanayakam Pact (Sri
    Lanka, 1957)   181
Bangladesh, migration of Rohingyas to   8, 16
Barisan Nasional (BN, Malaysia)   12, 150, 155,
    156–158, 159, 160, 217
Batbayar, B. (Baabar)   139–140
BBS (Bodu Bala Sēna, Buddhist Power Army,
    Sri Lanka)   15, 186
Beetham, David   27
behavior of populist leaders see popular
    leadership
Bersih 2.0 (Coalition for Free and Fair
    Elections, Malaysia)   156, 157
Bersih Five rally (Malaysia, 2016)   156
Beyrer, Chris   66
Bharatiya Janata Party (BJP, India)   11, 100,
    102, 110, 111, 112, 223
Bhutto, Zulfikar Ali   84
Bihar (India)   109
BIMARU states (India)   108–109, 109n52
Biver, Emilie   203–204
BJP (Bharatiya Janata Party, India)   11, 100,
    102, 110, 111, 112, 223
blasphemy, case against Ahok
    (Indonesia)   13, 14, 17, 165–170, 169n3,
    172–173, 174–175, 216
Blasphemy Against Religion (video)   165
Blasphemy Law (Indonesia)   14, 167

Blue House (Cheongwadae, Seoul)   31, 32, 35
BN (Barisan Nasional, Malaysia)   12, 150, 155,
    156–158, 159, 160, 217
Bodu Bala Sēna (BBS, Buddhist Power Army,
    Sri Lanka)   15, 186
Bolia, Nomesh   116
bots, for spreading spam and fake news   68
bottom-up populism   6–7, 9, 17, 39, 225
  impact on democracy   38
  see also progressive populism; South
    Korea; Taiwan
Brexit   1, 5n9, 103
bribery see corruption
British imperialism   179, 216
Bröning, Michael   28
Buddhist monks (sangha)
  in Myanmar   198, 202–204
  in Sri Lanka   179, 184, 186
Buddhist nationalism/populism see
    Myanmar; Sri Lanka
Buddhist Power Army (Bodu Bala Sēna, Sri
    Lanka)   15, 186
Buddhists
  in Indonesia   13
  in Malaysia   152
  in Myanmar   14, 15
  in Sri Lanka   14, 15, 179
build-operate-transfer (BOT) projects
    (Taipei)   47–48, 55–56
Buku Harapan ("Book of Hope", election
    manifesto, Pakatan Harapan,
    Malaysia)   156–158
Bumiputera (Malay ethnic group)   151, 152,
    153f, 217
Buni Yani   165
Burma see Myanmar
Bush, George W.   30
Business Today   117

CAG (Comptroller and Audit General of
    India)   107, 116
Calida, Jose   74
candlelight movements/protests (South
    Korea)   24, 27, 29, 34
  Choi Soon-sil Gate and Park
    Impeachment Candlelight Protests
    (2016-2017)   31–33
  Mad Cow Disease Candlelight Protests
    (2008)   31

INDEX

229

SOFA Revision Candlelight Protests (2002-2003) 29–30
Canovan, Margaret 168–169
Carandang, Melchor Arthur (Overall Deputy Ombudsman, Philippines) 73
Case, William 5
cash transfer programs (Mongolia) 139–140
cast inequalities (India) 11, 100–101
Ceasefire Agreement (Sri Lanka, 2002) 181
censorship *see* freedom of press/speech
Centre for a Better Tomorrow (think tank, Malaysia) 150
Ceylon Citizenship Act (1948) 180
chaebols (family conglomerates, South Korea) 28, 217, 218
Chakravartty, Paula 102
Chaudhry, Iftikhar Muhammad (Chief Justice, Pakistan, 2005-2013) 9, 80, 81, 82, 88, 89
cheap labor, transition from agricultural to manufacturing/service sectors 212–213
checks and balances system 25, 51–52, 55, 214*t*, 225
  in Malaysia 13, 158
  in Mongolia 141
  in Myanmar 199
  in Pakistan 220
  in Philippines 63, 76, 77
  in Sri Lanka 181, 188, 189
  in Thailand 134–135
Cheng Wen-tsan 47
Chennai Corporation (municipal corporation) 108, 115, 116
Chennai (Tamil Nadu) 107
Cheongwadae (Blue House, Seoul) 31, 32, 35
Cherif, Reda 213
Chettyars (trading caste, South India) 200
China 213
  globalization 69
  regional influence of 39, 42–43, 43*f*, 44, 45*f*
  Sri Lanka-China relations 188
  Taiwan-China (economic/cross-strait) relations 9, 38, 40, 42–46, 43*f*, 45*f*, 49, 50, 52, 54, 55, 56, 57–58, 217, 218, 221, 224
Chinese
  in Malaysia 152, 217
  in Myanmar 199, 200
  in Taiwan 42, 221

Choi Soon-sil 32, 34
Choi Soon-sil Gate and Park Impeachment Candlelight Protests (South Korea, 2016-2017) 31–33
Cho Kuk (Law Minister, South Korea) 35
Christians
  in Indonesia 13
    see also Ahok
  in Malaysia 152
  in Myanmar 14, 15
  in Sri Lanka 14, 179, 185
Citizenship Law (Myanmar, 1982) 201
civic activism (South Korea) 28–29
civil political participation
  in India 118, 119–120
  in South Korea 26–27, 28
  in Taiwan 48, 48n21, 51, 53, 55, 56
  in Thailand 123, 129, 130
civil service reform (Thailand) 124*t*
civil society organizations 17, 39
  in India 119–120
  in Myanmar 209
  in South Korea 26–27, 217
  in Taiwan 38, 40, 44–45, 46–49, 50, 52, 57, 217
    see also bottom-up populism
"Civil State" (*pracharat*, poverty reduction program, Thailand) 121, 123, 129
clientelism 222n5
  in India 17, 100
  in Mongolia 143
  in Thailand 17
Coalition for Free and Fair Elections (Bersih 2.0, Malaysia) 156
Code of Conduct and Ethical Standards for Public Officials and Employees (Philippines) 73
colonial governance
  in India 102, 112, 118
  in Myanmar 199–200
  in Sri Lanka 179, 180
Commission on Appointments (Philippines) 75–76
Commission on Human Rights (CHR, Philippines) 10, 72–73, 78
common people *see* ordinary citizens
Communication and Multimedia Act (Malaysia) 156

INDEX

communications technology *see* Internet; social and electronic media

community kitchens/cooked food subsidies (India)   11, 106–108, 115, 116–117

community village funds (Thailand)   11, 121, 123, 124*t*

competitive authoritarian regimes (Malaysia)   155

Comprehensive Dangerous Drugs Act (2002, Philippines)   67

Comptroller and Audit General of India (CAG)   107, 116

computers
 free laptops for students (India)   108–111, 117, 212
 free tablets at primary schools (Thailand)   123, **128**

conglomerates, family (*chaebols*, South Korea)   28, 217, 218

Congress Party (India) *see* Indian National Congress

consolidated democracies, unconsolidated vs.   25, 52

constitutions *see under individual countries*

corruption   9
 in India   11, 17, 102, 108, 111, 112
 in Malaysia   12–13, 152, 154, 155, 156–158, 159, 160
 in Pakistan   84, 85, 86–87, 219
 in South Korea   28, 31–33, 34, 36, 218
 in Sri Lanka   188–189, 191
 in Taiwan   38, 47, 218
 in Thailand   11, 17, 124*t*, 127, 131, 135

criminality (Philippines)   10, 62, 67
 see also drug wars

Cross-Strait Service Trade Agreement   46
 see also China; Taiwan

Curato, Nicole   65

cyberspace *see* Internet; social and electronic media

Dalits   109, 114

Dangerous Drugs Act (Philippines, 1972)   67

Davao City Investment Code   62–63

Davao City (Philippines)   10, 62–63, 65

Daw Khin Wine Kyi   206

decentralization of government   132, 133, 158

Delhi   107

democracy
 consolidated vs. unconsolidated   25, 52
 direct   39, 48–49, 53, 56, 61, 217, 225
 impact of populism on   16–17, 51–52, 78, 86, 97, 113–120, 138, 139, 225
  authoritarian populism   214*t*, 220
  bottom-up populism   38, 43, 52–57
  ethnic/religious/rightist populism   18, 21–22, 209–210, 214*t*, 225
  progressive populism   214*t*, 218–219
  redistributive/economic populism   17, 18, 119, 125, 130, 214*t*, 215, 225
 participatory   1, 18, 28, 28n14, 214*t*
 populism as form of   1, 61, 177
 sustainability of   69
 see also civil political participation; representative democracy

Democracy Index 2017 (EIU)   16–17

democratic institutions   75
 performance of   225
 weak   10, 61–62, 64, 75, 77

Democratic Party (US)   2

Democratic Progressive Party (DPP, Taiwan)   45, 46, 46n20, 47, 48, 50, 52, 53, 54, 55, 218

democratization, (rise of) populism and   2, 6, 16–18, 51, 220

demonetization (India)   11, 111–113, 117–118, 212

demonstrations *see* protests

Department of Statistics Malaysia   151–152

Destradi, Sandra   102

Dhanagare, D.N.   101

Dharmapāla, Anagārika   179

difference in differences (DID) methodology   104

The Diplomat   205

direct democracy   39, 48–49, 52, 56, 61, 217, 225

Dobama Asi-ayone (the We Burman Association)   200

Doctrine of State Necessity (Pakistan)   83

Doner, Richard   213

DPP (Democratic Progressive Party, Taiwan)   45, 46, 46n20, 47, 48, 50, 52, 53, 54, 55, 218

drug wars
 in Philippines   10, 66–67, 73, 74, 219, 222
 in Thailand   66

INDEX   231

Duterte, Rodrigo   64, 71, 222
   anti-drug/criminality campaign/drug
      war   10, 66–67, 73, 74, 219, 222
   anti-elite ideologies/populism of   65–66
   elections/election campaign (2016)   10,
      62–63, 64, 75, 77
   erosion of independent institutions
      by   72–74, 77–78
   marginalization/bypassing of
      opposition   10, 221
Dutt, Yogender   110
Dutugamunu (King of Sri Lanka, r. 161-137
   B.C.)   15, 183
dynastic rule (Sri Lanka)   183, 187

Eastern Europe, rightist populism in   5
economic populism   6, 11, 122–123, 137, 212n1,
      222, 222n5
   impact on democracy   225
   Latin America vs. Asia   223–224
   see also India; Malaysia; Mongolia;
      redistributive populism; Thailand
The Economist   80
Economist Intelligence Unit (EIU)   16–17
The Edge (Malaysia)   155
education/educational support
   in India   108–111, 117, 212
   in Philippines   70–71
   in Thailand   121, 123, 124t, 126, 128, 130, 212
Egorov, Georgy   3
Egypt   171–172
EIU (Economist Intelligence Unit)   16–17
Elāra (ancient Tamil king)   15, 183
Election Commission of Pakistan   88
elections/election campaigns   52, 72,
      104, 110
   populist appeals   16, 139–140
   redistributive populism in   11, 12, 18
   use of social media and trolls in   68
electoral politics   5–6, 180
electronic media see social and
      electronic media
elite see anti-elite/anti-establishment
      ideologies/populism; political and
      urban elite/establishment
employment guarantee (India)   104–106
equivalential logic concept (Laclau)   23
Erdogan, Recep Tayyip   97

establishment see anti-elite/anti-
      establishment ideologies; political and
      urban elite/establishment
Estrada, Joseph   63, 222
ethnic/religious populism   6, 8, 13–16, 18,
      214t, 215–217, 221, 222
   impact on democracy   18, 214t, 225
   North America/Europe vs. Asia   224–225
   roots/sources of   14, 214t, 215–216
   targets of   13, 214t
   see also Indonesia; Myanmar; Sri Lanka
Europe   147
   exclusionary/rightist/ethnic populism
      in   4, 5, 21, 26, 36, 64, 160, 224
European debt crisis (2012)   4
Europeans, in Myanmar   199, 200
European Union
   anti-EU sentiments/
      Eurosceptics   4, 5, 5n9
   see also Brexit
exclusionary populism   4, 6–7, 18
   see also ethnic/religious populism;
      Indonesia; Myanmar; Philippines;
      rightist populism; Sri Lanka

fake accounts   68
fake news   31, 53, 68, 78
farmers/farmer movements (India)   11, 100,
      101, 212
financial crisis (Asia, 1997)   121
fiscal impact of populist measures
   in India   100, 107, 110, 116, 119
   populism and   11, 17, 211, 215, 225
   in Thailand   122, 131, 133, 134, 135
Fisher, Max   33
flawed democracies   16–17
   see also India; Indonesia; Malaysia;
      Mongolia; Philippines; South Korea; Sri
      Lanka; Taiwan
Foa, Roberto Stefan   21
food programs, subsidized prepared
      (Tamil Nadu, India)   11, 106–108, 115,
      116–117
Fourth Wave Asian Barometer survey
      (ABS)   39, 42–43, 43f, 44, 45f
FPI (Islamic Defenders Front, Indonesia)   14,
      166, 169, 170
France   5n9, 97

232 INDEX

Freedom House, *Freedom in the World 2018* 155
Freedom Party (Austria) 5n9
freedom of press/speech
in Malaysia 155–156
in Myanmar 209
in Philippines 10, 72
in Sri Lanka 184–185
in Taiwan 52, 53
Free Irrigation Service Act (2017, Philippines) 71
Free Laptop Yojana (Uttar Pradesh, 2018) 108–111, 110, 117
free trade agreements *see* China; Taiwan

Galle (Sri Lanka) 186
Galston, William 55
Gandhi, Indira 11, 100, 101
Gandhi, Mahatma 11, 100, 223
see also Mahatma Gandhi National Rural Employment Guarantee Act
Gandhi-Nehru family 102
Gandhi, Rahul 102
Gascon, Jose Luis Martin 73
General Appropriations Act (Philippines) 71
General Council of Buddhist Associations (GCBA) 200
general will of the people (*volonté générale*, Mudde) 2, 3, 24, 61, 69, 148, 151, 177, 197, 198
Ghaziabad (India) 109
Gilani, Yousaf Raza 84
Gintota (Sri Lanka) 192–193
globalization
in Asian countries 2, 7, 69, 224, 225
effects of 69
as source of populism 1, 4, 61, 64, 69
see also Taiwan
Global Monitor 207
GNPF (National Fatwa Guards Movement, Indonesia) 166
The Godfather (Mario Puzo) 86
Goods-and-Services-Tax (GST, Malaysia) 150, 154–155, 154f, 157, 159, 160
governance, "good governance" government (Sri Lanka) 176, 188, 191–194
government, populism in opposition vs.
in 25, 52

Govindarajan, Vinita 107
Gram Sabha (fulcrum of Panchayati Raj and village development, India) 105, 114–115
grassroots activism/movements 6, 12, 17, 32, 68
Gravers, Mikael 202
Great Britain
Brexit 1, 5n9, 103
British imperialism 179, 216
Greece, leftist economic populism in 4
Grillo, Beppe 97
GST (Goods-and-Services-Tax, Malaysia) 150, 154–155, 154f, 157, 159, 160
The Guardian 204
Gujarat (India) 11, 101n17, 102–103
Gulf Cooperation Council countries 8, 221

Habib Rizieq Syihab 168–169, 173
Hadiz, Vedi, *Islamic Populism in Indonesia and the Middle East* 171–172, 174
Hageman 115
Haiyan (super typhoon, Philippines, 2013) 65
Hajj scam (Pakistan) 81
Hall, Stuart 148
Hanif, Mohammad, "Pakistan's Judges Are on a Mission. But What Is It?" 80
The Hankyoreh (newspaper, South Korea) 32
Harriss, John 98
Hasanov, Fuad 213
Hazare, Anna 101
healthcare schemes (Thailand) 11, 121, 123, 124t, 125, 130, 134
hegemonic populism *see* Sri Lanka
Himalayas 101
Hindus
in India 103, 223
in Indonesia 13
in Malaysia 152
in Sri Lanka 14, 15, 179
Hitler, Adolph 137
horizontal populism 7, 13, 36
House of Representatives (Philippines) 73, 75–76
Hubbard, Thomas 30

INDEX

Human Rights Commission (Sri Lanka)   184
human rights organizations   65
   condemnation of drug war
     (Philippines)   66
Human Rights Victim's Memorial
   Commission (Philippines)   73
human rights violations
   in Myanmar   204, 209, 210
   in Philippines   66, 72–73
   see also drug war
Hungary   5n9
Hung Chung-chiu   45
hybrid regimes   16–17, 155
   see also Malaysia; Pakistan; Thailand

ICMI (Indonesian Muslim Intellectual
   Association)   168
ideational (approach to) populism   2–3, 4,
   148, 149
identity-driven politics/populism   61
   in India   102–103
   in Malaysia   13
   in South Korea   33
   in Sri Lanka   180
IFMR LEAD   117, 117n79
Iglesias, Pablo   4
immigration *see* migration/immigration
impeachment
   in Philippines   74, 78
   in South Korea   26, 32–34, 37
imprisonment of public officials (South
   Korea)   34–36, 37
INC (Indian National Congress)   11, 100,
   102, 200
inclusionary populism   2, 4, 6
   see also bottom-up populism; leftist
     populism; progressive populism
income traps   213, 214t
independent institutions, erosion of
   (Philippines)   72–74, 77–78
India
   anti-elitist ideologies/populism   11, 17,
     100, 102, 119
   caste inequalities/cast mobility   11,
     100–101
   civil political participation/civil society
     organizations   118, 119–120
   clientelism   17, 100

colonial governance   102, 112, 118
Constitution   223
corruption   11, 17, 102, 108, 111, 112
economic developments   101, 117–118, 213
education/educational support   108–111,
   117, 212
elections/election campaigns   102, 106,
   109–110
environmental damage/struggles   11,
   100, 101
ethnic/religious populism   223
farmers/farmer movements   11, 100,
   101, 212
history/roots and rise of
   populism   11, **99–103**
liberal reforms (1990s)   11, 101
migration/immigration   8, 16
ordinances bypassing parliament   112,
   112n62, 118
pluralism/anti-pluralism   11, 102, 223
populist measures   103–104
   cash allowances to farmers   212
   demonetization   11, **111–113**,
     117–118, 212
   fiscal impact of   100, 107, 110, 116, 119
   free laptops for students in Uttar
     Pradesh   **108–111**, 117, 212
   guaranteed wage employment in rural
     India   102, **104–106**, **113–116**
   impact on democratic
     governance   **113–120**
   projects run by women   106–108, 115
   subsidized prepared food in Tamil
     Nadu   11, **106–108**, 115, 116–117
poverty reduction   100, **104–106**, 114, 213
redistributive/economic populism   6, 11,
   17, 98, 119, 212, 213, 214t, 215, 222
secularism   102, 223
self-sufficient agro-artisanal villages
   (Mahatma Gandhi)   11, 100
sub-national identity-driven
   populism   102–103
India Against Corruption (movement)   101
India Human Development Survey-II   114,
   114n67, 116
Indian National Congress (INC)   11, 100,
   102, 200
Indians, in Myanmar   199, 200

234 INDEX

Indian Statistical Institute   117
Indo-Burman conflicts   200
Indonesia   5, 17
  anti-elite/anti-establishment
    ideologies   168, 170, 171–172
  blasphemy case/rallies against Ahok   13,
    14, 17, 165–170, 172–173, 174–175, 216
  democracy/democratization   5, 17, 220
  demographic composition/ethnic and
    religious groups   13, 165
  elections/election campaigns   63, 167, 168
  ethnic/religious populism   6, 13–14, 17,
    214t, 216, 220
    Islamic/Muslim populism   14, 167, 170,
    171–175, 216
  Islamic vs. political/national identity
    in   167, 172, 174
  political reform (1998)   168
  redistributive/economic populism   222
  social media   221
  support from Gulf countries   221
  ulama   166, 172–173
Indonesian Muslim Awakening Party (Partai
    Kebangkitan Muslim Indonesia)   168
Indonesian Muslim Intellectual Association
    (ICMI)   168
Indonesian Ulama Council (MUI)   14,
    166, 172
Indo-Sri Lanka Accord (1987)   182
institutions, weak   10, 61–62, 64, 75, 77
International Organization for Migration   7
Internet   45–46n18
  see also social and electronic media
Inter-Services Intelligence (Pakistan)   86
intra-party populism (United States)   1–2
Ipsos, What Worries Malaysia in 2017?
    (survey)   152
Iran   68
Islamic Defenders Front (FPI, Indonesia)   14,
    166, 169, 170
Islamic Defense Action Movement
    (Indonesia)   166, 173
Islamic Party of Malaysia (PAS)   160
Islamic populism (Indonesia)   14, 167, 170,
    171–175, 216
Islamic Ummah Party (Partai Umat Islam,
    Indonesia)   168
Italy   97

i-voting (online polling platform, Taipei)   48,
    48n21, 53, 56

Jaipur Literature festival   103
Jakarta   14, 17, 63, 165, 166
Jamisola, Leonardo   65
Janatha Vimukthi Peramuna (JVP, Sri
    Lanka)   182
Japan   132
  migration control   8
Jāthika Hela Urumaya (JHU, National
    Heritage Party, Sri Lanka)   186, 190
Jayalalithaa, J. (Chief Minister of Tamil
    Nadu)   106
JHU (Jāthika Hela Urumaya, National
    Heritage Party, Sri Lanka)   186, 190
Johns Hopkins Bloomberg School of Public
    Health (Baltimore)   66
Joint Investigation Team (Pakistan)   86, 87
Jokowi (Joko Widodo)   63
judges, abuse of authority and persecution
    (South Korea)   34–35
Judicial Populism 2.0 see Pakistan
judicial populism   11
  contribution of social/electronic media
    to   84, 86, 221
  see also Pakistan
judicial reform (South Korea)   34–35
Justice and Development Party (AKP,
    Turkey)   171
Justice Trust   208
JVP (Janatha Vimukthi Peramuna, Sri
    Lanka)   182

Kaltwasser, Cristóbal Rovira   4, 7, 25, 26, 39
Kandy (district, Sri Lanka)   193
Karachi   81, 85
Karen (ethnic minority group, Myanmar)   14
Karnataka (India)   101n17, 107
Kaur, Nehmat   103, 118
Kazin, Michael   51
Kejriwal, Arvind   101
Kenny, Paul   4, 5–6
Khan, Imran   91
Khan, Tikka   88
Khera, Reetika   115
Khosa, Asif Saeed Khan   86
Khyber Pakhtunkhwa (Pakistan)   91

INDEX 235

Kim Dae-jung 30
King Prajadhipok's Institute (Thailand) 131
Klinken, Gerry van 208
KMI (Kuomintang, Nationalist Party,
    Taiwan) 38, 40, 41, 42, 44, 44n14, 45,
    46, 46n20, 50, 52, 53, 55, 57, 217, 218
Knight, Allan 169
knowledge institutions, role in educating
    for democracy/rules-based
    governance 78
Korean War (1950-1953) 29–30
Ko Wen-je 46, 47, 50, 53, 55–56
    see also White Force
Krungthai Bank (Thailand) 130
K Sports Foundation (South Korea) 32
Kukrit Pramoj 123
Kuomintang (KMT, Nationalist Party,
    Taiwan) 38, 40, 41, 42, 44, 44n14, 45,
    46, 46n20, 50, 52, 53, 55, 57, 217, 218
Kyaukse (Myanmar) 203

labor transition, between agricultural
    and manufacturing/service
    sectors 212–213
Laclau, Ernesto 22–23, 51, 171, 173
Lakha, Salim 106
laptops see computers
Latin America 139
    anti-globalization and anti-immigration
        sentiments 64, 223
    economic populism 223–224
    (inclusionary) populism 4, 26, 36
    Latin American vs. Asian
        populism 223–224
Law on Political Parties (Mongolia) 146
Lawyers Movement (Pakistan) 10, 81
leadership see populist leadership
Lee Myung-bak 31, 34
leftist populism
    Asia vs. Latin America 223
    in Southern Europe 4–5
Le Pen, Jean-Marie 5n9
Le Pen, Marine 5n9, 97
Levitsky, Steven 52
Liberal Party (Philippines) 75–76
Liberation Tigers of Tamil Eelam (LTTE) 15,
    182, 183, 184
Lima, Leila de 74

Loxton, James 52
LTTE (Liberation Tigers of Tamil Eelam) 15,
    182, 183, 184

Ma Ba Tha (ultranationalist Buddhists,
    Myanmar) 197, 201–210, 216
Macapagal-Arroyo, Gloria 76
McDonnell, Duncan 137–138
Mad Cow Disease Candlelight Protests (South
    Korea, 2008) 31
Madhya Pradesh (India) 107, 109
Maduro, Nicolás 97
Mahana (Buddhist institution,
    Myanmar) 15, 202
Maharashtra (India) 100
Mahathir Mohamad 147n1, 149, 217
Mahatma Gandhi National Rural
    Employment Guarantee Act
    (MGNREGA, India) 102, 104–106, 212
    audits 105–106
    electoral benefits 106
    positive and negative implications
        of 105, 113–115, 116
Mahāvamsa ("Great Chronicle", Sri
    Lanka) 179–180, 183
al-Ma'idah (Q 5:51) 13, 165–166
Malays 151
Malaysia
    anti-elite/anti establishment
        ideologies 13, 157, 158
    anti-racist ideologies 157, 159, 160
    checks and balances system 13, 158
    as competitive authoritarian
        regime 155, 217
    current trends in populism 156–158
    definition of populism in 148–151
    democracy/democratization 17, 155
    demographic composition/ethnic and
        religious groups 151–152, 153f, 217–218
    economic development/status 150,
        154, 213
    elections/election campaigns 149, 152,
        156, 159, 160, 217
    federalism/decentralization 158
    foreign capital and cheap labor 213
    freedom of speech/press 155–156
    institutional and political
        reform 157–158

Malaysia   (*cont.*)
　national identity/identity-driven
　　populism   13
　pluralism   13, 151, 151–152, 158
　populist measures,
　　free public services   212
　　(fuel) price controls   150, 154, 212, 222
　redistributive/economic populism   6,
　　212, 214*t*, 222
　socioeconomic and political
　　issues   151–155, 153*f*
　　corruption   12–13, 152, 154, 155, 156–158,
　　　159, 160
　　governance   152, 155
　　inflation   152, 159
　　Malay-Muslim rights   159, 160
　　migration/immigration   8, 152, 154
　　taxes   152
　　(un)employment   152
　taxes
　　Goods-and-Services Tax (GST)   150,
　　　154–155, 154*f*, 157, 159, 160
　　Sales and Services Tax (SST)   159, 160
　see also Pakatan Harapan
Malaysia Agreement (1963)   158
Malaysian Chinese Association   150
Malaysian Islamic Party   13
Mandalay (Myanmar)   203, 208
Manichean dualism (Taiwan)   38, 47
Manila   66, 67
Manila Bay   10
manufacturing sector, shift of labor from
　　agricultural sector to   212–213
Maragatham, M.   115
Marcos, Ferdinand   67
Marcos Jr., Ferdinand   75
Maria Chin Abdullah   156
market regulation   224
Maʻruf Amin   173
Mathur, Shobit   116
Ma Ying-jeou   9, 38, 42, 44, 45, 50
MBC   31
media   45–46n18
　judicial populism and   84, 86, 221
　as platform for political
　　support   68, 78–79
　populist leaders and media criticism   78
Medialdea, Salvador   73

Mendoza, Ronald   65
Merdeka Center   159
　Malaysia General Election XIV Outlook
　　(survey)   152
#Me Too movement (South Korea)   33
Mexico   68
MGNREGA *see* Mahatma Gandhi National
　　Rural Employment Guarantee Act
Miaoli Dapu land case (Taiwan)   45
migration/immigration   21
　in Asia   7–8
　in Europe   5
　Europe/North America vs. Asia   224–225
military
　coalition with urban elite (Thailand)   215
　connection with judiciary (Pakistan)
　　10–11, 83, 86–87, 88, 89, 91, 219–220
　cooperation with nationalists
　　(Myanmar)   **202–205, 206–207**, 210
military coups/interventions
　in Myanmar   201, 202
　in Pakistan   10, 83, 84, 89, 219
　in Thailand   12, 17
Military Intelligence (Pakistan)   86
military rule
　in Myanmar   15, 202, 206
　in Pakistan   10–11, 83–84, 89
Mindanao (Philippines)   62, 66
Minsaya (mentor of a king, Myanmar)   199
Mir Foundation (South Korea)   32
Modi, Narendra   11, 102, **111–113**, 118, 212, 223
Moffit, Benjamin   170
Mongolia   6
　checks and balances system   141
　clientelism   143
　Constitution   146
　democracy/democratization   17, 136, 139,
　　142, 144
　elections/election
　　campaigns   139–140, 142
　inflation   139
　mining revenues   139, 140, 212
　populist measures,
　　cash transfer programs   139–140
　　fiber optic communications
　　　network   139
　　transformation into economic
　　　powerhouse   139, 212

INDEX

unrealistic/unnecessary/short-term
promises/measures 139–140, 141
positive vs. negative populism 141–142
reception of populism/image of
populists 138, 140–141, 145
redistributive/economic populism 12,
212, 214t, 215, 222
(social) media 136, 145
(socio)economic development 138, 141,
142, 143
(trust in and view of) political
parties 142–146
monks see Buddhist monks
Mookherjee, Dilip 104–105, 106
Moon Jae-in 29, 32, 34
Moors (ethnic minority group, Sri
Lanka) 14, 179
Moulmein (Myanmar) 203
Mounk, Yascha 21, 97
Mudde, Cas 2, 4, 7, 24, 25, 26, 39, 122, 143–144,
148, 170, 197
Muhammadiyah (Islamic NGO,
Indonesia) 168
MUI (Indonesian Ulama Council) 14,
166, 172
Mukhriz Mahathir 149
Müller, Jan-Werner 2–3, 98, 122
Munro-Kua, Anne, Autocrats vs. The
People: Authoritarian Populism in
Malaysia 148–149
Muntinlupa (Metro Manila) 74
Musharraf, Pervez 10, 81, 83
Muslim Brotherhood (Egypt) 171–172
Muslim populism (Indonesia) 14, 167, 170,
171–175, 216
Muslims
in India 223
in Indonesia 13, 220–221
in Malaysia 151, 152
in Myanmar 14, 15, 202, 203, 204–205,
206, 208–209, 210, 216
in Sri Lanka 14, 15, 179, 185–187
Mussolini, Benito 137
Myanmar
authoritarian rule 17, 197, 198
Buddhist institutions 15, 198–199,
201–205
Buddhist nationalism 15–16, 197

historical development 198–201
rise of populism based on 201–206
under NLD rule 206–209
checks and balances system 199
civil society organizations 209
colonial-capitalist 199–200
Constitution(s) 198, 201, 205
democracy/democratization 16, 197, 209,
210, 220
demographic composition/ethnic and
religious groups 14, 199–200, 201
economic development 199–200
elections/election campaigns 197,
198, 207
ethnic/religious populism 6, 14, 15–16,
201–206, 214t, 215, 216, 220
anti-Christian and anti-Hindu
movements/sentiments 15
anti-Muslim movements/
sentiments 15, 202, 203, 204–205,
206, 208–209, 210, 216
role of media and education in lifting
religious sentiment 205, 206
freedom of speech 209
human rights violations/violence/ethnic
cleansing 16, 17, 204, 209, 210
liberalization 197
migration/immigration 8, 199–200, 201
military coup (1962) 201, 202
military rule 15, 202, 206
cooperation with Buddhist
nationalists 202–205, 206–207, 210
populism as discourse vs. political
strategy 201, 202–203
pre-colonial 198–199
religious/ethnic conflicts 197, 200, 201
Rohingyas 8, 16, 17, 201, 216
sangha (Buddhist monks) 198, 202–204
see also Ma Ba Tha

NAB (National Accountability Bureau,
Pakistan) 88
Naga Min ("Dragon King", military operation,
Myanmar) 201
Nahdlatul Ulama (NU, Sunni Islam
movement, Indonesia) 168, 173
Najib Tun Razak 12–13, 155, 156, 158
Nandhi, Mani Arul 115

Narayan, Swati 114
Narmada dam (India) 101
National Accountability Bureau (NAB, Pakistan) 88
National Council for Peace and Order (NCPO, Thailand) 121, 123, 129
National Democratic Alliance (NDA, India) 111
National Fatwa Guards Movement (Indonesia) 166
National Freedom Front (Sri Lanka) 190
National Front (France) 5n9
National Heritage Party (Jāthika Hela Urumaya, Sri Lanka) 186, 190
national identity 1, 2, 9, 15
  see also identity-driven populism
National Investigation Agency (India) 117
National Irrigation Administration (Philippines) 71
nationalization 223
National League for Democracy (NLD, Myanmar) 15–16, 197, 198, 201, 209, 216
  religious nationalism under NLD rule 206–209
National Movement Guards Fatwa (Indonesian Ulama Council) 14
national populism 103, 103n25
National Public Security Act (Taiwan) 53
national socialism 137
National Welfare Scheme Card (Thailand) 129–130, 132
NCPO (National Council for Peace and Order, Thailand) 121, 123, 129
NDA (National Democratic Alliance, India) 111
Nehru-Gandhi family 102
Nehru, Jawaharlal 100, 223
New Bilibid Prison (Philippines) 74
New Delhi 11, 103
Ne Win 201, 202
New Masyumi Party (Partai Masyumi Baru, Indonesia) 168
New Order (Indonesia) 168
New Power Party (NPP, Taiwan) 9, 38, 45–46, 47, 50, 52, 54, 57
  promotion of direct democracy 48–49, 53
  on Referendum Act 49

New Straits Times (newspaper, Malaysia) 149, 150
New York 205
New York Times 33, 80
New Zealand 155
Nielsen 154
Nigeria 139
Nilsson-Wright, John 33
Nisar, Saqib (Chief Justice of Pakistan, 2016-2019) 10, 80, 84
NLD (Malaysia) *see* National League for Democracy
Noida (India) 109
North America
  anti-globalization and anti-immigration sentiments 65
  ethnic/religious populism 224
  immigration/refugees 224
Northeast Asia, Southeast Asia vs. 6
North Korea, North Korea-South-Korea relations 23, 24
Norway 156
NPP (Taiwan) *see* New Power Party
NU (Nahdlatul Ulama, Sunni Islam movement, Indonesia) 168, 173

Obama, Barack 66, 122
Occupy Wall Street (2008 Great Recession movement) 157
Odisha (India) 107
Office on Missing Persons (Sri Lanka) 191, 192
Office of the Ombudsman (Philippines) 10, 73
Official Language Act (Sri Lanka, 1956) 180
Official Secrets Act (Malaysia) 156
"One China, Two Interpretations" policy (1992 Consensus, Taiwan) 42
One Tambon One Product (OTOP, entrepreneurship stimulus program, Thailand) 11–12, 121, 124t, 125–126
Open Society Forum 142
opposition 76
  marginalization/silencing of (Philippines) 74–76
  populists in power vs. populists in 25, 52
Orban, Viktor 5n9
ordinary citizens 22

INDEX 239

"corrupt elite" vs. "pure people"
(Mudde)   24, 61, 70, 144, **148**, 151, 170,
177, 197, 198
as target group for populists/reception of
populism by   138–139, 142, 143
OTOP (One Tambon One Product,
entrepreneurship stimulus program,
Thailand)   11–12, 121, 124*t*, **125**–126
Oxford Handbook of Populism   2

Pakatan Harapan (PH, Malaysia)   12, 147, 149,
150, 151, 154, 158–159, 160
Buku Harapan ("Book of Hope", election
manifesto)   156–158
Pakistan   6
authoritarian populism   214*t*, 219
checks and balances system   220
Constitution(s)   82–83, 92, 93
corruption   84, 85, 86–87, 219
democracy/democratization   11, 17, 81, 84,
86, 87–88, 89, 90
education   85
elections/election campaigns/elected
government   83, 84, 87, 91, 220
health care   85
judicial populism   10–11, 80–81, **84–89**,
92–93, 219–220
impact on democracy   81, 86,
87–88, 89, 90
reversal of   92–93
suo motu power/notices   10–11, 81, 82,
84–85, 86, 87, **89–91**, 92–93
judiciary   80–81
(appointment of)
judges   88–89, 92, 93
classes of courts   82, 85, 92
jurisdiction   82–83
pending/backlog in cases   80–81, 82
public opinion on/trust in   90, 90*t*, 92
right of appeal   82, 87, 92
see also Supreme Court of Pakistan
martial law   83, 219
migration/immigration   8
military,
coups/interventions/military
rule   10–11, 83–84, 89, 219
military-judiciary connection in   10–11,
83, 86–87, 88, 89, 91, 219–220

role of military in   10–11, 91
trust in   90, 90*t*
public opinion on/trust in
governance   85, 90–91, 90*t*, 92
social media   84, 86, 221
Pakistan International Airlines (PIA)   85
Pakistan Muslim League-Nawaz
(PML-N)   88, 91
Pakistan Tehreek-i-Insaf (PTI)   91
Palli-Sabha (voters of revenue villages,
India)   105, 105n33, 114
Panamagate/Panama Papers scandal (Nawaz
Sharif)   86–87
Park Chung-hee   33
Park Geun-hye, impeachment of   32–**34**, 37
Park Young-soo   33
Partai Kebangkitan Muslim Indonesia
(Indonesian Muslim Awakening
Party)   168
Partai Masyumi Baru (New Masyumi Party,
Indonesia)   168
Partai Umat Islam (Islamic Ummah Party,
Indonesia)   168
participatory democracy   1, 18, 28,
28n14, 214*t*
Partido Demokratiko Pilipino-Lakas ng Bayan
(PDP-Laban)   76
PAS (Islamic Party of Malaysia)   160
Patel, Sardar Ballavbhai   223
PBNU (Pengurus Besar Nahdlatul
Ulama)   173
PD Diary (MBC program)   31
PDP-Laban (Partido Demokratiko
Pilipino-Lakas)   76
PDS (Public Distribution System, India)   105
peasant movements *see* farmers/farmer
movements
Pengurus Besar Nahdlatul Ulama
(PBNU)   173
pension retirement schemes/elderly
allowances (Thailand)   121, 123, 124*t*,
126, 130, 212
People's Alliance for Democracy ("Yellow
Shirts", Thailand)   12
People's Power Party (Thailand)   12
Perikatan Nasional (Malaysia)   147n1
Peronists (Argentina)   97
Pew Research Center   63

240 INDEX

PH *see* Pakatan Harapan
Pheu Thai Party   12, 127
Philippine Dangerous Drugs Board   66
Philippine National Police (PNP)   67
Philippines   61, 76, 147
  anti-elite/anti-establishment ideologies/
    populism   62, 64, 65–66
  anti-pluralistic populism   17
  authoritarian populism   9–10, 214*t*, 219
  checks and balances system   63, 76, 77
  Constitution (1987)   75, 76–77, 78
  criminality/crime rate   6, 67, 219
  democracy/democratization   5, 16, 17, 61,
    63, 64, 76–77
  drug war   10, 66–67, 73, 74, 219, 222
  elections/election campaigns   62–63,
    64, 75, 77
  erosion of independent
    institutions   72–74, 77–78
  freedom of press   10, 72
  human rights violations   66, 72–73
  impeachment   74, 78
  marginalization/silencing of
    opposition   74–76
  political turncoatism   75–76, 77
  populist measures,
    free irrigation   10, 71
    salary increase/incentives for police
      and soldiers   10, 71
    subsidized/free education   10,
      70–71
  redistributive/economic populism   10,
    212, 215, 222
  (social) media and bots   68, 78–79, 221
  see also Duterte, Rodrigo
Phule, Jyotirao   100
Phyo Min Thein   207
PIA (Pakistan International Airlines)   85
PILDAT Score Card on Perception of Pre-Poll
    Fairness (Pakistan)   90, 90*t*
Plagemann, Johannes   102
pluralism   3, 7, 98, 148, 177
PML-N (Pakistan Muslim
    League-Nawaz)   88, 91
PNP (Philippine National Police)   67
Podemos (leftist party, Spain)   4, 5
Podujana Peramuna (PP, Sri Lanka)   193
political marketing (Thailand)   125, 132, 133

political participation *see* civil political
    participation
political parties/institutions
  failure of mainstream   143–144
  undermining legitimacy and power of/
    destabilization of   2, 51–52
    see also democracy, impact of
    populism on
  weak institutions   10, 61–62, 64, 75, 77
political populism   2, 3, 4, 8, 9–11, 122
  see also Thailand
political turncoatism
    (Philippines)   75–76, 77
political and urban elite/establishment
  coalitions/connections with military
    10–11, 83, 86–87, 88, 89, 91, 215, 219–220
  "corrupt elite" vs. "pure people"
    (Mudde)   24, 61, 70, 144, 148, 151, 170,
    177, 197, 198, 214*t*
  redistributive populism and   130–131
  see also anti-elite/anti-establishment
    ideologies/populism
popular "fandomism" (South Korean
    phenomenon)   23
populism
  Asian vs. Western and Latin American   2,
    223–225
  concepts and functions of   22–25
  countering of   119–120
  definition/concept/approaches to   2–4,
    22–25, 26, 39, 61, 97–98, 99, 122, 137, 144,
    147, 148–151, 169–171, 174, 177, 197, 225
  as form of democracy   1, 61, 177
  impact on democracy   16–17, 18, 21–22,
    25, 38, 51–57, 78, 86, 97, 113–120, 118–119,
    130, 138, 139, 177, 209–210, 225
  origins/causes for rise of   4, 5–8, 61, 97,
    138, 143–144
    democratization   2, 6, 16–18, 51, 220
  as political strategy vs. discursive style vs.
    ideology   3, 197–198
  populists in opposition vs. in power   25
  positive vs. negative populism/
    implications   137–138, 141–142
  types of   4–5, 6, 8–18
    mixed models   222–223
    see also authoritarian populism; bottom-
    up populism; ethnic/religious

INDEX

populism; political populism;
progressive populism; redistributive
populism; top-down populism
populist leaders/leadership
appeal of populist leaders 64–65
leadership style,
direct identification with sentiments
and morality 169
techniques and behavior 169–170
leadership style, techniques and
behavior 64, 78, 98, 119, 143, 170–171
direct identification with sentiments
and morality 98, 138
tactics for maintaining power 3
unrestricted executive power of 63–64, 98
populist movements *see* social movements
post-communist states 136
see also Mongolia
poverty reduction 11, 12, 17
in India 100, **104–106**, 114, 213
in Thailand 121, 123, 124*t*, **129**, 130
power
legitimacy of 27–28
unrestricted executive 63–64, 98
PP (Podujana Peramuna, Sri Lanka) 193
Prabhākaran, Vellupillai 183
pracharat ("Civil State Cooperation",
Thailand) 121, 123, **129**
pragmatism, politics of skepticism vs.
politics of 169
Pramuka Island (Indonesia) 165
Prayut Chan-o-cha 123, 124*t*, **128–130**, 132
Printing Presses and Publications Act
(Malaysia) 156
progressive populism 6, 9, 51, 214*t*,
217–219, 225
impact on democracy 214*t*, 218–219
roots/sources of 214*t*, 218
targets of 214*t*
see also South Korea; Taiwan
protests 217
in Indonesia 14, **166–167**, 169n3, 170, 171,
174–175
in South Korea 18, 22, 24, **27–33**, 34, 35,
37, 218
in Taiwan 38, 40, 44–45, 57
Provisional Constitutional Order (PCO)
judges (Pakistan) 88–89, 93

PTI (Pakistan Tehreek-i-Insaf) 91
Public Distribution System (PDS, India) 105
public money
preemptive spending of 11
see also redistributive populism
public participation *see* civil political
participation
Public-Private-People Partnership
(Thailand) 121
public reliance/dependence (Thailand) 131,
132, 135
Pulse Asia 77
Punjab (Pakistan) 85, 91
"pure" people *see* ordinary citizens
Purnama, Basuki Tjahaja *see* Ahok
Putinism 64
Puzo, Mario 86
Pyi Thar Yar ("Clean and Beautiful Nation",
military operation, Myanmar) 201
Pyi Thu Hluttaw (House of Representatives,
Myanmar) 198

Quimbo, Romero 76
Quran verses, Al-Ma'idah, verse 5:51 13,
165–166

Race and Religion Protection Laws
(Myanmar) 207
Rai, Suyash 117
Rajapaksa, Basil 183
Rajapaksa, Chamal 183
Rajapaksa family 183
Rajapaksa, Gotābhaya 183, 186
Rajapaksa, Mahinda 15, 176, 182, 189–190,
192, 193–194, 195
regime (2009-2014) 176, **182–190**
anti-minority violence 185–187, 190
authoritarian populism 183–184
dynastic rule 183, 187
electoral defeat 187–188, 189–190
opposition 184
Rajapaksa, Namal 183
Rajasthan (India) 107, 109
Rakhine (ethnic minority group,
Myanmar) 14
Rakhine State (Myanmar) 16, 201, 204, 206
rallies *see* protests
Rampton, David 178

Rangoon 199, 200, 207, 209
Rappler (online news platform, Philippines) 72
Rashtriya Swayamsevak Sangh (RSS, India) 112
Ray, Suchetana 108–109
RBI (Reserve Bank of India) 112–113, 118
redistributive populism 8, 11–13, 17, 70, 211–215, 212n1, 214*t*, 221
 elites and 131
 fiscal impact and ineffectiveness 11, 17, 100, 107, 110, 116, 119, 122, 131, 133, 134, 135, 211, 215, 225
 impact on democracy and economy 17, 18, 119, 214*t*, 215, 225
 Latin America vs. Asia 223–224
 roots/sources of 212–213, 214*t*, 222
 short-term poverty reduction and 18
 targets of 214*t*
 see also economic populism; India; Malaysia; Mongolia; Philippines; Thailand
Red Shirts Movement (Thailand) 12
Referendum Act (Taiwan) 48–49, 54
refugees/refugee crisis 5, 13, 16, 224
religious and ethic populism *see* ethnic/religious populism
religious nationalism *see* Indonesia; Myanmar; Sri Lanka
Reporters Without Borders (RSF) 155–156
representative democracy 7, 219
 in Mongolia 142
 in Pakistan 11
 in Philippines 61, 63, 64, 76, 77
 in South Korea 18, 24
 in Sri Lanka 177
 in Taiwan 18, 38, 47, 48, 54, 55, 56, 57
 see also democratic institutions
Republican Party (US) 1–2
Reserve Bank of India (RBI) 112–113, 118
Rice Pledging Scheme (Thailand) 121, 127, 131, 132, 212, 213
rightist populism 1
 in Europe 4, 5, 21
 in United States 21
 see also ethnic/religious populism
Right to Information Act (India, 2005) 105
Roberts, Kenneth M. 169

Robredo, Leni 75
Rohingyas (ethnic group, Myanmar) 8, 16, 17, 201, 204, 216
Rome, Ancient 97
Roxas II, Manuel 62
Roy, Srirupa 102
RSF (Reporters Without Borders) 155–156
RSS (Rashtriya Swayamsevak Sangh, India) 112
rural and agricultural development
 in India 102, 104–106, 113–116
 in Thailand 12, 121, 123, 124*t*, 125, 127, 129, 130
Russia 68

Sabah (Malaysia) 158
Salem (India) 115, 115n72
Sales and Services Tax (SST, Malaysia) 159, 160
Salleh Said Keruak 150–151
Samajwadi Party (SP, Uttar Pradesh) 109–110
Samak Sundaravej 124*t*
Same-Sex Marriage Act (Taiwan) 49n23
Sanders, Bernie 2, 68
sangha (Buddhist monks)
 in Myanmar 198, 202–204
 in Sri Lanka 179, 184, 186
Sant Maral Foundation 142
Sarawak (Malaysia) 158
Sarawak Report (online news resource) 155
Sasanabai (head of Buddhist monks, Myanmar) 198–199
Satya Shodhak Samaj (Truth Seeker Society, India) 100
Saudi Arabia 68, 221
Second Anglo-Burmese war (1852-1853) 199
SEC (Securities and Exchange Commission, Pakistan) 72
Securities and Exchange Commission (SEC, Pakistan) 72
Security Offences (Special Measures) Act (Malaysia) 156
Sedition Act (Malaysia) 156
Self-Respect Association (India) 100
self-sufficient villages (Mahatma Gandhi, India) 11, 100
Senanayake-Chelvanayakam Pact (1965) 181

INDEX
243

Sen, Sunny   108–109
Seoul   29
separatist nationalism (Sri Lanka) *see*
  Liberation Tigers of Tamil Ealam
Sereno, Maria Lourdes   74
service sector, shift of labor from agricultural
  sector to   213
Shan (ethnic minority group, Myanmar)   14
Sharif, Nawaz, disqualification of   84, 86–89,
  91, 219
Shrivastava, Piyush   109
Shukri Shuib   150
Shwedagon (Rangoon)   200
Shwe Phi, *Mawlawi and Yogi*   200
Singapore   8
Singhalese Populist Party   15
Sinhalé (name of Sri Lanka as ethno-
  religiously homogeneous state)   187
Sinhalese (language)   180
Sinhalese/Sinhalese Buddhists   179–181, 182,
  183, 185, 187, 190, 192, 195, 216
Siraj, K.H. Aqil   173
Sirisena, Maithripala   188–191, 193–194, 195
Sitagu Sayadaw   204
skepticism, politics of pragmatism vs.
  politics of   169
SLFP (Sri Lanka Freedom Party)   180, 188,
  191, 193
Smith, Anthony   179
social and electronic media   45–46n18,
  61, 221
  contribution to judicial populism   84,
  86, 221
  as platform for political support   68, 78
social movements   2
  in South Korea   22, 24, 33
  in Taiwan   38, 40, 46–47, 52
  see also civil society organizations
socio-cultural (approach to)
  populism   2, 3–4
SOFA Revision Candlelight Protests (South
  Korea, 2002-2003)   29–30
SOFA (Status of Forces Agreement, South
  Korea)   29–30
Solo (Indonesia)   63
Sonin, Konstantin   3
Southeast Asia, Northeast Asia vs.   6
Southern Europe, leftist populism in   4–5

South Korea   17, 22
  "accumulated evils" reform (persecution/
    imprisonment of public
    officials)   34–36, 37
  anti-elite ideologies/populism   6, 18,
    23–24, 26, 27–28, 32, 36, 224
  bottom-up populism   9, 17–18, 24, 27–33,
    37, 217, 218
  civil society organizations/civic
    activism   26–29, 217
  corruption   28, 31–33, 34, 36, 218
  democracy/democratization   16, 23, 24,
    26–27, 213, 217
  direct individual political
    participation   26–27, 28
  economic development   33, 37, 213, 224
  equivalential logic concept   23
  impeachment   26, 32–34, 37
  inequality in   27–28, 33, 37
  migration/immigration   8
  North Korea-South Korea
    relations   23, 24
  peaceful mass protests   18, 22, 24, 29, 35,
    37, 218
    candlelight protests   24, 27, 29–33, 34
  political dichotomy   23, 24, 28
  popular "fandomism" (popularity of
    political commentators)   23
  progressive populism   6, 214*t*, 217–218
  redistributive/economic
    populism   26, 222
  representative democracy   18, 24
  rural population   213
  social media/bots   68, 221
  social/popular movements   22, 24, 33
  Supreme Court   34–36
  top-down populism   27, 34–36, 37
  US-South Korea relations   9, 24, 29–30, 31
  youth   33
Spain   4
SP (Samajwadi Party, Uttar
  Pradesh)   109–110
Sri Lanka   176
  (British) colonial rule   179, 180
  Buddhist nationalism   15, 176, 178–182,
    184, 185, 187, 188, 188–189, 193, 194–195
    by non-state actors   192–193
    state reform vs.   192

244 INDEX

Sri Lanka (*cont.*)
  centralization/decentralization 181, 192
  checks and balances system 181, 188, 189
  China-Sri Lanka relations 188
  Constitution(s)/constitutional crisis 181,
    184, 187, 188, 191, 192, **193–194**
  corruption 188–189, 191
  democracy/democratization 17
    liberal democratic politics/
    values **188–191**
  demographic composition/ethnic and
    religious groups 14, 179, 180
  elections/election campaigns/electoral
    politics 180, 183, 186, **187–190**, 193,
    194, 195
  ethnic/religious populism 6, 14, 15, 214*t*,
    215, 216
    anti-minority/Muslim politics and
    violence 15, **185–187**, 190, 192–193, 221
    anti-Western ideologies 184
  fertility rates 185
  foreign policy 188, 192
  freedom of press/censorship 184–185
  "good governance" government
    (*yahapālanaya*) 176, 188, **191–194**
  identity politics 180
  political dichotomy 184
  political elite/establishment 177–178, 181
  Rajapaksa regime (2009-2014) 15, 176,
    182–190
  sangha (Buddhist monks) 179, 184, 186
  semi-presidentialism 181
  Tamil separatist nationalism/conflict 15,
    176, 181–182, 183, 185
  transitional justice program 191, 192
Sri Lanka Freedom Party (SLFP) 180, 188,
  191, 193
State Bank of Pakistan 87
Status of Forces Agreement (SOFA, South
  Korea) 29–30
Suarez, Danilo 76
sub-national populism (India) 102–103
Suharto 168, 220
Su Mon Thazin Aung 208
Sunflower Student Movement (Taiwan) 41,
  43, 45, 49, 52
  occupation of Parliament (2014) 46, 54, 55
  see also New Power Party

suo motu power/notices (Supreme Court of
  Pakistan) 10–11, 81, 82, 84–85, 86, 87,
  89–91, 92–93, 219
Supervision Act (Taiwan) 53
Supreme Court of Pakistan
  autonomy of 81, 89
  connection with military 10–11, 83, 86–87,
    88, 89, 91, 219–220
  disqualification of Nawaz Sharif 84,
    86–89, 91, 219
  involvement in public affairs 9–10, 84–86
  jurisdiction 10–11, 82–83
  pending/backlog in cases 80–81, 82
  representative institutions and 89, 92
  suo motu power/notices of 10–11, 81, 82,
    84–85, 86, 87, 89–91, 92–93, 219
  *Zafar Ali Shah v. General Pervez
    Musharraf* 83
Supreme Court of the Philippines 74, 78
Supreme Court of South Korea 34–36
Surayut Chulanont 124*t*
Swamy, Arun Ranga 98
Syihab, Habib Rizieq 168–169, 173
Syria 68
Syrian refugee crisis (2015-2016) 5
Syriza (leftist party, Greece) 4, 5

tablets *see* computers
Tacloban City (Philippines) 65
Taekeukki (national flag) rallies (anti-
  impeachment protests, South
  Korea) 33
Taipei
  build-operate-transfer (BOT) projects/
    urban renewal 47–48, 55–56
  civil political participation/i-voting 48,
    48n21, 53, 56
Taiwan 17, 215n3
  anti-elite/establishment ideologies 6, 18,
    38, 40, 41, 43, 44, 45, 46, 50, 224
  authoritarian rule 43–44
  autonomy 42, 53
  Blue-Green divide 41–42
  bottom-up populism 9, 17–18, 38, 52, 57,
    217, 218
    impact on democracy 38, 43, 52
  build-operate-transfer (BOT) projects/
    urban renewal 45, 47–48, 55–56

INDEX 245

China-Taiwan (economic/cross-strait)
relations 9, 38, 40, 42–46, 43*f*, 45*f*,
49, 50, 52, 54, 55, 56, 57–58, 217, 218,
221, 224
civil political participation 48, 48n21,
51, 53, 56
technocratic governance vs. 38, 48,
54, 56, 57
civil society organizations/social
movements 38, 40, 44–45, 57, 217
absorption in political system 9, 45–46,
47, 50, 52, 57
populist issues and agendas 46–49
corruption 38, 47, 218
democracy/democratization 16, 44, 48, 217
direct democracy 39, 48–49, 53, 56, 217
liberal democracy/values 42–43, 46,
52–53, 57
representative democracy 18, 38, 47,
48, 54, 55, 56, 57
economic development/economic
policy 38, 40–41, 43–44, 46, 50, 56,
213, 224
(youth) unemployment and
underemployment in 41, 50
elections/electoral politics 6, 49–50, 54
environmental protection/
management 40, 44, 47, 53–54, 57
freedom of press/fake news act
proposal 52, 53
manufacturing sector 56
migration/immigration 8, 221
national identity 9, 58
national security 49, 53
progressive populism 6, 214*t*, 217–218
redistributive/economic populism 222
referendums 48–49, 53, 54
rural population 213
social media 221
Taiwan Foundation for Democracy,
2015 Democratic Governance
survey 39, 41, 43
Taliban, destruction of Buddha statues in
Afghanistan 205, 208
Tamil (language) 180
Tamil Nadu 11, 100, 101n17, 114
subsidized prepared food in 11, 106–108,
115, 116–117

Tamil National Alliance 192
Tamils 14, 179, 180, 187, 189, 216
Tamil separatist nationalism 181–182, 185
Liberation Tigers of Tamil Eelam 15, 182,
183, 184
Taoyuan (Taiwan) 47
Tea Party movement (Republican
Party, US) 1
Technical Education and Skills Development
Authority (TESDA, Philippines) 70
Teehanke, Julio 66
TESDA (Technical Education and
Skills Development Authority,
Philippines) 70
Thailand 17
agricultural and rural development 12,
121, 123, 124*t*, 125, 127, 129, 130
checks and balances system 134–135
civil political participation 123, 129, 130
civil service reform 124*t*
clientelism 17
Constitution (1997) 121, 123, 130, 133, 135
corruption 11, 17, 124*t*, 127, 131, 135
decentralization 132, 133
democracy/democratization 5, 16, 17,
215, 220
democratic elections/electoral system 17
drug war 66
economic development 123, 125, 127,
132, 213
elections/electoral system 17, 131
foreign capital and cheap labor 213
migration/immigration 8
military coups 12, 17
political marketing 125, 132, 133
political populism 122, 123, 131, 134
populist measures 124*t*
30-Baht healthcare scheme 11, 121,
123, **125**, 134
300-Baht minimum wage 121,
123, **128**
2000 Baht Aid Check 126
Civil State project 129
community village funds 11, 121,
123, **125**
First-time Car Buyer Policy 127, 135
fiscal impact of 122, 131, 133, **134–135**
free education 121, 126, 212

populist measures *(cont.)*
    free tablets at primary schools 123, 128, 135
    launch of 500-Baht banknote 135
    One Tambon One Product program 11–12, 121, **125–126**
    pension retirement schemes/elderly allowances 121, 123, **126**, 130, 212
    positive and negative effects of 127, 130–133, 134, 135
    Rice Pledging Scheme 121, **127**, 131, 132, 135, 212, 213
    sustainability of 132, 133, 134–135
    Thai Niyom Yangyuen project 121, **129**
    welfare benefits/welfare scheme card 123, **129–130**, 131, 132, 134, 135
populist policies under different governments 121–122, 123
    Abhisit Vejjajiva (2009-2011) 121, 123, 126, 132
    Prayut Chan-o-cha (2014-2018) 123, **128–130**, 132
    Surayut Chulanont (2006-2007) 124*t*
    Thaksin Shinawatra (2001-2006) 121, 122, 123, **125–126**, 132
    Yingluck Shinawatra (2011-2014) 121, 123, **127–128**, 132
    poverty reduction 121, 123, 124*t*, **129**, 130
    redistributive/economic populism 6, 11–12, 17, 121–123, 130–131, 134, 212, 214*t*, 215, 220, 222
Thai Niyom Yangyuen ("Sustainable Thainess") program 121, **129**
Thai Rak Thai (TRT) 121, 123, 130
Thaksin Shinawatra 11–12, 66, 121, 122, 123, 124*t*, **125–126**, 130, 132, 212
Thein Sein 197, 198, 207, 209
Theravada Buddhists (Myanmar) 14
Thompson, Neil 205
Thousand Islands (Pramuka Island, Indonesia) 165
Time Magazine 202
top-down populism 6, 7, 39, 169, 221, 225
    see also authoritarian populism; ethnic/religious populism; India; Malaysia; Mongolia; Pakistan; Philippines; redistributive populism; South Korea; Thailand

Transparency International's Corruption Perception Index 152, 154
tribalism, political 22, 72
Trillanes IV, Antonio 73
trolls, use in and after election campaigns 68
TRT (Thai Rak Thai) 121, 123, 130
Trump, Donald 2, 5n9, 68, 122
Trumpism 22
Truth Seeker Society (Satya Shodhak Samaj, India) 100
Tsai Ing-wen 44n14
Tsipras, Alexis 4
Turkey 68, 97, 137, 171–172
TV Chosun 32

UMNO (United Malays National Organization) 12, 13, 147, 147n1, 150–151, 156, 157, 158, 160
unconsolidated democracies, consolidated vs. 25, 52
Union Solidarity and Development Party (USDP, Myanmar) 15, 201, 204, 206, 207, 210
United Arab Emirates 84
United Development Party (Indonesia) 168
United Front for Democracy against Dictatorship (Red Shirts Movement, Thailand) 12
United Malays National Organization (UMNO) 12, 13, 147, 147n1, 150–151, 156, 157, 158, 160
United National Party (UNP, Sri Lanka) 180, 188, 191, 193, 194
United Nations 65, 66
United Nations Human Rights Council (UNHRC) 191
United Nations Office of Drugs and Crime 66–67
United Progressive Alliance (UPA) 104, 106, 111
United States 1–2, 147, 149, 160
    2016 elections 68
    anti-US protests (South Korea) 29–30
    democracy in 21–22
    rightist populism 21
    South-Korea-US relations 9, 24, 29–30, 31

INDEX 247

Universal Access to Quality Tertiary
  Education Act (Philippines)   70
Universiti Utara Malaysia   150
UNP (United National Party, Sri Lanka)   180,
  188, 191, 193, 194
UPA (United Progressive Alliance,
  India)   104, 106, 111
urban elite *see* political and urban elite/
  establishment
USDP (Union Solidarity and Development
  Party, Myanmar)   15, 201, 204, 206,
  207, 210
US imperialism   66
US Military Tribunal (South Korea)   29
Uttar Pradesh (India)   11, 109
  free laptops for students in   **108–111**, 117, 212

Vaishnav, Milan   113
Varieties of Democracy Index   28n14
Varma, Pavan   103, 103–104n27, 118
Venezuela   68, 97, 223
Vera, Eugene de   76
vertical populism   6–7, 13, 37
  see also bottom-up populism; South
    Korea; top-down populism
Vietnam   213
villages
  community village funds (Thailand)   11,
    121, 123, 124*t*
  guaranteed wage employment in rural
    India   102, **104–106**, **113–116**
  self-sufficient villages (India)   11, 100
volonté générale (general will of the people,
  Mudde)   2, 3, 24, 61, 69, 148, 151, 177,
  197, 198

wages
  guaranteed wage employment
    (India)   102, **104–106**, **113–116**
  minimum wages (Thailand)   121, 123, 128
Walton, Matthew   205

weak institutions   10, 61–62, 64, 75, 77
We Burman Association (Dobama
  Asi-ayone)   200
Wenlin-Yuan urban renewal project
  (Taiwan)   45
Western Europe, rightist populism in   5
Western populism   1–2, 21–22, 176, 223–224
West, The   65
Weyland, Kurt   169, 198
White Force (WF, populist party, Taiwan)   9,
  38, 45–46, 47, 50, 52
  see also Ko Wen-je
Wickremesinghe, Ranil   188, 191, 193–194, 195
Widodo, Joko (Jokowi)   63
Wirathu, Ashrin   202, 204, 205, 206, 208, 209
Wisconsin   97
Woods, Dwayne   39
World Migration Report 2018 (International
  Organization for Migration)   8–9
World Press Freedom Index   155–156

xenophobia   64
Xi Jinping   58, 221

Yadav, Akhilesh   110
Yadav, Mulayam Singh   109–110
yahapālanaya ("good governance")
  government (Sri Lanka)   176, 188,
  191–194
Yang Seung-tae (Chief Justice, South
  Korea)   34–35
"Yellow Shirts" (People's Alliance for
  Democracy, Thailand)   12
Yingluck Shinawatra   12, 17, 121, 123, 124*t*,
  127–128, 132
YMBA (Young Men's Buddhist Association,
  Myanmar)   200
Yoon Seok-ryul (Attorney General, South
  Korea)   35
Young Men's Buddhist Association (YMBA,
  Myanmar)   200

Printed in the United States
By Bookmasters